WHAT I KNOW

(so far)

ANTHONY RONDEAU

Published by Mindstir Media, LLC
45 Lafayette Rd | Suite 181| North Hampton, NH 03862 | USA
1.800.767.0531 | www.mindstirmedia.com

Printed in the United States of America
ISBN-13: 979-8-9861392-1-0 (paperback)
Library of Congress Control Number: XXXXXXXXXX

CONTENTS

FIRST THINGS FIRST

Dearest children,

While I may be liberal in my application of the word "dearest," I mean all four of you, not just my favorite(s). Immediately, I apologize for beginning this book with an awful dad joke.

This volume is a collection of perspectives, opinions, and observations from the viewpoint of your experienced, but incredulous dad who has previously and willingly shared knowledge with you. Sometimes you will sense déjà vu all over again because I will be repeating life lessons I've already dispensed. I do this because I'm not terribly confident you paid attention the first (second or third) times I've said it.

As the title of the book indicates, my own proficiency is ongoing. As if what I have learned about life makes me constantly feel like I am several credits short in my continuing education.

The book is in four parts:

- I Am Who I Am, Your Dad
- Intimate and Other Relationships
- My Best Guesses
- My Best Advice

The intentionally voluminous and potentially infinite volume is a set of non-sequential insights. The discernments are the same guesses and advice I have offered or contemplated because of you. From guidance with kid gloves to assistance by tough love, the book is written from the perspective of a "seasoned" dad who realizes his maturing children may not have—and probably didn't—listen to him while they were young.

Believe it or not, this manuscript began as a letter to you. It has been compiled from the notes, observations, and stories I have been writing down for more than thirty years in my handwritten speckled notebooks and Word files on my computer. Admitting I have preserved these documents should indicate the depth of my love for you—or that I am a hoarder who can't throw anything away. I decided to assemble the collection in the form of a letter for two reasons: 1) neither you, a social media message, nor your mother can interrupt me, and 2) you can't ignore me. Well, at least you can't roll your eyes and disregard me to my face.

While it is beyond paternal mandates of customary astuteness like "make your bed" or "eat your vegetables," it developed from my many dad speeches of my own ouch-ful experiences and I'm-wide-awake-in-the-middle-of-the-night contemplated rhetoric. To make it easier for you, it is styled in a tone, manner, and voice you should recognize: with authoritative dad bluster, astonished wonderment, and possibly a unique perspective. What you don't know is that sometimes the parental roaring was delivered while it felt like I was staring into the oncoming headlights of a speeding truck. If that doesn't make any sense, you'll understand what I mean when you have your own children, trust me.

Listen, I know some of my advice went unheeded, but I dispensed some top-notch and terrific legacy wisdom among the lessons you snubbed. I have counseled and consoled you with my been-there-done-that theories of how to survive a breakup, why boys are stupid, or why it's important to make a good impression. As your dad, like the proverbial fallen tree in the woods, I wonder endlessly if you paid attention at all or just heard a loud, discordant thud. Though I am just a tree, I am self-aware and know there are other trees in my forest wondering the same things I do. On behalf of my fellow, kindred, and unheeded dad forest mates, I wish I knew if I haven't just been pissing, spitting, or blowing into the wind.

The writing is unequally self-deprecating, authoritative, and humbling—kinda like the role of being a dad. It is a compilation of ponderables and pseudo-reflections throughout my life—as a know-it-all twenty-something who viewed the world as his oyster, to a stunned dad who cannot believe the cost of everything like clothing, education, food, and especially those same oysters that looked so good in my more youthful days.

Stunned, shocked, and stupefied are probably three of the top ten words to describe the role of a father. Dads get confused because our bedrock notions have shifted in our heads and under our feet. We wonder, *Am I supposed to be tough and show no emotion? Is this the time I'm supposed to be sensitive? Am I expected to always keep my mouth shut even when I feel like roaring?* I don't know if every other dad senses this, but I feel as if I've been asked to play a game with vague-ish rules, without an indisputable conclusive guidebook, and feeling like it-seems-as-though-I've-gone-through-the-looking-glass-where-two-plus-two-equals-Cheshire Cat. Despite the general challenges, I foot soldier on. I offer a dad-centric and everyman perspective—that is if every man/dad muses and considers the mundane, the strange, and the well-above-my-pay-grade topics my wife implies (not so subtly) I should leave for others to examine.

While I readily admit I am not the sharpest bulb in the knife shed, modestly, my cleverness surpasses my intelligence because I am unafraid to be passionate, I am undaunted by mistakes I will certainly continue to make, and I am brave enough to relentlessly ask questions until I understand. It's like I tell you, "Dust yourself off, rub some magic dirt on it and get back in the game." I implore you to ask questions, understand the crowd before you follow it, and find out how to live a life worth living.

I acknowledge I am flawed. Perhaps not as defective as you, Mom, my family, and friends believe I am, but I comprehend my own imperfection. However, I remain quixotic and cautiously unworried by my shortcomings because, like acne or a kidney stone, this too shall pass. I don't know why I chase wisdom like an errant knight. Possibly my lack of acumen frees me from rigid mental shackles and allows me to pursue ding-dong ideas constantly ping-ponging between my left and right brain.

Ultimately, I view this book as a testament and as a gift to you. You should know three things:

1) Dad was here.
2) I try my darndest to lead a good and well-lived life.
3) Abundantly and ten-to-the-nth-power tenfold, I love you.

I offer this on behalf of our shared hugs and smiles, and on behalf of the tears I have shed for you and with you.

To set your minds at ease, especially since I began with an awful dad joke, you are not required to read any of this. I would like you to make it past the introduction, but that's a request and not a demand. The days of demanding you, forbidding you, and forcefully instructing you are behind me. Now I look at life like this: I taught you how to ride a bike with and then without training wheels. Go ride your bike because my back is kinda sore. The road of wonderment is ahead of you. It has a few potholes, but you know how to maneuver around them. You might fall a few times too, but I taught you how important it is to get up one more time than you go down.

Also, to set your minds at ease, I am not dying. Hopefully you all take this as good news.

This book MAY improve your lives; then again, it MAY not. In it I share personal observations, experienced opinions, and thoughtful ideas up to this point in my life. Some of them MAY be fact-based and obvious. Some of it MAY be entertaining conjecture. And the book MAY help you avoid pitfalls I have already traversed and similar ones you MAY encounter on your journey through life. You're on your bike, keep riding.

This is not specifically a self-help book. If I had intended specific guidance and/or self-help hints, I would suggest:

1) Drink more water. (At least a half a gallon per day).

2) Pay attention to your body in the manner you regarded your mom and not the way you often dismissed me.

3) Change the things you can, accept the things you cannot, and be wise to the distinction between them.

4) Don't get old.

There are no life hacks or social hints on how to improve your life. Actually, there are, but I, your former eternally optimist dad, have become your slightly more realist dad. I have watched you grow from show-me-teach-me children to I-can-do-it-by-myself young adults. I have seen the triumphs and the mistakes when you did and didn't listen to me. Sometimes, you ride straight and true like you were born to be on a bike. Other times, you are a bit wobbly. I want to rush in and help, but I refrain. It is the hardest part of being a parent, just watching from the window. I get nervous because I taught you to ride on flat neighborhood pavement on a nice day; I could only warn you about uneven terrain. Life's path may be pitted, and the skies are not always sunny and clear. Read on and ride on but be careful. Through it all, I am proud. You continually dust yourself off and jump back on the seat of your bike.

I am writing this in the easy manner, style, and tone in which I speak; it should be discernible to you. Surprisingly to me, it was harder than I thought it would be. It was difficult having to stay focused and eliminate "umm" and "uh" from the sentence structure. It was challenging to remain linear and not go tangential as I am prone to do. It was made more strenuous without a dedicated font for sarcasm. (**Dad Note:** A sarcasm font is a great idea!) Most problematic was curtailing my desire/need to type IN ALL CAPITAL LETTERS when making a salient point; half of the book would have been published with this approach.

Throughout the book, I have added sidebars in the form of a Dad Note. Sometimes they're silly, snarky, and/or insightful. Hopefully they explain a rationalization or at least provide some entertainment value more emphatically than my usual dumb dad jokes. I offer a beginning, a middle, and an ending to each chapter based on the analysis of my beginnings, awareness that I am in the middle of it, and fully cognizant an ending is somewhere ahead of me. The chapters are broken down into sections. Obviously, the heading is the topic. I introduce my assertion. I support and/or defend my declaration in independent affirmations with pithy, precise marksmanship of my penmanship. Sometimes my aim is off and the explanations ain't so pretty, pithy, or precise. At the end of each chapter, I have added a summation of my humble opinion called "In My Humble Opinion."

The method of my manner is tinctured with dad madness/gladness. Regretfully, my sons, it is contagious. However, don't worry, it is a (mostly) non-life-threatening affliction. As soon as you become a father, the brilliant and inspiring thoughts in your head lose clarity and poignancy traveling out of your mouth. Actually, grown men without children exhibit symptoms of this disorder as well.

So be prepared to fill in the potholes of my not completely paved concepts, uneven analogies, and under construction logic. There is but little polish to my style, displayed in the less than graceful jumbledness of the way I converse; kinda like the way I dress—conservative, but with a flair for a bit of color. My tone, pitch, sound, and timbre may be difficult to detect. Assume the atmosphere is conversational and pleasant, but this being New England, wait five minutes and it could change quickly.

I started writing this letter/book before I was thirty years old, not much older than you are now. Actually, it was just a collection of topical paragraphs I collected in my numerous handwritten notebooks. (**Dad Note:** To my dear technologically advanced and technology-dependent children, a long, long time ago we placed a pen in our dominant hand, gliding west to east to dispense ink on a piece of paper to communicate thoughts, words, and ideas—shocking!) At that time, I had recently moved to Michigan and relayed some of the stories to an older woman whom I had befriended at the bank where we worked. Her enthusiasm and appreciation for my wit, ideas, and opinions seemed genuine. Perhaps she just enjoyed the notion that a not-quite-thirty-year-old human male thought he had figured out life's mysteries that have challenged others for generations/millennia.

Either way, her enthusiasm prompted me to compile this, and I will always be grateful to her and others who have inspired me.

This has taken a long time. I have written, proofread, rewritten, re-proofread, changed the format, re-rewritten, and self-edited this work many times. I question everything. As situations present themselves and questions pop up in my head, I apply reasoned but limited dad logic based on experience and previous patterns of dad thought and behavior.

To prove that this book is actively flexible as my resolved, yet nomadic reactions evolve, it is important to be able to insert those new feelings or recently acquired knowledge. Though this collection of words seems linear and sectioned, it is not. There was no epiphanic moment. There was no sudden realization or particularly intuitive revelation that had me sit down in front of a computer screen and type until all advice/opinions/impressions leeched from my thoughts onto a page in a book. Ideas form from contemplation and interaction; words, in a very non-sequitur manner, are the result. Since this book is titled *What I Know (So Far)*, it should transform as I develop. The resultant words are the license I have taken with my whimsically gauged intelligence and my locked and loaded dad-engaged rationality.

For more than twenty years, I have been your parent. "Parent" is easily defined as mother caregiver or father caregiver. Preface it with the word "your" and the definition becomes termed and distinct, but eel-like and slick. The job description is vague, but unambiguous. Duties are outlined as love, feed, clothe, shelter, nurture, and teach, but nothing identifies all of the obligations of being "your parent." The position requires no experience, all training is on-the-job, and no company handbook exists to categorize how to do the job flawlessly. I, like you, am a work in progress.

Early on in our relationship I watched with you and was your *Lion King* (complete with mighty roar), your sounding board, your punching bag, and a whole list of other roles in your life. I loved playing "alpha and omega" on your stage. Lately, I've had fewer callbacks and only supporting roles. I get it. I'm no longer leading man material and I'm okay with the bit parts. As you enter your more self-reliant years, I try to be a good role model and a better listener. I was, and am, grateful to have you in my life. I hope the feeling is mutual.

Love, Dad

Section 1

I AM WHO I AM, YOUR DAD

The best thing in my life is that you are my children. Hopefully, having me as your dad is on your list of the top ten best things in your life. (**Dad Note:** I will settle for top twenty, but no lower!)

When you were very young, you had many questions. I could answer all of them. As you aged, I couldn't answer them all. It's not that I wasn't up to the task, you seemed to get so darned smart so darned quickly. You demanded responses. I wasn't as swift. Unlike my sometimes-short fuse, my intelligence is more of a slow burn.

In this section, you will gain insight into why and how I am who I am. It should satisfy your curiosity about choices I have made and address a number of your adult "What the heck was he thinking!?!" questions.

ABOUT ME—WHAT YOU MAY OR MAY NOT KNOW

Many self-improvement and other desires remain with me on the north side of fifty years of age. The following statements may confirm what you already know about me. Some insights will give perspective about me, and others MIGHT reveal what you did not expect.

I Ask a Lot of Questions

Either because a) I'm not bright or b) I yearn to learn, I ask a lot of questions. (**Dad Note:** This is a statement. It is not a question. It's not even a rhetorical one. So please, put away your smartphone. There's no need to text me which letter you favor.)

I guess I could read more than newspapers and textbooks to satisfy my curiosity. It's come to the attention of your technology-challenged dad that someone invented a wireless mechanism where I can access information instantly via a thing called "the internet." Whoa, slow down with that wild future nonsense! Even if that were true, I still prefer to talk to people to acquire knowledge and insight. It is true my brain is loaded with useless trivia, movie quotes, and song lyrics, but I love to have conversations to exchange ideas and to discover why/how someone forms personal opinions. While I may not always agree with them, I appreciate differing viewpoints.

It has been brought to my attention OFTEN that people are SOMETIMES offended/insulted/upset by my inquiries. My interest is perceived as impolite, impertinent, and that I only engage to voice my own opinion. Listen, I am neither an expert in the Socratic method nor mischievous, I just like to know how someone else thinks.

I didn't always ask so many questions. When I was young, I was kinda shy. Perhaps I am making up for lost time. So, forgive my semi-intrusive behavior. I find the human mind fascinating as it searches, categorizes, and comprehends.

Two is My Favorite Number

I am certain you know this. You used this knowledge as inside information when I coached your youth sports teams. Whenever a tiebreaker was needed or to decide who went first in an agility drill, I would ask the group to guess a number between one and one thousand. Two was always my choice. Not surprisingly, two was the number you always "guessed."

As kind of a "dad experiment," I watched you strategize with this intimate information. When you were very young, you chose the number for yourself to bat or shoot first. As you matured, you shared the info with a teammate for a personal or common benefit. You were beginning to understand the power and value of knowledge. The "research" was invaluable to me; it indicated the development of personality, social adaptation, teamwork, and leadership skills. For me, the revelations were signposts of strengths and weaknesses along your life's highway. They suggested clues on how to raise you; when I should push and when I should back off. I learned a lot about you from my seemingly innocuous experimentation. (**Dad Note:** And you thought the only guinea pigs we had were kept in a crate!)

Two became my favorite number in my early teens. I was watching television and a commercial aired for the car rental company, Avis. (**Dad Note:** A brief historical commentary. When I was young, we watched entertainment, news, and sports on a television set [*thin gasp*]. We also watched the commercials during the breaks of our regularly scheduled programming [*slight gasp*]. Since we didn't have a remote-control unit with each TV [*full gasp!*], if we wanted to change the channel, we walked over and turned a knob or pressed a button [*double gasp!!*]. Also, we couldn't record a show to watch it later so we couldn't fast-forward past the commercials [*harder double gasp!!*]. And, we watched programming on the night it was broadcast or waited until it was re-aired in the summer. Are you still breathing!?!)

Anyway, I watched a television commercial for a rental car company. Thinking back, it was kind of strange I watched it because I wasn't old enough to drive a car, let alone rent one. During the advertisement, Avis referenced its number two market share position behind the Hertz rental car company. Avis recognized and embraced their second position to Hertz and developed a "We Try Harder" campaign. The main slogan was, "When you're only number two, you try harder. Or else." I fell in love with the slogan.

It zeroed in on my adolescent angst. It addressed feelings of being the largest square peg in a petite round hole of the world. I felt second-rate and I was tired of it. I immediately adopted the Avis catchphrase. I wanted to stop accepting the substandard mediocrity I believed I was. I wanted to embrace a new mantra. Being number two was now a challenge to improve, a springboard to shine. I felt like Moses in a rented dune buggy busting out of a desert after forty years of personal anguish.

At about age fourteen, I began to develop my burgeoning self-confidence. I was enrolled at Portsmouth Abbey School, a small, all-male Catholic high school run by English Benedictine monks. The environment was supportive, and I was making small, positive strides in the classroom and on the athletic fields because of my new "I'll try harder" outlook. I discovered faith in myself and my abilities. Instead of being overwrought by unyielding insecurities, I challenged myself to do better in all phases of my young life. I was elected class president and by the end of my sophomore year I had made the Dean's list once and played in some varsity games for football, basketball, and baseball.

Even with a few accomplishments, I maintained my underdog mindset. To succeed, I trained harder or studied longer than others did. If I wanted an extraordinary result, I had to do something extra past the ordinary. If I wanted to be the best, it wasn't enough to try; I had to take positive strides to make sure it happened. It was okay to doubt myself, but the uncertainty would no longer control me, and those negative thoughts now served as fuel for personal encouragement.

The truth is, I didn't always finish in first place or get an A on a test. Sometimes I won, but most often I didn't. Winning is great. It's an honor to be recognized as the best in your field, but **I discovered an equally rewarding achievement—personal satisfaction if I did everything I could to improve even if I didn't finish in first place.** When I tried my best and prepared the best I could, I was usually happy with the outcome. To this day, I remain inspired by the underdog mentality I created so many years ago.

Why I Cover My Ears

No, it's not because of my own singing, but I am afraid of loud, sudden noises like fireworks, balloons popping, or worse, a gunshot. This fear has a name. It's called *ligyrophobia*. I don't know why or how this developed. A loud, sudden noise startles me like it would anyone else, but then it feels sharp and burrowing. It invades my head and expands, shaking me from the inside out. It disorients me for a few seconds. I clench my fists and make taut my muscles until the feeling passes. I recover from the shock and sense the baffling feeling dissipate.

It is a bothersome condition. It doesn't interrupt my life, but it disappoints me that I might have been unable as a soldier to defend our country. It would have been difficult enough taking orders from someone besides your mother, but I would have been unable to cope if I ever had to witness gunfire around me, or worse, at me. It is why I sing our national anthem so loudly, proudly, and soundly off-key with my hand firmly over my heart. I respect all the men and women who can handle loud noises around them. I respect those who died or were wounded in defense of my country because of what those loud noises did. Further and most humbly, I have the greatest respect for those who experience what I do but perform their duties anyway.

My Greatest Fear

Fear of water is called *aquaphobia*. Fear of flying is called *aerophobia*. I struggle with an unnamed phobia: I am afraid to fly over large bodies of water, with you or without you. Perhaps it could be called *aerograndeaquaphobia*. If it becomes a medical condition, I'll take the credit and count it as my first invention. I am not a nervous flyer, per se. I think it's a great way to travel until teleportation becomes reality. When I was a kid, I saw the movie *Willy Wonka & the Chocolate Factory*. I always hoped that Wonkavision would become a real method of travel. When I was older, I wanted to travel via transporter like they did on Star Trek. (**Dad Note:** Not that you care or asked, but *Star Trek: The Next Generation* is my favorite series in the franchise. Love Kirk, but I'm a Picard guy.) I haven't given up hope, but like the rest of the world, I'm still waiting.

Simply, I do not like being in a plane where all I can see are two colors: white (clouds) and blue (sky or ocean). If the plane crashes into too much blue (a large ocean without a coast in view), it will be inhabited by too many hungry grays (sharks). My own gray matter (my brain) knows I can't swim far enough or fast enough through the blue (ocean) to get to the pale cream/golden/caramel shore (pink shore, if the plane went down near Bermuda) before my red (blood) becomes dinner for the grays (sharks) in the blue (ocean). At 30,000 feet in the air, if the blue of the water is in proximity to brown earth and green grass or trees below me, I can visualize seeing green for a short swim in the blue to the brown. I can envision landing in a pillowy group of green trees. Slightly black and blue from the fall, I'll recover and be in the pink soon.

I get nervous just thinking about flying over large bodies of water—my forehead and palms are sweaty as I am typing these words. My fear is nearly paralyzing. The condition intensified when I became a husband and a father. My thoughts crawl into dark scary recesses of my brain where I imagine your life without me and more horrifyingly, my life without you. I am glad to know none of you share this speck of crazy with me and I am pretty sure that phobias are not hereditary. Fortunately, you will travel and experience places my gray matter won't allow me to go.

I Don't Like Games of Chance (Like Sweepstakes or the Lottery)

If you asked, "Dad, have you ever bought a lottery ticket?" I would answer, "Yes I have, but probably fewer than ten in my lifetime." I'm not a fan of a game or contest which relies 100% on luck. I understand I have as good a chance as anyone else to win. I recognize the appeal of "But, what if I DID win?" Like anyone else, I can dream and visualize my list if my single ticket once-a-decade purchase has all the correct numbers.

- A forty-foot cabin cruiser
- 1965 Pontiac GTO convertible
- Hire Southern Culture on the Skids and The B-52s to play at my birthday party
- Book a family vacation every year to Bermuda (Well, at least every year with Mom.)
- A new first baseman's mitt, ten new maple baseball bats, and Red Sox tickets
- Whatever Mom wants (**Dad Note:** It may be wise to place this higher on the list.)

- Autographed and framed pictures of Eric Cantona, Dwight Evans, and Moses Malone

(**Dad Note:** If there's any money remaining, give me your Christmas list. Naughty or Nice is TBD.)

It is fun and easy to imagine winning gobs of money, but I still won't play. In my oddball way of thinking, playing a game of chance for the singular purpose of improving my life is counterintuitive to me. It would mean admitting to myself that I am not satisfied with the life I have. As if my life would become miraculously better if I had more money.

My grandfather always told me he was rich and happy as long as he had his family and two nickels in his pocket to rub together. I never understood what he meant until I became a dad. I don't measure being rich by how high I can stack a pile of money. I don't measure success that way either. Being rich and being successful are not arbitrary concepts to me. I have my own simple formula: + ([#PIL + #PLM] + [#PIR + #PRM]) * (#PHMB).

I take inventory of the number of people I love (PIL) who love me back (PLM), add that to the number of people I respect (PIR) and who respect me back (PRM), and multiply that number to the number who have my back (PHMB). Since it does not compute on my financial calculator, I don't know the actual number, but statistically and whole-heartedly, my life is good with or without gobs of money.

What Happens in Vegas, Stays in Vegas

That may be true, but I don't gamble either. I have been to casinos in Las Vegas and spent one night watching people pull handles on machines and sit at tables staring at cards. It was creepy that there were no clocks on the walls and that no one looked like they were having fun except for me at the buffet. My reasons for not gambling are similar to why I don't play lottery games—I love my life the way it is, and winning lots of money won't make me love it more; though a windfall of additional money would be helpful for home improvements, tuition payments, and gifts.

I am not immune to the charm of gambling. I get it—the allure of risk and desire to win causes a reaction in your brain producing cravings for more of the same. It is the combination of eagerness, anticipation, and thrill against a misty background of possibility. It happens to me, especially when I pitch playing baseball. I like the control of being on the mound and testing the combined probability of my strength and pitch selection.

But sometimes, actually most times, I want to throw a ball as hard as I can past a batter. My shoulder feels like a nail is being driven into it. My arm bounces between the second and seventh circles of hell as if it would prefer not to be attached to me rather than continue. I do it again and again disregarding the pain until I can't lift my arm, or your mother shows up to watch my game. The biochemical craving supersedes all rational thought. It is a compulsion to compete and win, and it scares me a little. Fortunately, I can control the urges and it doesn't seep into other areas of my life. I still love it when I win and want more, but now I'm okay when I lose.

I don't gamble because I don't want to find out if I have a personality addiction to it. Addiction leads to imbalance. Imbalance can lead to loss. To chance losing things I hold most dear, like family, friends, and especially your respect, is too great a risk for me.

I Suck!

I imagine you are nodding your heads in agreement when you read that line. "I suck!" is attention-grabbing and has more marketing allure than what I really wanted to write: "I LOVE to vacuum!"

I'm probably the only non-OCD dad in America, possibly in the whole world, who would make this statement. (**Dad Note:** The announcement that "I love to vacuum'" not "I suck!") Besides my other household chores of grilling meats, doing yardwork, and drinking beer, I love vacuuming. (**Dad Note:** Okay, drinking beer, even a quality crafted double IPA with a cool name, doesn't qualify as a household chore, but grilling and mowing should count.)

I love to vacuum for three reasons:

- It gives me a sense of accomplishment.
- It makes me feel like I contribute to the family's well-being.
- I do my best thinking while pushing that thing around the house.

Life is complex, intricate, and often you have to wait to know if you did things correctly. Vacuuming is easy and I am instantly gratified. I have a simple task and claim small victories room by room.

All of your lives, your mom did/does so much for you. I couldn't/can't keep pace with her. She bought your clothes. She fed you healthy meals. She gave you great advice. She manages our household more efficiently and effectively than any U.S. president's chief of staff. Heck, even her printed schedule calendar was precisely color-coded! (Honestly, how could I compete with that?) The bar was set too high and grilling a few burgers and cutting the lawn don't measure up well on the yardstick of familial duties. So, I added cleaning the house to my shortlist of things I can help with. (**Dad Note:** I'm not a huge fan of dusting, especially baseboards, folding laundry, or washing windows. Doing dishes and scrubbing toilets are acceptable tasks though.)

Even as a kid, I liked to vacuum. It appeals to the simplicity of my nature and the logic is clear.

There is dirt.
There is a dirt-sucking machine.
Turn on dirt-sucking machine.
Push dirt-sucking machine over dirt.
Result: no more dirt.
Repeat as often as required.

Now I do it to comfort and support Mom's rational, psychological, and emotional stability; Mom fears chaos and disorder and the well-being of society may collapse if things are unkempt or crumbs remain on the floor. So, in the name of decency and for unity, I schlep around the ol' dirt inhaler to prevent bedlam and dust bunnies. I keep societal disarray as far from our door as a Jehovah's Witness from a house with a "Beware of Vicious Devil Dog" sign on it.

Also, while pushing and pulling the vacuum around from room to room, I do some of my best thinking. I have come up with many ideas/thoughts for this book while vacuuming. In case that doesn't impress you, I have also formulated business ideas, developed jokes, conceived inventions, thought of things I should say to people, and repressed other things I should not say to people. I am convinced this is an inherited trait. My mom said she did her best thinking in the shower. Water whooshes out of the showerhead like the white noise of the motorized din of a vacuum cleaner, blocking out everything else while you concentrate on a task you can do on autopilot. There is a mind freeing-ness in being in the moment to think, to gain a small victory of completing a task, and to help Mom prevent society from crumbling by keeping our house in order. (**Dad Note:** I am a tiny bit sorry if my vacuuming ever woke you or interrupted you while you were watching television or doing something. The low rung "dad work" and "dad thinking" needed to be done.)

I Pick Things Up and Put Them Down

I really, really like sports. I sense additional head nodding, some eye-rolling, and a sarcastic muttering like, "No duh! My dad likes sports—what a shocking revelation!"

Watching, coaching, or playing, I love the competition of an event. I especially like watching, coaching, or playing team sports. I appreciate the commitment in training, both personally and for the benefit of the team, which precedes an event. I love to see players strive towards a common goal through well-executed plays. I revel in witnessing the amazing and understand the hard work that goes into the most routine of plays.

Here's a multiple-choice quiz for you.

"Dad loves sports because_____":
  a) of the trophies and awards he has received.
  b) athletics teaches many great life lessons.
  c) of the way he was raised.
  d) at his age, he gets to hang out with friends and drink beer.

The correct answer is b). However, you receive credit for c) and d) also; those responses are mostly true. If you chose a), I am honored you recognize my accomplishments, but disappointed you think that's why I played.

I received athletic awards. I am proud of what I did to earn them. Some are very dear to me because I remember what it took to get them; I own no participation ribbons. But trophies were never the reason for me to participate; I wanted to excel. Sometimes I wanted to prove to others I was better than they thought I was. Often I challenged myself because I wanted to see how good I could be.

Athletics, especially team sports, forces you to learn valuable life lessons including teamwork, dedication, optimism, and time management skills. I say "forces" because not all of the lessons are positive.

Life isn't fair.
Some people will cheat to win.
Sometimes luck goes against you.
Some people have advantages you do not possess.

It can be frustrating not playing on even terms, but I have learned that if I prepared well enough to win and I competed to the best of my ability, then I am not disappointed with the result. I may grumble a bit, but I am generally at peace with a decision.

Anything You Can Do, I Can Do Better

I was raised in a competitive environment. One of my cousins once said that my brother, your Uncle Bob, and I couldn't set a table unless it was a competition. (**Dad Note:** We even had our parents buy a mini ping-pong set which fit onto the dinner table.) We invented many games to play inside and outside our house. One of our favorites was a summer game of Wiffle ball in our cousins' pool—those contests were epic battles! In our own home, we broke enough furniture that my parents silently vowed not to buy new stuff until we were fully grown. (**Dad Note:** We were in our twenties before they finally did.) I still don't know why competing with each other gripped us so tightly. Our mom and dad were not overbearing. They never demanded we play at a high level. They expected us to do our best. They were always pleased with our efforts and proud of our accomplishments, and perhaps happy that most of our sports were outdoors.

Competition appeals to me. It is a way to measure your effort against a result. It doesn't define me but is a big part of what makes me tick. So I hope you understand and have forgiven me for those hats I gave you one Christmas that read "Team RONDEAU—We Didn't Come Here To Lose!"

My Personal Epiphany

When I was fourteen—that wonderful age when you are unsure of everything in life except that you're smarter than your parents—I had my first self-aware vision of how I wanted things to be. I was a tall and husky kid, which is a nicer way of saying I was big and fat. I didn't suddenly get husky, I always felt that way. Because of it, I felt bullied, ostracized, and not good enough. The teasing wasn't always overt and may have been entirely in my own head, but I felt like an outsider. Until then I had suffered the stings and arrows, but never did anything about it. It seems kind of odd that I was bullied especially since I was bigger than most kids my own age, but trust me, I was. Despite a great and supportive family environment, those burdens of social, intellectual, and physical anxiety felt very heavy, and they were all mine.

I don't remember the single event which crossed the line in my emotional sand. One day, I had just had enough. I quit blaming others for my perceived shortcomings. I quit justifying why something didn't work out the way I wanted it to. I accepted it was my perception that mattered, not what I thought someone else was thinking. I allowed myself to offload the bags full of negative thoughts and unhelpful feelings which I wore everywhere.

Fortunately, I never lashed out or reacted (too) negatively to those around me. I had a soul-searching epiphany that my fourteen-year-old brain could grasp: **If I gave maximum effort in anything I did, there is no way I could consider myself a failure.** Initially, this realization didn't make me any smarter and didn't make me any better of an athlete, but it gave me a new self-assurance and cognizance that my life was mine to manage; the direction of my life was all up to me. I didn't become an all-star athlete immediately, but I gained confidence in myself. My newly discovered confidence inspired me to understand I was as good as anyone I competed against or with. It inspired me to understand that if I wanted better grades, I had to study more. If I wanted to be faster, I had to run. If I wanted to be stronger, I had to lift weights. It was the beginning of a physical and intellectual odyssey. One that challenged me to learn what it takes to be better than my opponent, to want to be better than I was the day before, and to **gauge my own success by my own standards**.

I'm Not as Dumb as You Think I Am

Well, at least I hope I'm not. I may misspeak often or forget the correct word to use, but I am not brainless.

I am not breaking any "guy codes" here and I think you are all old enough to learn some inside information about men, especially about dads.

Our intelligence surpasses the questions we would not/could not/cannot/ will not answer for you. Our knowledge transcends current social mores, political incorrectness, and can't be measured by traditional standards. Our conventional acumen actually exceeds our conventional views and clothing. We are not dumb, just "dad dumb."

Being dad dumb is not a self-inflicted malady, like a "dad bod." A dad bod is identified as the shape only a dad can have AND appreciate. As he looks in a mirror, he hopes his mate is as impressed as he is and loves what HE sees, not what SHE sees. My dad bod condition is mostly my own fault through genetics, time, beer, and gravity. Mom's great cooking has played a modest part, but no one ever forced me to have a second helping. So, the overweight guy you hug every once in a while is my creation. But don't worry, there is a remedy. It's called "dad vision." The man you see looks very different to me. I see brown hair, no wrinkles, a killer smile, and a fabulous personality. My vision is selective and it's all in my mind's eye. The glass reflection of what I'm staring at is stark, but fortunately, dad vision cures it.

Anyway, back to what dad dumb is. When you were very, very young, I was at the height of my intelligence and popularity in your view. I may not have been the center of your universe like Mom was, but I was a big planet in the system like Jupiter or had cool rings like Saturn. You were constantly amazed at how dad big, dad strong, dad funny, and dad smart I was. The run lasted a few revolutions around the sun and then you changed and went all supernova on me.

You began to see the world, and your place in it, as limitless. You became aware of other planets besides me. You were maturing and questioning everything. Frankly, you asked more questions than I could or would answer. I can't pinpoint when all this happened, but I knew I was in trouble when you were in 4th or 5th grade. You asked questions about Santa Claus, "new" math, and where babies *really* come from. I was in trouble—I never even knew "old" math disappeared. You asked about subjects I didn't want to touch with a 39½ foot pole. You elevated your enquiries and wanted to know why some people are mean or get angry with other people because they're different. I could only offer opinions on subjects I still don't understand.

It's not an oxymoron, but there is such a thing as "dad intelligence." It is different from standard male intellect. (**Dad Note:** That's not an oxymoron either!) Our thoughts and actions are manipulated by our role as a parent and protector. We know one day we will have to address sensitive issues with you, but the first time you ask, you always seem waaay too young. We see you through the lenses of our dad vision and emotions influence the thoughts we are prepared to offer. A dad is equipped to tell you when "i" comes before "c," but not why a "p" goes into a "v."

I thoroughly enjoyed your affection and adoration when you were little kids, and despite some uncomfortable questions I am proud that you have become inquisitive and intelligent. Some stuff you learned from me and some stuff you had to learn for yourself because I could not or would not help you.

I never intended to seem dumb to you. I answered what I could. I preferred to watch you dream, plan, and discover with limited interference from me as you circled the sun. I, and the planet formerly known as Pluto, are very proud of you.

I Know How to Apologize - Mea Culpa

I am sorry for embarrassing you when you were young. I know it is unacceptable to apply a blanket apology for past offenses, but I hope we are at the age in our relationship where we look back and laugh rather than carry grudges. In your mind, the list is very long. It probably begins, and ends, with my sense of humor. So, to you, your boyfriends/girlfriends, classmates, teammates, amusement park attendants, sales associates in stores, waiters/ waitresses in restaurants, and anyone else you think I embarrassed you in front of, mea culpa.

I should note that I am not whole-heartedly sorry and some of the blame is actually yours. You outgrew me so quickly and my relevance faded in the blink of an eye. One day you are sitting on my lap. I'm making silly sounds reading a Dr. Seuss book for the umpteenth time. The next day, it seems, you are sitting behind the wheel of a car driving off to college. It is a very difficult proposition to fathom as a parent, going from being your "everything" to being your "seldom-needed thing."

Sometimes I intruded just to interject myself into your lives. I was never terribly worried about embarrassing you. I raised you to be strong-willed, to think for yourselves, and to have a sense of humor. I knew you would recover and hopefully forgive my intrusion. I wasn't worried about repercussions or reprisals from you; you would get over it and forgive my indiscretion. My only concern was that someday I might be irrelevant to you. And that is something I could not handle.

So here's the deal. You promise to forgive and never forget me, and I promise I won't ask anyone to pull my finger at any of your weddings. Deal?

I Ain't No Willy Shakespeare

I have always wanted to be a writer. I realize the irony as I tap a keyboard and words appear on the screen in front of me. No, I'm talking about writing professionally. I love to make up and tell stories, to entertain, and to inspire people with my words. I would love it if I got paid to do it.

A very long time ago, my English teacher for my junior year in high school was Father Ambrose Wolverton. With unyielding patience and an equally unyieldingly soothing voice, he taught me how to write. I remember him telling me, "In every story you will write there is a beginning, middle, and an ending. Think small—construct your sentences with easily understood words. Keep it simple." To this day, I am convinced he really wanted to say, "Anthony, keep it simple, stupid! Stop trying to impress me with long and winding sentences. It looks like crap!" Fortunately for me and my ambition to write, he was always kind. His message got through and I try like heck to keep it simple. When I find my words begin to swirl and clog, I spur myself with the words I imagined he wished to say to me: "Keep it simple, stupid!" (**Dad Note:** Father Ambrose passed away while I have been writing this book. I intended to show it to him when it was completed. He was one of those special and reserved individuals who probably had no idea how many lives, like mine, he positively influenced.)

Thanks to Father Ambrose, some other teachers, and my own curiosity, I know the basics of writing. With 100% certainty, I've never placed an "e" before an "i" except after a "c" and I (try to) write simple and readable sentences. Plus, I am mildly entertaining, sometimes interesting, and can usually tell a good story. So why haven't I ever attempted to assemble my thoughts into words for others to read? There are two reasons: I need encouragement and I have been too fearful.

I do well as a self-starter, but I thrive when someone is pushing me to do my best. Spurred on by someone who believes in me I feel like a superhero ready to leap tall buildings in a single bound, or at least short buildings because of my age, weight, and knees. I need the push. I tend to doubt myself when I am on uncertain ground. Even when I am confident in my idea and my ability, my brain plays "What if?" with me as if it's a table tennis game. My mother was an ace at encouraging me past the mental ping-ponging. She was the perfect combination of patronage: 70% bulldozer and 30% safety net. She could push, inspire, and challenge. She could steady my hesitation by asking one question: "What's the worst that can happen?" Inhibition seemed silly after I resolved that. I always felt compelled to re-evaluate my insecurity, find an angle or proposition I had not considered, and propel myself wearing her "I-know-I-can" rose-colored glasses and her admiration. Even draped in her approval I had to get past the fear. Three questions always nagged me: What if my best isn't good enough? What if it isn't appreciated? What if I am misunderstood?

When I was younger, they were difficult to answer as I was often concerned with others' opinions of me. I needed to know if I was understood. I wanted positive, instant feedback. Writing to entertain, inform, or impart wisdom offers none of that. Worse still, any effort could easily be ignored.

Now, being older, I still have doubts, I still hesitate. For this book, I have overcome my fears and conjured my own support. The fears were easier to alleviate; I'm wider, wiser, and I don't give a flying firetruck as often as I used to. My support is manufactured from encouraging words I imagine my mom would have said and the heaps of experience I maintain as my life's reference points. I'm no Shakespeare and I'm cool with that now. I hope you are too.

IS THERE ANYTHING I WOULD CHANGE ABOUT MY LIFE?

It may not happen every day, but often enough I spend time contemplating my existence here on Earth. Perhaps it is a trademark of aging, like needing reading glasses, getting gray hair, and having an AARP card in your wallet. I reflect on what I have done, and I review my plans going forward as a resident of this planet. I do this for three reasons:

- I am getting older.
- I am getting older. (Oops, I already said that!)
- I forgot what number three is. (See numbers one and/or two.)

In those contemplative moments, I ask myself a lead question or two to consider. As recently as this week, I pondered:

- OMG, why aren't I in better shape?
- Am I a good role model?
- Would a young me be proud of who I have become?
- Did I hold true and dear to my ideals, or did I alter them for convenience?
- Should I get a new phone?

- If I add more Hungarian paprika to my "Wait For It!" dry rub recipe, will it be too spicy? (**Dad Note:** Is "too spicy" even a real thing?)

I am truly unenlightened and easily sidetracked. I ruminate like a hamster on a wheel chasing the pea zipping unpredictably through my neurons. I try to focus. I don't waste time on what I cannot or could not control. I try to answer honestly while avoiding "what ifs" and "do-over" pitfalls. My thoughts zig, then zag, then zig again colliding into the ideas banging off the walls of my cranium. I chase them around my brain as if I were in a bumper car with a bumper sticker that reads "No Regrets."

Presently and persistently, two other questions routinely plead for answers like dogs begging for bones.

- Is there anything I would have done differently?
- Is there anything I would have changed if I could have?

My answers didn't actually surprise me, but I thought I would share them with you as helpful and possibly impactful. I've also provided a mindset and basis for my processing of an idea. This won't be as fun as learning how to make fudge or as informative as being taught how to change a tire, but don't be afraid. Just buckle up in my bumper car and remember, no regrets!

The Mindset to Answer the Questions

The mindset is obvious; it's how I began this chapter. I'm old. Mindset is about attitude, outlook, and approach. In order to satisfy the two questions, reference points from when I was young(er) needed to be established. My discoveries fell into two private, personally identified music genres.

1) A Single Guy's Life (The Wishes of an Unmarried Man). Playlist identified by the songs "No Shoes, No Shirt, No Problem" by

Kenny Chesney, "Boom" by P.O.D., and "Hoochie Coochie Man" by Muddy Waters. In my care-freer days, my desires and cravings were tinctured with a here-and-now attitude. The impetus was self-centered, not egoistically inconsiderate. I cared about my fellow man and the environment, but a cool car and a great stereo were more absorbing. I was peripherally attracted to politics and societal improvement, but more attentive to self-interests like saving money, investing for the future, and buying even cooler cars. I have always been fair and conscientious of others, but, simply and unapologetically, it was all about me.

2) The Life of a Married Guy with Children (Hopes and Dreams of Those Counting on You). Playlist identified by songs "Calm Like a Bomb" by Rage Against The Machine, "The Best Part of Me" by Lee Brice, and "You've Got a Friend in Me" by Randy Newman. While I would love to have assembled a "Married to My Best Friend Before We Had Kids" playlist, I have never held that distinction. My eldest daughter was born before I was married. When I did marry, I married a woman with two small children. I gained another daughter and a son instantly. Then, we had a son together. This is my family; I wouldn't change it or my playlist for anything. Dearest children, you are the soundtrack of my life.

The Basis to Answer the Questions

I remember my life before you. It is filled with colorful stories of attempts, triumphs, and failures. The era was remarkable in that there was more joy than sadness and more ups than downs. However, to answer most questions based on my life before you fails in impact because of context—you are part of my framework now. You nuance my perspective. You influence my environment. Nothing will change that.

When I answer if there is anything I would have done differently, my entire lifetime serves as my research library. When I answer if there is anything I would have changed if I could have, I am limited to the You-In-My-Life platinum information only.

To be honest, the questions were easier to answer when you were young. I was in the midst of raising you and any misstep by me was easily correctable as you were a "work in progress" without far to fall. Now that I am older, when these two questions surface, I try harder to concentrate and try harder to eliminate guilt from the equation. No parent enters the gray tunnel of raising a child and comes out unchanged on the other side. My biggest concern about the vamoosing section of the passageway is if I added enough substantial value to your lives.

As I age, I wonder what impact I have made on the lives around me. Like most people, I am considerably insignificant on a large scale. I have concluded that no ink or breath will be wasted discussing my historical (in)significance when my physical life finally concludes. Beyond close friends and family, my importance will not register more than a tearful blip when I die. Honestly, I am okay with my irrelevance. I really am. I never invented anything, saved a life, or solved a major social dilemma. I never helped avert a national crisis, won a beauty pageant, or appeared on TV. In the annals of the banal and (in)significant history of things, I have eaten a four-pound cheeseburger (with fries!), won a few championships in sports, and expelled an inordinate amount of carbon dioxide. Woe, though, is not me. I have learned, observed, and participated. Life isn't fair and tends to be bumpy, but I have mostly enjoyed the grooves, flow, and rhythms of my life. I am confident there have been more successes than failures. And like a stone thrown into a pond, I have made an impact. Perhaps the ripples don't reach the shore, but I made some waves; I am sure of this. I have reestablished a relationship with God. I have a good idea of my connection to the universe. I have helped raise the four of you. And though your mom may debate the consistency, I am an excellent best friend and ever-improving husband.

I am older and, surprisingly, (a little bit) smarter than I was. I accept that I cannot force things to bend to my will or to my way of thinking. I acknowledge that change is as much a part of my life as you are. I choose to live a well-lived life and hope I have been a good role model.

Is There Anything I Would Have Done Differently?

"Yes ..." is the very easiest of answers. "Yes" probably should be in all caps, preceded by an outcry, and followed by at least three exclamation points as in "OMG, YES!!!" (**Dad Note:** Putting the letters in **bold** would have been too obvious and over the top, right?)

In no particular order, I would have:

-   Not eaten so many cookies in the middle of the night. (**Dad Note:** Another too obvious one, right?) The math is downright scary. Six per night over the last thirty years amounts to 65,700 cookies consumed. That might possibly be a low number and doesn't factor in leap years. I am depressed just thinking about it. Thankfully, I don't eat cookies because I am depressed or that number would skyrocket. By the way, Nabisco executives and shareholders, you're welcome.
-   Walked more often. How could I have not fit in twenty minutes each day to walk a mile? Over a thirty-year period, I would have walked nearly 11,000 miles—the equivalent of walking from our house in Rhode Island to the Grand Canyon and back twice. I certainly would have burned off a few more of those cookie calories presently residing around my waist.
-   Always stretched before exercising. When I was young, it seemed like a waste of time. "Let's play" was my motto. Let me tell you from the bottom of my heart and every other aching muscle, the recovery time from soreness to normal adds a week with every decade. In your teens, a strained anything will hurt for a few hours, maybe days, but you played anyway. In your twenties, it is one week, two max if it's serious. In your thirties, it's two weeks. By the time you get to your fifties, you're entering the "fuhgeddaboudit" stage

of recovery. Same principles apply to sprains, breaks, and tears on any other part of your body. (**Dad Note:** These are medical facts. I would have presented clinical evidence except that I sprained my dialing finger while eating cookies last night.)

- Gone to more music concerts, especially classical ones. I don't really know why, but I wish I had. I have attended a lot of concerts. Your mom can attest to this fact since I annoyingly point out which groups I have seen live whenever a song of theirs comes on the radio or shuffled from a playlist. Unlike eating too much ice cream, I think your brain, via your ears, can handle way more input than your stomach can, via your mouth. I love listening to music and listening to music at a concert isn't just about the music, it's about the experience. Each experience forms a memory and good memories are the only thing you take with you into heaven according to my mom. Whether you believe that or not is irrelevant. The point is that I may have improved my life by accumulating more positive feelings from additional events and encounters. I am not a religious scholar. I don't know if memories travel with your spirit through the membrane that is Saint Peter's gates. I am not a scientific scholar, so I don't know how chemically stored messages in your brain get transferred to your soul's MP3 player. Heck, you know I am no scholar of any kind, but I would like to think that my mom was telling me life is about making good memories more than anything else.

- Learned to play cribbage. Everyone in my family plays except me. I really don't know why I didn't want to learn. The games I witnessed always seemed spirited and fun. I guess I got to a point in my life where I was too stubborn to ask someone to teach me. Don't let this happen to you. Participate in family games, as silly as you might think they are, because the fun memories will last you a lifetime— and perhaps beyond.

- Learned to ski and play golf earlier in my life. Skiing, because your mother is sooo much better at it than I am. (**Dad Note:** I'm being petty.) Golfing, because I could have spent more time with my dad. He's a wonderful man and father. He's honest and considerate. He has a lot of friends who like and respect him. He worked hard to support his family. He also has a terrible singing voice and an even terribler sense of humor. He's full of quirky and annoying ways, but he's the only dad I have.

- Tried harder at ice-skating. (**Dad Note:** Actually, I take it back. I'm cool without this in my skillset.)

- Gone to the doctor/dentist more regularly. I can't really defend myself here. However, it seems like doctors never give you good news. Like most people, I don't like hearing bad news. Also, in my warped way of looking at things, I figure if you have any level of pain in your life it means you're still alive. I can deal with living; I'm still working on the getting-used-to-dying-someday part of my life.

- Studied and mastered Spanish. Instead I had three years of high school French. French was the "in" foreign language when I was in high school. And with a last name ending in "-eau," I don't think I had much of a choice.

- Acted on my instincts and bought stock in Google, Priceline, and Netflix in 2004 when I first started tracking them. The $30,000 I would have invested then would be worth more than $1,000,000. Sorry about the hit to your inheritance. Before you curse me, take a deep breath, think good thoughts, and remember how much fun we had when you were young. (**Dad Note:** You're still thinking about the $1,000,000, right?)

- Liked to have better relationships with each of you. There is a wide and blurry line between being your parent and being your friend. **Being your dad is the greatest present God ever gave me.** Unfortunately, the present didn't come with an instruction manual. (**Dad Note:** Not that I would have read it anyway.) When you were young, I was very protective of you. I didn't want you near harmful things or to be in harmful situations. I would do anything to keep you safe. I imagine all parents are like that. As you got older, I didn't realize my role as your father was supposed to evolve. I didn't know I should let you experience some of the things I tried to protect you from. It was difficult because there isn't an expiration date on the youthful phase of your life. It's more difficult because skinned knees became broken hearts and skateboarding accidents became car accidents at an indistinct lightning-quick pace right in front of me and I didn't notice the transformation. It is most difficult because I'm just not wired to let go. Fortunately for me, I'm going to try. Fortunately for you, I will never be too far if you ever need your protector dad.

I want you to grow up healthy and unscathed by the physical ailments I have had. I want you to grow up to be well-liked and able to handle all social situations, something which I wasn't able to do early on in my life. I want you to deal with success and loss with equal grace, something I still struggle with daily. I want you to be successful in whatever field you choose and not meet with the doubts I had in my business career(s). I guess I want you not to experience pain as I had or at least deal with it better than I did. However, pain is part of life just as joy is. I once read that in order to truly appreciate light, you must experience darkness. I think there is some truth to that, but please, for my sake, stay out of too many dark spaces.

Is There Anything I Would Have Changed If I Could Have?

This seems like an easier question than asking if I would have done things differently. Doing things differently implies a concerted effort on my part to commit to a process that might have altered my path in life. Some of those I just answered. But, if a genie appeared before me and offered to grant me a wish to change anything in my past, what would I choose to alter? From any angle, I would pass on the opportunity and not change a thing. It may seem like a sappy answer, and it might shock the genie, but

"Not one thing" would be my reply, lock it in, final answer. **Knowing what I know now, I am 100% positive I wouldn't have done things any differently if there was any infinitesimal chance I wouldn't have you in my life.** I figure, for as long I am given the chance to plant daisies rather than push them up, I have the opportunity to change things every day on a go-forward path only.

In My Humble Opinion

Yes, I have regrets and there are a few things I would/could/should have done differently. But to wonder or worry about what might be if I had done something else is wasted energy. Well, not entirely wasted—it is fun to consider what might have been had I done something else, but I don't dwell on it or let it control my life; I would be paralyzed by procrastination if I did.

If you really want to know if there is anything you would have changed from your youth, wait until time travel is invented. I'm sure the technology to transport through time will be an app on your smartphone in the near future. Until then, change the things you want to change, accept the things you cannot, and pray for wisdom to know the difference. If you are destined for greatness on a large scale and can make strides on issues plaguing mankind, then use all of your powers of good to help make a better world. If your life is destined to be simpler like mine is, choose to make your own life and those whom you love better for you being a part of it. I know if I make someone else feel appreciated, comforted, smart, or improved for having met me, then I know I have played my minor part in making the world a better place to live. Most people tend to magnify their own importance or position and think they are a whole lot more substantial and necessary to a larger social fabric. I realize I am but a single woven thread in that fabric. I am important to the overall effect, but nothing singled out for significance. And honestly, I am "collector car" cool with that.

Section 2

INTIMATE AND OTHER RELATIONSHIPS

A relationship is easy to identify and define. It is a connection from one living thing/person to another living thing/person. An inanimate object can provide comfort and support, but you can't form a relationship with it—not a healthy one, not a reciprocal one. It takes at least two carbon-based forms to tango, tangle, or tie.

Relationships can occur naturally, like between you and your mom when you were born. They can develop symbiotically as we've seen on reefs between algae and coral. They can happen for mutual benefit, like between you and your employer.

Relationships can ensue out of respect, from fear, and for profit. They can result intuitively, innately, and instinctively. They can emerge to provide assistance, by force, and for use. Relationships can materialize through weak links and strong bonds; they take root in many forms along the temperamental and emotional spectrum of love.

Though I stated a relationship is easy to define, I found it difficult to differentiate the stages and levels of a relationship. I tried to come up with a couple of clever anecdotes or references to illustrate my point. My analogy of a relationship and a person applauding was inadequate. Sure, a relationship needs at least two parties like the sound of clapping needs two hands, but those same hands may not work in tandem to produce the desired effect or can remain silent if they have different goals. I then recalled a jokey quote by Ben Franklin to express the intimacy of a relationship but thought "three may keep a secret if two of them are dead" was not the angle I was aiming for. I decided relationships fall into the murky, circumscribed category of "I know it when I see it."

For better or worse, richer or poorer, and in sickness and in health, relationships are connections. An intimate relationship resides at a higher level; it involves trust, respect, commitment, and most often love. To form bonds enhanced by mutual esteem/regard and fueled on faith is my "X marks the spot treasure." And if I am indeed fortunate enough, there will be lots of Xs in tandem with lots of Os.

It is my opinion that the world would be a better place if people spent more time cultivating and maintaining intimate relationships. Too often we stand on the edge of the beach afraid of the water or worrying about getting sand between our toes. Have confidence in being a bit unsure of the temperature or what lies beneath your own vulnerability. There is risk, but the prize is the best feeling you can imagine.

LOVE

Before I offer enlightened rhetoric, educated opinion, or a thought-provoking body of evidence, let me say this: Love is soup.

Before you assume a spellcheck function rearranged my words, before you assume you misread my three-word statement, or before you ask a doctor to evaluate my mental health, allow me to restate: Love is soup.

Before you presuppose every word under the chapter title "Love" is dad-discerned crap, before you deny them three times as less than spiritual claptrap, before you imagine each thought is dad-garbled from the two marbles slothfully bounding against the cobwebbed corners of my brain, and before your suspicion about my diminished intellectual acuity is finally confirmed, I declare: Love is soup. Love is soup. Love is soup.

LOVE IS SOUP. LOVE IS SOUP. LOVE IS SOUP.

I am joyful and comforted having voiced it (okay, written it) repeatedly. I am centered and so exuberant I highlighted my breakthrough in bold and in all caps. (**Dad Note:** Please notice I didn't underline it, increase the size, change the font, or add an exclamation point; those modifications would have been excessive even by my low standards of what constitutes actual hyperbole.)

Before Before

Before I explain why love is soup, I'd like to share my winding, specious, and tangential journey towards my revelation so hang in there until the end of the chapter. I promise if my explanation doesn't make sense by then, I'll go willingly with the nice men in white coats whom you send to collect me.

I figured I must already know what love is because a) I am married, and b) I have children who adore me. I also assumed that since I grew up within a loving family, I must know what love is and what it is to be loved. I will examine my own relationships for answers.

I have read extensively, though not specifically, about love. Your mother seems to rip through romance-y books like I do a food buffet. Not the salad bar part, but the sizzling chicken, spicy side dishes, or carved meats section. I must have read somewhere, something about love.

Within the thousands of songs I have listened to, specifically and repeatedly, the word "love" is in the lyrics. Therefore, and mostly by osmosis, I must have retained detailed insight about love.

I have watched a lot of movies and television shows and not all of them featured a superhero with a special ability, a hero who defends or corrects injustices, or an anti-hero who fights an oppressive, wayward system. I am sure—well, at least I am pretty sure—I have seen a romantic film that doesn't contain violence. (**Dad Note to Self:** Furtively, slyly, and covertly ask my wife if I have actually watched, and not slept through, a movie about love.)

When I was younger, I wrote poetry and short stories. I still write short stories from time to time, but I gave up writing poetry when I couldn't find a word to rhyme with "orange." Kidding aside, I have even tried/attempted to write a sweet-ish country song called "Forty Candles, But Just One Flame." I must have written something in one of my speckled notebooks about love.

Mostly and mainly, I enjoy posing questions to myself for late-night contemplation. Reasoning deductively, inductively but somewhat unsystematically about ideas significantly above my mental paygrade makes me feel like I can justify my midnight snack runs to the kitchen. It makes sense I should start here; I am confident I have ascertained some notion of love. (**Dad Note:** Okay, I admit it. It is the middle of the night, and those cookies aren't going to eat themselves.) However, I do believe notions and ideas about love from my relationships, from what I have seen on a screen, from what I have listened to or written about will present themselves with a bit of mental elbow grease.

In my attempt to educate and entertain you, I have reminded myself of the numerous, weighty issues I have contemplated throughout my lifetime.

- Is there life after death?
- Why does the couple on the next street always buy matching cars?
- Do things really happen for a reason?
- What is the best advice I ever received?
- What is love?
- Which really did come first, the chicken or the egg?
- How would I describe a "perfect day" for me? (**Dad Note and Zen Koan Corollary:** Is your mother's "perfect day" the same as mine? Further, does hers even include me?)
- Is there ever an appropriate time to say "I told you so?"

The answers I have discovered/uncovered and the opinions I have formed are the basis for this book. Guesses, presumptions, and discernments never occurred quickly; I solved nothing in a single sleepless night or after consuming a solitary sleeve of cookies, or even during a lengthy, multi-state car ride in my convertible. The one thing I have learned is that solutions, views, and estimations—especially for grand observations—take time to acquire, and even then there's no guarantee my reasoned affirmations will ever reach the top shelf of grandness. I may never fully solve or even conceptualize some of the questions I ask my two brain marbles to contemplate, but I do try and usually produce a workable theory. By the widest of margins of my dad-induced errors, the dumbest, the most nearly unworkable question I ever asked myself was "What is love?" To alleviate the pressure on my agitated brain agates of developing a comprehensive answer to such a cumbersome conundrum, I have reposed and repositioned the question often and in many ways. Here's an example of some notes I jotted and/or remembered from a contemplative post-midnight session a few years ago.

- What's love really got to do with it?
- Is love really like oxygen? (**Dad Note to Self:** I'm thinking it's more like nitrogen.)
- Seriously, why can't I help falling in love with you? (**Dad Note to Self:** Really dumb question.)
- Will love really keep us together? (**Dad Note to Self:** Love is really more like glue than oxygen.)
- Love will find a way. (**Dad Note to Self:** Really? Love has a navigation app?)
- Do I really give love a bad name? (**Dad Note to Self:** Never ask a question if you can't cope with an honest answer.)
- I'm not really sure there are fifty ways to leave your lover. (**Dad Note to Self:** I've been broken up with at least that many.)
- Does anyone really think all you need is love? (**Dad Note to Self:** What about soup? What about nitrogen? Where's my Love Shack?)

Usually, the following morning, my petri dish musings wither under the sensible-but-not-so-intensible light of day microscope. I realize my big-picture reflections of the meaning of love were not as pondered as I had expected. The tangents and offshoots of the question "What is love?" were neither entirely helpful nor revealing. Plus, on that night, my thoughts were heavily influenced because I had been listening to my "All You Need Is Love" playlist. It was also very middle-of-the-night evident that I am really, really, really prone to hyperbole and even more obvious that "I love rock 'n' roll, always ready to put another dime in the jukebox" for all kinds of music. (**Dad Note:** It's a paraphrased lyric from Joan Jett's song "I Love

Rock 'n' Roll." I sense you knew that because I played it loudly during your youth, but you have no idea what a dime is or what a jukebox is and why you would put one into the other. Well, to answer your small, picturesque questions, go do an internet search. I'm busy with soup, with love, and I get too easily distracted.)

I mentioned previously that the one thing I have learned is that solutions, views, and estimations—especially for grand observations—take time to acquire. I actually learned two things. After I puzzled and puzzled 'til my puzzler was sore, I am grateful I don't get headaches. Nights of deliberate assessment of "What is love?" and other equally game-changing but brain-draining personal queries have compelled me to offer compassion to all of you headache sufferers. (**Dad Note:** Is it so unbelievable I've never had a headache? Oh, it's not that. You can't believe I can be, or have ever been, compassionate.)

With my mastery of light-hearted mockery and barely veiled contempt for stupidity, I'll admit the notion that I can be considerate and caring can be difficult to grasp. I'll also admit my human interactive conversational history is bursting with the salt-rubbed wounds of sarcasm; however, and surprisingly, I can be compassionate.

Perhaps I am not kind, caring, or gentle, et cetera—sometimes. But I am bona fide sensitive to the concerns of others—sometimes. **Compassion is a virtuous feeling of mercy. It is a desire to help or improve the status quo of another's condition**. I am willing to do this ad infinitum. Ipso facto, I am as ad hoc compassionate as anyone else. Not only did I score pretty well on the National Latin Exam, but I am also sympathetic, and I am empathetic.

To prove my point and display advanced knowledge besides my fixation on a dead language, I know that sympathy and empathy are two forms of compassion.

Sympathy is a shared feeling, usually between a person who has experienced what someone else is experiencing presently. It is commonly associated with grief, disappointment, or distress. When sympathy or compassion is expressed, it is intended to bond as a confirmation of support in an

I-know-what-you're-going-through way. For example, I can be compassionate and sympathetic towards a person who has suffered the loss of a family member to cancer because it's happened to me. I can sympathize with a candidate rejected for a job they really wanted. I sympathize with the anxious person moving far from a place they've called home for most of their life. I am sympathetic to the nervousness and unease surrounding "Big Day" good events like graduation, the first day at a new job, a first and/or blind date, or a wedding ceremony. I feel sympathy also for Big Day dubious events like being called into the principal's office or getting a whopping speeding ticket.

Empathy goes further, and a bit sideways, in the sense that it stems from the attempt to place oneself in the position of the affected party. For example, I can only try to empathize with someone agonizing over the loss of a loved one in a manner I have not experienced, like when a high school classmate of mine was killed in the Twin Towers terrorist attack on September 11, 2001. I cried the whole time while I wrote a letter to his parents to express my condolences. I sympathized with their loss but could only imagine what they went through. Also, I am empathetic for the person dealing with life-altering addictions, mental illness, or depression. Daily, I count my blessing and say prayers for them and the families challenged, anguished, and suffering.

Brain Pain

However, and to a much lesser degree and manner of compassion, I feel bad for those of you who get headaches. But much like the some-to-none compassion I have for the bug I am about to squish, I cannot be sympathetic because I've never had one and I refuse to be empathetic by imagining trading places with a headache sufferer or the death-sentenced insect. (**Dad Note:** While I never shared your fear of creepy-crawlies, I was considerate of your feelings. I was kind and tolerant when you asked me why I didn't set the insect free instead of crushing it under the sole of my size 14 shoes or pinching it in a paper towel.)

While I have some-to-none compassion for an errant insect scouting for food, a mate, or better digs, I do have it for two groups of people: anyone who gets headaches and anyone who has tried to explain what love is. Not surprisingly, the two groups are not mutually exclusive; plus, contemplating an explanation of love certainly increases the odds of joining the community of cranium sufferers.

I researched headaches recently. Yikes! My exploration indicated I would prefer to trade places with an about-to-be squished bug before inviting an incapacitating sensation into my head. Every indication is that they are difficult to bear. Even the onomatopoetic synonyms and adjectives to describe them are harsh sounding: throbbing neuralgia, piercing megrim, crushing hemicrania, pounding migraine, bilious headache. (**Dad Note:** Who the heck was in charge of naming rights for headaches? Jack the Ripper? Vlad the Impaler? Cruella de Vil?) It is estimated that 95% of humans experience headaches. With a world population of 7.8 billion people, that means nearly 7.41 billion currently have or have had a headache—ouch! Fortunately, I exist pain-free in the 5% minority of non-sufferers. Coincidentally, I also reside in another unique minority community: I am left-handed. Only 10% of us on the planet are. Concentrically to the two clusters, it's me and a (left) handful of others worldwide who are sinisterly dexterous and not ever vexed in the head. The odds grow exponentially infinitesimal when you add another category to the mix: dads who are truly funny. Essentially, I am one of a kind!

Pounding and painful, but like giving birth or being good at ice skating, I have no experience. I've never popped a pill for relief of pain between my temples or sat in a dark room to dismiss a disorienting discomfort. From my no-familiarity perspective, you become very un-you. I am fairly confident there are times when you and some/most of my friends wish I would/could be "un-me." If I could transform and become un-me—or at least less me—it wouldn't be because of an ache in my head. Actually, if you had paid any attention to my life, you would know I don't like to take medication for any ailment. I can count on one hand the number of pain relief pills I have placed in the other hand to put in my mouth to help my body. In my non-sequitur brain, pain is a feeling; if I feel, I am alive. However, headaches must really suck and might alter my zero pill-popping policy.

Love Is ... ?

So, here are some facts you may have overlooked or not known about your dear old dad. (**Dad Note:** Emphasis should be on "dear," not "old.")

- I know what compassion is.
- I can conjugate verbs and decline nouns in Latin.
- I feel empathy and sympathy.
- I have squished a lot of bugs so you didn't have to.

Ergo, it must be agreed that I am sensitive, and I have feelings. Another lesser-known fact about me you may have been unaware of: I sense and will express troubled sadness for any chump, idiot, or poor sap who has contemplated AND then tried to explain the meaning of love. (**Dad Note to Self:** Sensitivity awareness and demonstrations of kindness may need to be revisited.)

The sheer number of dupes—I mean people—who have devoted time to this subject is mind-boggling. Low-brow, low-level theorists like Beavis and/or Butthead, Homer Simpson, and I have tried. Higher-brow, multi-level thinkers like Socrates, Shakespeare, Taylor Swift, and Valentine's Day greeting-card writers have endeavored as well. A staggering number of IQ points from all sides have been exhausted to explain what love is. For hundreds of years, thousands have tried and written millions of pages about an unfathomable and infinitely suspect subject. Based on the heart-and-soul commitment to the issue of love, two suppositions can be easily assumed. It is either:

- important for the heart and soul of a person forging an intimate relationship, or
- philosophers, theorists, and guys like me are suckers.

Until I learned that love is soup, I did not fully grasp what love is. I tried to conceptualize, to describe, and to explain. I tried to neatly package my thoughts and feelings into words. I theorized and tested. I failed. Not so much failed, but I kept returning to near square one in the process.

- Is it passion? Is it friendship? Is it affection, adoration, devotion, or worship?
- Can I express a sensation I cannot properly describe, label the combined action/reaction of an emotion, and define its value?
- Further, I know and sense I am loved, but am I repaying it equivalently?

Before my "love equals soup" epiphany, I had more questions about it than answers. I barely felt confident explaining what little I did know. But I am your dad and willing knight-errant. I should do my best to explain what love is. As Don Quixote jousted windmills, I am duty-bound to unsheathe my less than sharp intelligence to battle mysterious, ethereal concepts. The Man of La Mancha was resilient; he was beaten and suffered head trauma. With all of my other saddling faults, at least no mind-numbing migraines will slow me on my journey. I will expose what love is, and further, I will reveal what it is to be truly loved. Commencing my quest, I dream the impossible dream.

I Forgot How Much a Hand Cramp Hurts

My vision was grand, but it needed a plan. I thought about a binge-watching marathon of romantic comedies; I even dared to consider viewing the myriad of syrupy sweet Hallmark Channel movies Mom has recorded and saved on our cable DVR list. (**Dad Note:** There is no anger/derision/ disdain in my tone. Mom loves watching predictably patterned, everyone-can-see-you-two-belong-together-so-it-all-works-out-in-the-end two-hour romance films. She says they make her feel good. I, on the other hand, have recorded an overabundance of I-already-know-the-final-score-but-I-will-watch-it-again-and-again Manchester United matches. Like Mom, it makes me feel good to watch them again.)

I contemplated revisiting a romantic novel or book I had read to understand love but remembered I hadn't even perused one unless I count *Frankenstein* or *Gone with the Wind* as love stories. I considered rereading poems and stories I had written previously in hopes that I had stumbled across the meaning of love in my youth. I decided against it. I might have depressed myself exposing how young and dumb I was. I considered sourcing information online but presumed it would be cheating. Instead, I found a stack of index cards left over from your middle school and high school days. If you don't remember, stacks of them sit on a shelf next to half-filled orange-capped white glue plastic bottles, hundreds of half-used magic markers, and thousands of half-sharpened No. 2 pencils. With my own pen, I wrote the word "LOVE" on the first line of a bunch of them. I printed in all capital letters to signify the importance of my mission. Relying on my own wits and effort, I decided to freely associate three to five thoughts per card. I would write/scribble under the heading "LOVE" any words, ideas, phrases, song lyrics, movie quotes, and names as they flowed from my head through the ink in the pen.

I was certain this was the perfect genesis for my mission. As certain as a broken clock is right twice per day, this was flawless. I thought, *This is going to be easy.*

I wrote "my children" on one card. I wrote Mom's name on another. Then I wrote each of your names on separate cards. It took some time and thought. Then I printed the names of close family members, both those still with us and those who have passed away. I paused before I grabbed a second stack of index cards to decide if the names of friends should be included. I asked myself, *Do I love them or just really, really like them?* I scribbled a bunch of friends' names; I figured the feeling of "like" is in the spectrum of "love" and if I've made a mistake, I'll remove the card. I mean, really, which one of my friends is gonna know whether or not they made my "People and Things I Love" list?

I moved on from my dilemma. I added teams, items, objects, ideas, and things I loved. Not surprisingly, next were:

- The Boston Red Sox, but especially the 2004 team. In 2003 I cried tears, the saddest tears, when "we" lost to the New York Yankees in the ALCS. In 2004, I cried most wonderfully when "we" finally beat the Yankees and eventually won the World Series. To win four straight playoff games against the Yankees when "we" were down three games to none in a seven-game series should be all the evidence any one doubter needs to prove there is a God. Well, at least a God who finally favored New England.

- The 1985-1986 Boston Celtics. Along with the 2004 Boston Red Sox, this is my all-time favorite professional sports team with a 40-1 home record. The squad featured five players who would be inducted into the Hall of Fame. I even have a basketball signed by each member of the team. The only negative associated with this memory is that the Celtics didn't get the chance to beat the Los Angeles Lakers in the NBA Finals because they were beaten by the Houston Rockets.

- A half-pound+, hand-made, medium-rare cheeseburger on a lightly toasted, buttery brioche bun. Add lettuce (iceberg or romaine), a thick slice of tomato, and seasoning from my private stash of dry rubs. Hold the pickles, onions, and don't let ketchup, mustard, or relish within a half-mile of my burger. And yes, I'll have fries. Not the side salad, not the fresh fruit alternative, but the fries.

- A cast iron seared, evenly smoked, droolingly buttery, fire-kissed rare ribeye steak. With this meal, I would like a side salad, but Mom's bacon and egg spinach salad with the lemony homemade dressing. Fries would be a good addition here as well.

(**Dad Note:** It took seven full index cards to complete these first four entries. I admonished myself for my protracted daydreaming. I smiled, but my hand hurt from writing. As I wiped the drool from my chin I said, "Concentrate, Anthony!" I decided to be less specific or else I would hyper-focus on sporting moments or favorite foods. I'd accomplish nothing because I would head to the television to re-watch those games or head outside onto our deck to warm up my grill and/or smoker.)

I continued.

- Manchester United, including but not limited to, Eric Cantona's majestic disdainful stare towards an opponent, his iconic turned-up collar as he doubles down on his disdainful stare, his poignant-in-any-language quotes, and his kung fu kick. A pinpoint perfect Paul Scholes long pass, a yellow card tackle by Scholesy, you beauty of a ginger ninja. The songs and the chants about the club and players. The splendor of Old Trafford. The '99 Treble Winners. "Ole, get in!!!" Sir Alex Ferguson, the wonderment of scoring a game-winning goal during never-ending "Fergie Time."

- I love the memory of mid-autumn sunsets I watched from the patio of my parents' home on Narragansett Bay. As the sun would disappear, the sky became an illumined natural canvas splashed with intense purples, vivid pinks, and dazzling burnt orange streaks. The contrast looked like the colors had been shot upward from a canon packed with found-only-in-nature colors. The memory is enhanced and the "love" factor increased as I remember the accompanying sound of hissless, popless, and sweeter-than-sweet music coming from a favorite, never-been-touched-by-human-hands, vinyl-pressed recording of the album *Francis A. & Edward K.* floating from the stereo in my old room. The recollection reminds me that I am grateful for my eyes, my ears, and that there is a God in heaven who appreciates a just-dipped-over-the-horizon sun and the sounds of Frank Sinatra and Duke Ellington.

Four more index cards later, I reminded myself, *For the sake of your cramping hand, focus, Anthony!!!*

Expeditiously and more succinctly, I continued again with a list of what I love.

- The number two
- An exceptionally tasty and potent double IPA
- A great, evenly burning cigar
- Playing baseball
- Drinking beer with my softball teammates, though not necessarily playing softball with them
- Using my smoker
- Eating meat I have smoked
- I love our dogs, Cinder and Rooney
- My 1965 Ford Mustang convertible

I continued to write furiously. I added other free-form thoughts and ideas related to love. As quickly as I harvested them from the manured loam inside my head, I hurled them at index cards like lobbing paint against a pristine wall.

- "Love is Strong," a Rolling Stones song
- Spending the Fourth of July with family
- Love is passion, fondness, tenderness, affection, friendship …
- Love is blind?
- The Feast of the Seven Fishes on Christmas Eve
- The feeling I get each time I twist my wedding ring around my finger.
- Love can destroy like Thor's hammer.
- Love can connect emotions like an Erector Set.
- Love is also a comic strip (*Love Is* …) and a television series (*Love Is* _____).

- *The Love Boat* was another television series from the late 1970s to the mid-1980s.
- Love makes me smile. Love can make me cry.

There were some others, but they were scattered like comets across the vacuum of the universe. My hand began to throb psychosomatically. The thoughts swirled in my head, increasing in a backlog. I have no filter when I speak or think, but my darned pen dammed up the words fomenting in my brain. I paused before the ideas gushed over the barrier. I took a deep breath and remembered a line I had written down years ago in one of my many notebooks and wrote it on an index card.

"One word frees us of all the weight and pain of life. That word is love."

About 2500 years ago, Sophocles, the Greek tragic dramatist, presumably said these exact words, though presumably not in English. I was pleased to have recalled such a beautiful quote. I was calm. I was centered. However, suddenly, my brain shifted back to the storm. The hand-cramped dam broke, and the charming moment passed. My brain fast-forwarded a couple of thousand years and "Love is Like Oxygen" by Sweet and the movie *Love Actually* came racing ahead of my mind's other music flotsam and movie jetsam. I wrote furiously, and messily, for the next fifteen minutes.

I reviewed thirty-two index cards. I could easily read and track my thought processes on twenty-two of them; the remaining pieces of paper needed a forensic audit for legibility. Eventually, I reached a few conclusions.

- I noticed that I easily named people and things I love. Some were incredibly easy to recognize as most dear to me. While I couldn't rank all of them, I recognized the commonality of positive emotion. Each input made me feel good; therefore, love must be a feeling.
- The words I read affected me in varying degrees. I loved some things more than others. The levels of the feeling indicated depth.

- Love is based on factors. It is composed of emotions, thoughts, and reactions, not a single feeling.
- I enjoyed the sensation of recollecting the positive. It made me happy. If I want to be happy, it is necessary to involve, surround, and connect myself to more love.
- Love is a level of commitment past the stage of "like." I can walk away from like. It's not so easy to untether from love.

(**Dad Note:** I had made progress, but I wasn't entirely satisfied with my discoveries. I felt stuck somewhere between dime-store philosophy and senior thesis. I was convinced there was more to love than I had surmised so far, more hidden treasure to expose to the light of day. I doggedly pressed on.)

Am I A Hoarder?

Not one to quit so easily, I changed tack slightly. I decided my quest required a more scientific approach—I should examine what others have said about love. I put down my pen, rubbed my aching hand, and sat quietly in my comfy chair. I took a deep breath and mentally climbed into the scattered, rusty-dusty attic in my brain. It is a wonderfully lusty library of songs I have heard, books I have read, and negligible facts I have retained. It exists veritably recessed but hardly repressed. It is my private and astonishing stash of insignificant and marginal knowledge. If I correctly choose the precise synapse pattern, delightful data gems are instantly available.

Your mother would describe my brain differently. I can visualize her mouthing the words "crappy cesspool," "abominable garbage heap" or, my favorite, "hoarded trivia wasteland." Whether treasure trove or rubbish collection, my debatable knowledge rests like coins hidden under couch cushions, a lot of good stuff is buried between my ears.

I'll Take Song Titles For $200 Please, Alex

Music is a good place to start. I scanned the RAM and ROM storage parts of my mind for locked-away lyrics and/or song titles. It's the busiest of a pretty busy section. They reside alongside the TV Show Trivia Knowledge, Sports Statistics, and Notable Movie Quotes. These four sections take up so much space inside my head it's too bad it isn't print-ready or in a down-loadable format here in this document-free library! To begin, my brain queued an initial playlist with "love" in the titles.

- "Love Shack" by The B-52s (descriptive adjective)
- "Love Machine" by The Miracles (descriptive adjective)
- "Lovely Rita" by The Beatles (form of the word as a descriptive adjective)
- "Love Spreads" by The Stone Roses (noun)
- "Love Stinks" by J. Geils Band (noun)
- "Love You 'Till the End" by The Pogues (verb)
- "I Love Rock 'n' Roll" by Joan Jett and the Blackhearts (verb)

(**Dad Note:** Hmmm … I don't know what was being revealed about the concept of love by my first selections, but "Love Shack" was a splendid choice to start because it was one of two songs Mom and I chose for our solo dance at our wedding. The other was "December, 1963 (Oh, What a Night)" by the Four Seasons. It would be a safe bet in the history of all wedding receptions ever that no other newly married couple has chosen those two songs as their starter set statement of their eternal devotion to each other. **Further Dad Note:** My sub-chapter title reference was a nifty tip of my pen cap to Alex Trebek, the long-time television host of *Jeopardy*. He was still alive when I first wrote the clever tribute line, "I'll take song titles for $200 please, Alex." He has since passed away from pancreatic cancer, the same disease my mom died from. She handled her final days with effusive love and dignity, and he appeared to do the same. R.I.P. Mr. Trebek.)

From the song titles, I noticed love can modify as an adjective and be modified to produce other adjectives. It is a noun. It is a verb. I also summoned other songs where love is a crazy little thing, a many splendored thing, a battlefield, a street, and a train. It walks in, is strong, will keep you together, and loves L.A. Love is a busy word. ☹

My mind wandered to a favored music library list in my head: 90s Alternative Music. My head began to rock, bob, and thump. Thank goodness there is no head Head Librarian here to shush me or tell me to turn down the volume because it's getting loud in here. "Sabotage" by Beastie Boys, "Bullet with Butterfly Wings" by The Smashing Pumpkins, and "Cumbersome" by Seven Mary Three soon drowned out any lingering song notes of the love-titled first few. I knew there was nothing insightful to rely on, but I remembered how much I love alternative music. I sat there for a few moments imagining deep bass and thrashing nearly discordant sounds. I thought to myself, *How is it possible you've never had a headache with all of this noise up here?*

Getting back on track I accessed songs with heavy doses of the word "love" in the lyrics. I listened to "Hawkmoon 269" in my head. It's one of my favorite U2 songs. Lead singer Bono passionately and repeatedly states at the end of each verse he needs love. As I hummed and sang the tune, I noticed a bunch of similes and metaphors for how badly he needs it, but no mention of what it is even though he sings the word "love" at least fifty times. ☹

I searched specific genres: Soft/Light Rock, Adult Contemporary, and Country. I pressed play on my brain's MP3 player to hear random selections from the first two categories. A slow ballad song by Foreigner, "I Want to Know What Love Is," started. I fell asleep in my own head thinking, *Yeah, well, so do I.* ☹

I awoke from my inner cranium catnap to hear "Achy Breaky Heart" by Billy Ray Cyrus. In my mind's eye I pictured mullet-coiffed Billy Ray twanging, "Don't tell my heart, my achy-breaky heart." I chastised myself. I thought, *Really, this selection? That's the best song you can come up with and he doesn't even mention the word love?* To this day I still don't know what an achy breaky heart is, but kudos to 90s country music icon and denim dude BRC for staying relevant in my head all these years. ☺

(**Dad Note:** This exercise was helping a little. It also reminded me I should definitely update and edit my Spotify library and my iPod. ☺)

The Correct Response Was "Romantic Comedies"

I shuffled over to the Movies and Notable Movie Quotes section of my brain. I scanned for lines denoting romance. I recalled one of Humphrey Bogart's famous lines from a favorite movie, *Casablanca*: "Here's looking at you, kid." It indicated admiration and playfulness but put me no closer to explaining love. Next, Jimmy Stewart spoke to me as George Bailey in *It's a Wonderful Life*: "What is it you want, Mary? What do you want? You, you want the moon? Just say the word and I'll throw a lasso around it and pull it down." The line had depth and promise, but I searched further. I found Hugh Grant's opening remark in *Love Actually*: "If you look for it, I've got a sneaky feeling you'll find that love actually is all around." I gave that some thought in the context of my quest. *If love is all around, then why isn't it easy to define?* I mean, the sky is all around and if you asked me to describe it, I could. I might not get the technical meteorological terms correct, but I could tell you its color, its sounds, and probably make a good guess as to what it will do next. I am not sure I can be so precise in describing love, even though Hugh Grant tells me it is supposedly all around.

Perhaps my own ignorance stumbled upon something. I cannot discern exactly what love is. I think I recognize it, but perhaps love is a definitive non-definable thing. It's like standing in the dark on a beach at midnight and being enveloped by a warm breeze on a cold night. I don't know where the warmth came from specifically, but I am sure glad it's around me because why the heck am I standing here wearing only a swimsuit? Further, love is personal in nature. A person standing next to me on that same beach might have a different sensation of the same and sudden change in temperature. They might be wearing more clothing and possibly not even notice or enjoy what I am experiencing.

I headed off towards the peculiarly retained aisles within my head: Books, Television Series, and Trivia. Like the rest of this attic in my brain, the shelves here are overflowing with randomly spoken and seldom-used knowledge. There's not much wisdom concerning love that I can recall in the Books section. I have read a lot of books, but nothing exceptional comes to mind. Literally, I cannot recall literary works concerning the topic of love I have read. Sure, there are Shakespearean couples, like Romeo and Juliet and Rosalind and Orlando, who should merit attention. However, I don't remember any of the great lines. Besides, if the book was good, it probably was made into a movie like *The Hunt for Red October* by Tom Clancy and *Christine* by horror/suspense god, Stephen King. If so, it's already cataloged in another part of my head.

Moving on to Television Series proved as fruitless. There were TV shows depicting couples in love, but I never watched them. I do remember some characters from the soap opera, *Days of Our Lives*. I sometimes watched it while eating lunch at my grandmother's house. But love only seemed to be interchangeable as the characters were with a different partner every time I visited. By my own choice, *Moonlighting* with Cybill Shepherd and Bruce Willis was as close as I came to a show I watched with romance in it, but supposedly they didn't like each other in real life so I moved on. ☹

The Trivia section was packed to overflowing. It sits there messily waiting to be used as a game show lifeline answer or non-sequitur addition to a conversation/argument after a few beers. (**Dad Note to Self:** Tidy up the Trivia segment of the cranium library; it's messier than my kids' rooms when they were teenagers!)

God Is Love

As I ventured toward another aisle where the Religious Education Files were stored, I made a zig-zagged pit stop into Cool Monologue Speeches.

There in my mind's eye, I could imagine Alec Baldwin as smarmy super salesman Blake admonishing a group of real estate agents in a meeting scene from *Glengarry Glen Ross*: "Put that coffee down! Coffee is for closers only!" I could almost sense Jack Nicholson's disdain as Colonel Nathan Jessup during a court-martial in *A Few Good Men*: "You can't handle the truth!" I could almost see Mel Gibson in *Braveheart* as William Wallace, passionately inspiring his troops: "I am William Wallace!!!" I smiled but realized none of the quotes helped to explain love, but they did put me in a more positive mood because of the kick-ass dialogue! (**Dad Note:** I further realized for the umpteenth time plus one, that my friends, my family, and especially your mother are correct—my head is filled with crap. ☺)

The Religious Education Files were less crowded, but I have been stockpiling this section lately. It seems natural as I age to contemplate life's meaning, my existence, and the role of spirituality. I was provided a good foundation of rote material early in my life but stuttered adding stuff here while you were growing up. My life revolved around family, work, friends, and not much else. Plus, I had unanswered personal questions about religion and with God. The sector is growing again as I age. I have reread parts of the Bible, read other faith-based texts, and continue to contemplate above-my-pay-grade ethereal concepts.

I located an open-ended, disputable tidbit of religious-philosophical debate: "God is love." Biblical scholars have proposed that God is all-encompassing goodness, therefore God is love. On the surface, the statement seems so obvious and simplistic that I should easily understand it. But with pervasive negativity abound within all social structures, "God is love" is easily contested as well. At my age and though my faith is strong, I feel uncomfortable stating and defending a simple position that "God is love." It suggests a platitude worthy of being a mortar range target for intellectual non-believers. God may indeed be what love is, but I hardly feel comfortable divulging my interpretations of a monotheistic deity as the model for love. Further, God has been identified as "good" and "great" and a heap of other positive adjectives, but I am focused on what love is and being able to explain it to you.

I reached a few more conclusions—or at least hypotheses—about what love is. Deduced and discerned from the piles and piles of files upon files of song titles, music lyrics, movie and television quotes, excessive trivia minutiae, moderate book knowledge, and inadequate work-in-progress spiritual comprehension, I estimate that love is:

- complex. It exists in many formats of the root word.
- viewed differently by context.
- an emotional catalyst.
- acts as the impetus to do something or to make choices.
- both a cause and an effect; it instigates affection.
- seemingly limitless and unconditional, but I have doubts.

Okay, I Cheated!

I climbed down from my mind's dusty old attic. I needed a break. I made a few notes, especially about a serious spring cleaning for the Trivia section. I located a few valuable thoughts up there in my brain's library, but nothing definitive or succinct. I came away with the understanding that love is an emotion comprised of many parts. It is hard to identify, but you know it when you feel it. It has depth and degrees.

I sat at my desk. I had hoped to be typing something laconic and revealing for you, but my fingers didn't move on the keyboard because inspiration remained hidden in my head. Nervously, I fidgeted with the mouse. Since no thoughts were coming to me, I moved the cursor towards a search engine icon. I cheated and went online. With access to billions of bits of information, there must be something I could use. I typed the word "love" into my web browser.

I should have been more precise and much, much more specific; I didn't receive any motivation on the subject I intended, but Google, MSN, and Yahoo offered me many fee-based websites for sexual stimulation and nearly gave my computer a virus. Apparently, all internet service providers know what "love" is, that is, if I want to pay for it. The answers I hoped for remained elusive and now, the concepts to love and to be loved were sullied. In a shameful way I felt kinda dirty, so I headed upstairs to take a second shower for the day. While toweling off, I reminded myself that even if my inquiry was solved by an online search, the list of potentially unverified answers and dubious websites wouldn't be my definition of love. That is the key and remains my goal. Frustrated, I admonished myself. At this point in my life, I should know something. I am in love with your mom, and she loves me. A long time ago, I carved our names on a tree to prove it. Have I learned nothing since then to tell you what it is to love and to be loved?

Love Is a Feeling

Still convinced and confident the answers to what love is were within me, I returned to the mountain of unused index cards to write down more thoughts. I marveled once again at the hundreds of unused lined cards remaining. I pondered skeptically, *No one uses paper. No one writes by hand. Yet, we have so many. Was there a 2-for-1 warehouse sale? As a precautionary measure against nuclear attack, did the federal government warn families to stockpile 5x8 100-pound cardstock?* Most likely, as young students, you conveniently forgot to look for them each time you begged Mom to shop for more. I've seen fewer ants surround a honey-coated picnic basket filled with crumbs and sugar! When I am finished with this chapter, I plan to use the remaining cards to build a replica of the Eiffel Tower—not to scale, but the actual size! (**Note to Future Dad Self:** When I have grandchildren entering middle school, offer the residual index cards. The kids will have to take them, it's part of their inheritance.)

I wrote down specific memories or examples that made me feel good.

- My wedding day
- Watching the Boston Red Sox win the 2004 World Series

- Witnessing childbirth
- Mom's hug when my mother died
- Making the Dean's List in college
- Watching *The Great Mouse Detective*
- Teaching my children how to hit a baseball
- Hitting my first and only Little League home run
- Buying my third Volkswagen Beetle (The red convertible—it is my favorite!)
- Reading my name in the Sports section of the newspaper

These are very good memories. It feels good to remember them. In each instance I felt a positive emotion I would classify as love. Love was shared on my wedding day. It was there in our den when I cried watching my beloved Sox finally win the Series as my eight-year-old son asked me why I was weeping. It was present each time I watched *The Great Mouse Detective* while my eldest daughter cuddled and giggled on my lap. Love was at hand in the delivery room when I saw with my own bewildered eyes my youngest son enter this world. It was in our driveway as I watched a determined daughter not back down as I hurled fastball after fastball for her to hit. It was there in my parents' hearts when I opened the envelope to read I had made the Dean's List after a rough start in college. Perhaps it was pride and not love when I hit my only LL home run, bought my favorite VW Bug, or read my name in the newspaper, but it felt so, so good.

In two entries, I noticed something extra special: On my wedding day and in the hug from your mom when Rebe died, love was not only expressed, it was reciprocated. I loved and I was loved. AND because I love, I can be loved. Even on the day when my mom died, when love drained from my soul and it felt like a piece of me was forever removed, I sensed, I knew, I could still love and be loved.

Love Is Soup

You might presume I was in the kitchen when I had my epiphany that love is soup. I was indeed in there, but only to refill my water bottle and to retrieve my reading glasses. While I waited for the 24-ounce container to fill with slow-moving filtered water, my mind raced with what to do next. Unlike your mom who writes down everything she plans to do, I kind of mentally jot down action items on a vague canvas inside my head. Thoughts pinged with calls, chores, and appointments I had better not forget, but I was so giddy with excitement that I had possibly distinguished what love is and what being loved is from my most recent index card entries. My glee shifted to gloom as I was pretty confident I was going to forget something on my "honey-do" list and then be reminded by your mom, *for the thousandth time*, why I should put lists in writing and not pin them to an imaginary corkboard in my head. I arrogantly doubled down on my time-tested presumption that I need not jot. I went over my mental list again and realized I had forgotten a dinner I promised to make. Tomorrow I would be making my world-famous (okay, more like "house-famous" … okay, okay, precisely that "only I think it's famous") 15-bean soup. I made three more mental sticky notes and attached them to my messy mental chalkboard.

1) Retrieve secret soup recipe from speckled notebook.
2) Wash and soak the beans needed overnight.
3) Don't forget the dog's grooming appointment; she kinda stinks.

With my bottle filled with 24 ounces of water and my head filled with more than 24 scattered other ideas I am sure I would forget, I raced to my office desk to find my notebook. It's the one titled *Smoker Journal*. It's a continuing log of what, when, prep work, cooking length of time, and other notes for improving my techniques next time. The log entries even include the day's weather, the temperatures outside the box, inside the box, and the internal temp of the meat recorded throughout the process. Including the cleanup, it is a time-consuming commitment. (**Dad Note:** And you thought I just threw hunks of meat into a hot smoky box for hours so I could drink beer and smoke a cigar, didn't you?) Anyway, back to the speck-led notebook, it also contains recipes for dry rubs I've found and created, for basic "meat-and-potatoes" recipes for, well, meat and potatoes, but also poultry and plank-smoked fish. Stuffed way in the back of the notebook are hand-written pages of my "world-famous-okay-more-like-house-famous-okay-okay-precisely-that-only-I-think-they're-famous" soups.

Before I retrieved the 15-bean soup recipe I re-read one of my favorite creations: Yellow Split Pea and Smoked Italian Sausage. This one, along with my Green Split Pea and Ham are two of your mother's least favorites. I wondered, *How could one person like/love something another person dislikes/detests? Was it a single ingredient? Is it too spicy? Too blah? Too hot? Too much meat? Not enough meat? Is there one ingredient I could add or subtract to make it more appealing?*

I began to dissect/analyze/examine what I could change to improve her appreciation/satisfaction with my "world-famous-okay..." soup. While scrutinizing ingredients, combinations, and temperature settings, I had my "Love is Soup" epiphany. Soup begins with a single basic ingredient: water. Heated, it's just hot water. Add something, like salt, and it's hot salty water. Add more and it changes again. Eventually, you hit upon an appealing formula and method. As desirable and tempting as it may be for me, it's impossible for it to satisfy and please everyone. There is a combination of ingredients that charms me to gastronomic ecstasy which may result in someone else's misery or disgust. It's kind of like the Square Peg/Round Hole theory with an added twist: Not all square pegs fit or are destined for square holes. In other words, the attraction and complement aren't sin-gular or formulaic. In other, other words, let me provide a quick example. Chocolate is a sweet, tasty treat. You, your mom, and millions, perhaps bil-lions, of people love it. I am in a unique and microscopic minority. Like never having experienced a headache or being left-handed, I don't like the taste of chocolate. It is marginally acceptable to me in certain formats, but mainly, I don't like it. Nothing is gonna change my mind or taste buds and just because millions/billions love it doesn't mean I have to. What is appealing to some may be disconcerting to others.

Love is the same way. There are many "ingredients" to the profile which provide instant, long-term, and recurring attraction. Some may describe looks as most important for a successful coupling. Others might be more inclined towards sensitivity, status, wealth, a sense of humor, or a teaspoon of marjoram. Then, those factors need to be determined for mutually agreeable satisfaction. How sensitive of a mate am I looking for? How significant is a high/low level of wealth or status? How much will my sense of humor repel or attract? Should I use a tablespoon of marjoram instead of a teaspoon? These are just basic, uncomplicated examples. There are so many influences at so many levels at so many intensities that the arrangements are endless; no single sequence or recipe is desirable perfectly. But there is a recipe that attracts and holds me, and hopefully your mom and I are on the same page on this.

I've read the poems, stories, essays, etc., about love. I've heard the songs, hymns, carols, etc. I've watched the rom-coms and Hallmark movies. Love is layered and good and work and sacrifice and as important as breathing. Love is never having to say you're sorry, but smart enough—especially if you're married—to know you should. Love is ... Love is ... Love is a million and many splendored thing, but hopefully now you realize it is a combination of ingredients like soup is. It doesn't have to be perfect because nothing ever is, and it doesn't have to win over everyone because nothing ever does. It has to allure. It has to bond. It has to inspire and be inspired.

In My Humble Opinion

Love takes many forms and is important. Like so many things and situations, a single word cannot describe or define them. Early Greek philosophers postulated at least four different kinds of love from romantic to empathetic. Psychologists have added their own interpretations over the millennia. Without my argument or encouragement, it is obvious that love is not a single emotion; I am not reinventing the wheel here. But the best way I can explain it is, love is the response to distinctive optimistic and encouraging stimuli. It is a feeling comprised of an assortment of input. Love takes multiple forms as many, supposedly, as the Inuit word for "snow." It can be personal or shared. **Love is positive. It has a potentially limitless vertical range; anything below the least thing you love or are indifferent to falls into the equally limitless category of hate**. To one degree or another, you can love any person or thing you know. Because it is a feeling, it cannot be wrong. Because it is a feeling, it can inspire you to do and experience wondrous things; also, because it is a feeling, it can be dangerous. I do not want to focus on the negative aspects, but suffice it to say, it is adverse only as a result of excess. If you love a person or a thing too much, your life will be out of balance and no lasting good will come of it. Your focus will be consumed by short-term gratification. Think of it like this: I love beer. I love cheeseburgers. I love fries. For a few days, I would be happy if each meal were cheeseburgers, fries, and beer. Past that, it would be excessive. I would be a cholesterol-infested, kidney-failing mess. **Balance is the key**. As you will be able to recognize love, you will also be able to recognize if all of your attention is aimed at a single thing or person.

To truly love is spectacular. I imagine Dr. Seuss would have called it "supersplendiferous awesome-osity." And all the Whos down in Whoville would sing that truly loving is surpassed by only one "fahoo foray dahoo doray-ingest thing," and that is to be truly loved. To be truly loved is the most wonderful sensation you can experience. Empirically and quantifiably, your head and heart hit a stride of harmonic, cosmic, and karmic resonance. Okay, so I don't know if that's scientifically true. I do know it is most special in the best of ways. For me, it's like a favorite roller coaster ride—slightly unequal parts of scary, fun, and safe, but the best part is I am first in line, all the time. However, the ride is not free. The price of the ticket is dear; it will cost you valuable parts of your inner self. Don't worry—there is no personal surgery to perform like offering a spleen or gall bladder. The yourself-part of you which you must pay is your privacy and disclosure of weaknesses. In order to be truly loved, you must share yourself and you must be vulnerable. There are intimate pieces to the love jigsaw puzzle of which you are made. Not just your smile, but why and what makes you grin. Not just your fears, but why you are scared. Not just your laugh, but what's so darn funny. You must be open to the uncomfortable comfortableness of allowing someone else to see what you see and feel what you feel.

Sounds kinda scary, right? I promise it is worth it. There is nothing greater than opening up and trusting someone and having that reciprocated. Complete confidence in loving and being truly loved is the key. Bruce Springsteen sang a favorite line of mine regarding love. In the song, "Brilliant Disguise," he states, "God have mercy on the man who doubts what he's sure of." The best way I can relate to you that feeling is to imagine playing the Trust Game with your partner. It is an intimacy exercise. Two people stand in a line facing the same direction and the person in front stretches out their arms to the side and falls backward, hoping the person in the back catches them before they hit the ground. To me, this is my proof. If you believe in your heart that your partner will do whatever it takes to make sure you are safe, you are truly loved.

And know this: My love for you is at the highest end of the potentially limitless spectrum, well above what I feel for my beloved Sox and my beloved United. You can always count on that and believe I am there behind you always ready to catch you if you need me.

UNCONDITIONAL LOVE

It might seem peculiar and redundant to follow a chapter titled "Love" with one titled "Unconditional Love." As I read my children's collective thoughts, I sense them thinking, thinking for the millionth time, *Peculiar and redundant? Dad, you are the living definition of "peculiar and redundant." Why didn't you add the following paragraphs into the preceding chapter? OMG! You're such an idiot. Sometimes I can't believe we're related!*

Firstly, I know you would never verbalize those thoughts, or at least be considerate enough to mutter them under your breath so I couldn't hear you. You're smart to keep your thoughts to yourselves. There's no reason to insult a person from whom you might inherit a 1965 Ford Mustang convertible, an esteemed collection of sports memorabilia, or an incomplete assortment of shot glasses from around the world. It's like my grandmother always told me: "Anthony, they can't arrest you for what you're thinking."

Parrying your insulting jibes and casting aside those idiocy aspersions for the millionth time as well, I would agree with you that unconditional love is a form of love. In the interest of harmony and family unity, let me rephrase my accord: I WOULD HAVE agreed with you when I was young, dumb, and less jaded, like you are. (**Dad Note:** That is, I WOULD HAVE BEEN INCLINED to agree with you, when I was younger and dumber like you are, that my idea of unconditional love should have been included in the previous chapter on love. When I was younger and dumber, like you, I may have also agreed that unconditional love is possible and is a configuration of real love. My statement from my at-that-time [then limited] knowledge would have enhanced my interpretation of what love is, what love is not, and quite possibly improved the profile of what it means to be loved. I rarely agree with you that I am an idiot. I may very well be one, but I certainly don't need your stomp of approval to validate my lack of intelligence—I've got that covered all by myself.)

On the surface, unconditional love for another person, animal, or thing appears to be a subcategory of the notion of love. **Unconditional love is a status of the deepest commitment and condition of the highest obligation. To promise to love unconditionally is the boldest pledge.**

Pretty lucid and impressive statement for your (an) old man, right? Not so idiot-ish, huh?

Like some/most of my lucid and impressive thoughts, as well as some/most of my less coherent, unimpressive ideas, my statement concerning unconditional love occurred to me late at night. It was the contemplative session just after cookies in the kitchen and just before settling in to watch *Raiders of the Lost Ark* on the television in the basement. Unlike when I "invented" a gadget to hold and press my pants on a clothes hanger, I was pretty pleased with myself. However, my prideful glee turned sourer than expired milk. Even before Indiana Jones dodged the giant rolling ball, I decided unconditional love may exist in theory, but it cannot be produced. There are striking design flaws in the guarantee. The vow to love unconditionally is not only too great a burden for one person to have for another person, but it also has no practical application—I am convinced of that. Further, I am also convinced that graham crackers are a great snack, that *Raiders* is one of my top ten favorite movies, and that every relationship happens and/or endures with qualifications, restrictions, and stipulations.

Deficient Blueprint

In the previous chapter, if I didn't hit the bullseye shooting Cupid's arrow with my "Love is Soup" analogy or you found my explanation lacking, I apologize. I warned you that many have tried to explain it exactly, but there seems to be no standard answer. Even without my definition, you comprehend the concept sufficiently to recognize it easily; love, like soup, resides solidly in the amorphous "I-know-it-when-I-see-it" category. You also grasp the notion that human love for another does exist and is attainable just as you fathom that soup needs a spoon.

When you were kids, you loved playing board games with Mom and me. I especially liked the word ones, while you favored the games of chance like Sorry or Trouble. I was not a fan of messy games because no matter how much Mom and I indicated the post-game tidying was your responsibility somehow Mom and I completed the clean-up. Jenga, the piece-by-piece tower destabilizing game was as messy as it was tense. Love is like a Jenga tower. It needs a strong base. It is fabricated with many parts like friendship, trust, respect, and admiration to support the harmonious feeling and structure of love; a piece could be damaged or removed and love could still exist. Love is built on words and actions.

Unconditional love is built on quicksand. It is supported by unsound architectural concepts: blind devotion, unyielding adoration, and infinite passion. The weight of those commitments will easily bend, break, then crush the steadfastness of any relationship.

I tell you often that I love you. I mean it with all my heart and hope it has not lost its impact. What I feel for you is as perfect an emotion as I possess. It's hard to put into words the depth I feel for you. It's difficult to describe the perfect, blissful feeling. This is as close as I can illustrate my love for you with a "Nirvana for Dad" analogy: I am driving my convertible in a city during rush hour. I am calm, but sense I am going to be late to wherever I am going. At once, every other car pulls to the right so I can pass and drive as fast as I want, as if my sporty red VW Bug is an ambulance. No one gives me grief about my poor sense of direction. No one yells, "Turn that down!" as I blast loud, alt-rock music like Nirvana or Helmet. And of course, it's a beautiful day and the top is down.

When I say "I love you" I have no reservations. My feelings are tethered only to good thoughts about my past with you, our contemporary relationship, and the future I imagine for you. I would do anything to maintain that delicious, head-humming, heart-happy, soul-smiling feeling. But honestly, I cannot promise to love you unconditionally; it is smothering and poor parenting.

Humans have a distinct capability versus other living organisms: the ability to make choices based on reason and instinct. It distinguishes us from other living things whose decisions are determined by natural impulses. A maggot hatches and learns to fly without a flight instruction manual. A bee knows how to be a bee. Various animals receive some nurturing, but soon the parent squeaks, squawks, or barks to its offspring, "I'm finished regurgitating meals for you. For crying out loud, you're nearly six months old! And for the sake of Mother Earth, stop playing those damn video games, get out of the den, and go kill your own dinner!" A human child is predisposed to mature but needs guidance and assistance. To fully function in a society, it is essential to provide guidelines, set limits, and establish boundaries. The "restraints" should be concurrent with goals to inspire creativity, foster curiosity, and instill self-appreciation. Under the joint auspices of limitations and support, the nurturing will add to what Mother Nature has already designed.

Defective Electrical System

Unconditional love among humans is not real. I know I can love. I am confident I cannot love unconditionally. Faulty internal wiring leads people to believe in the fallacy of perfection and the ideal of hope.

Here is a shocking truth, especially to every grandparent on the planet: Children make mistakes. A child absorbs information from his/her surroundings in the form of parenting and what/he she observes. Despite well-intentioned instruction, a child will not grow up perfect. By choice or innocently, mistakes are made. If a child is absolved of all repercussions of a poor action or deed, no personal or emotional growth can occur. Further, if a child realizes there are no consequences to each decision, he/she will choose selfishly to benefit his/her own self-indulgence.

My high school economics teacher proffered a universal commercial truth: "There is no such thing as a free lunch." His opinion was that there are costs attached to each business decision and organizational venture. This applies to more than economic situations; there are strings attached to every choice we make including whom we love and why we love them.

Hope is a uniquely human perception. It is not an instinct, it is learned. An animal is predisposed to seek basic necessities like food and shelter. It does not wait expectantly for delivery of Omaha steaks or bushels of fruit; by design, it hunts or forages. A plant doesn't rely on hope either. If the sun does not shine, it adapts or dies. Humans are the only living creatures who can desire more than what was produced previously; historical information is just a reference point.

Hope convinces us to anticipate the likely, the improbable, and the impossible. That, despite all evidence to the contrary, something unexpected will happen. Unconditional love is constructed with unbridled and unwavering hope. If a relationship relies too staunchly on the concept of hope as a necessary detail, it is doomed. No matter how vigorously I hope, it will be cold in New England in the winter. No matter how relentlessly I believe that the Boston Red Sox will beat the New York Yankees each time, that Manchester United will win every match against its opponents, especially Liverpool, and that a rabbit will appear from a hat when I reach into it, it is impossible. My earnest hope might be met, hopefully more often than occasionally, but never to the pinnacle of my desire, never to 100%.

Love tempers hope because it allows for faith in unlikely occurrences; unconditional love demands it. Love binds tightly but is forgiving and allows for personal growth; unconditional love constricts but exonerates as it permits any behavior.

It Has No Off Switch

"I love you unconditionally" is an affectionate, tender, and bold statement. It is meant to convey deep and unreserved commitment. Whenever I hear it or read it, I laugh. Maybe not out loud, but trust me, I am chuckling on the inside. On the outside, my glee is revealed as a smirk. It's like when I recognize the humor of a meme or folly of a comic strip, I smirk. Just because I don't laugh out loud doesn't mean it's not funny. (**Dad Note:** By the way, "smirk" is one of my fifty favorite words; kudos to the person who came up with that splendid word.)

Unconditional love is like a hovering UFO outfitted with the brightest, most intense searchlight. At certain times, the beacon is appreciated. Imagine if the beam is constant, blindingly powerful, and follows you everywhere—there is no flicker, no twinkle, and no hiding from it. Love involves risk, but what risk is there if the radiance is unyielding? Love exposes weakness, flaws, and vulnerability to create a bond, but unconditional love sears and burns, and what person could produce or stand such scrutiny or attention?

Unconditional Love Is Unnecessary

Even an open-ended, less dedicated statement like "*I love you*" is loaded with tacit conditions and unspoken qualifications. Conditions provide a base for a relationship as they answer the what-ifs and stipulate guidelines. Qualifications allow for information to be absorbed and for emotional growth. Mistakes are part of the maturation process of life and of a relationship. In an environment with conditional love, self-improvement, acceptance, and tolerance are discovered. If no consequences are present, bad behavior persists and nothing is learned from mistakes. Boundaries are the model for what is and isn't acceptable in a relationship; unconditional love turns a blind eye.

You Want Answers?!?

So far, I have expressed thoughts and feelings about why unconditional love cannot exist in a relationship. I have been insightfully vague, but you want evidence of my conditions to love you. Here are a few examples to prove my point.

- I love you because you're my child. That bond has only strengthened as we have aged because pride, respect, and admiration are added to the mix. I have no illusions that you are perfect, but I never wanted you to be. Whether intentionally or not, you seem bound to my dad platitudes: to be the best you that you can be, to always be proud of who you are, and to never give up. If you were cloned here on Earth or a carbon DNA copy of you existed in a parallel universe, I couldn't love that person to the extent or in the manner I love you. If I could love unconditionally, the bough breaks if you are not mine. I have no relationship with your replicated twin.

Don't be sad for your doppelganger; remember, I only know you. And don't be happy either as I imagine you smirking as you contemplate an existence without my ceaselessly stupid dad jokes and relentless teasing. (**Dad Note:** Wow, I just used one of my favorite words to describe your reaction to me. I don't know how to feel right now ... I'm going to need a moment ...)

- I love you because you have not tried to kill me for all the stupid things I have done to embarrass you. And/or, if you have, you haven't succeeded. Besides murdering me, other obvious acts of atrocities would fall into this conditional category though I'd prefer not to identify them. (**Dad Note:** There's no need to provide you with any fanciful ideas for my demise.) Categorically, I will state it would be impossible to love you if I knew you had intentionally harmed, injured, or killed anyone or anything just for the pleasure of it. Commit these and you go on my naughty, do-not-pass-go-and-do-not-love list. Besides heartbroken, I would be vexed, perplexed, and my love would be annexed. However, in my heart and on the papers I signed, you are my child. I would try to forgive you for anything. For the sake of argument, let's not test this one.

- I love you because you love me back. It would be impossible to love you unconditionally if you have the capacity to love, but you do not. This rule precludes capability and competence. For instance, based on experience, I know you love me even though I don't see or talk to you each day. If for some reason you were incapable of expressing love you had previously communicated, I would love you devotedly because you are mine; the depth and/or pinnacle of our commitment has been achieved, but it cannot be furthered.

- In the previous chapter, I stated "Love is positive. It has a potentially limitless vertical range; anything below the least thing you love falls into the equally limitless category of hate." I've always wondered, can something be conditional and potentially limitless at the same time? I am no philosopher, but I do contemplate ideas way past my bedtime and extremely above my pay grade. The key to reconciling a love without limits and one with conditions is the word "potential." To solve my dilemma, I consider there is always the potential to love infinitely. But much like winning Megabucks without purchasing a ticket, the odds are stacked against me.

In My Humble Opinion, There Can Be Only One

To love unconditionally means to love without reservation. Here on Earth, it cannot be done, but don't despair entirely. It is not my intent to preach, but there is one relationship that manifests itself as unconditional: God's love for you. I am sure of this. I cannot provide you with facts, but it exists. You might consider as evidence the beauty you see in nature as a gift of

His love. You might think that the feeling your soul/heart senses when love is reciprocated by another is more evidence.

Conversely, you may consider the suffering of some from the oppression by others as proof that there is no God; therefore, there is no such thing as His existence and further, no such thing as unconditional love. Take a leap of faith with me because I know He is there, and His love is pure and without boundaries for you. The reason I know this is because you were entrusted with the greatest present you could ever receive—much better than any Christmas, birthday, Hanukkah, or other gift—you have free will. You have the ability to choose your own path in life. Having free will is proof enough to me that I am loved unconditionally. The composition of my life's decisions, choices, words, actions, inactions, etc., ... here on Earth will be judged. Even the intent of those assessments, resolutions, and outcomes will be arbitrated. I believe in the spiritual afterlife of heaven. I may make it there, but then again, I might not. It's up to me to use what was generously given, to use it wisely, and make this world, our world, a better place because I lived.

WHEN IT'S OVER, IS IT REALLY OVER?

(**Dad Note:** As clever as I try to be with the titles for the chapters, it's pretty obvious this one is about dealing with the pain caused by the death of a loved one. When I wrote this chapter, it was heavily influenced by what I learned about dying, death, and myself when my mom died. It was also guided by the mindset I needed to develop a better coping mechanism for what lay ahead for my first cousin and one of my best friends, Natalie, who was battling bravely against ALS, an incurable disease. It was the hardest chapter for me to write. I relived pains I thought had healed completely regarding the death of my mom; they have not. I allowed feelings to surface that I thought I had come to terms with regarding Natalie; I have not. I expose doubt and weakness. I do this because I love you.

Composing this chapter became even more difficult than I anticipated. Natalie, my dearest, sweet cousin and a best friend passed away on October 6, 2019. In the minutest of ways, I feel fortunate I did have the chance to read the preliminary construction of this chapter to her. She was my initial sounding board and maiden groundwork editor for most of this book. With her passing, there is a swirling void in my heart, and this chapter, this section, and this book become more difficult. Reviewing this chapter has also prompted me to alert you that sometimes throughout this book you will discover timeline inconsistencies. The explanation is simple, some of it was written before Natalie's passing. Rather than correct all past-tense flaws I hope you'll allow and forgive the imperfections. The meaning and the message of this chapter, and this book for that matter, reflect my own shortcomings when it comes to delivering a message—like me, they are rarely linear and not restricted by a timeline. Hopefully, you understand that the wisdom I dispense is more important than my own ungoodly grammar.

There is no bright side to this story, but perhaps a gray-streaked sky struggling for a clear horizon and clarity. I promised Natalie I would finish this book and then compile the multitude of stories I have concocted and submitted as hers on her personal social media page. I have added a few of the truth-challenged, fact-defying tales at the end of this chapter after "In My Humble Opinion." It is my hope to produce, market, and sell a book with these fictions/yarns/anecdotes and donate a pile of money to The ALS Association.)

I'm not a "bucket list" person. Sure, there are things I'd like to see and do before I die. Absolutely there are places I'd love to visit and/or re-visit, like Bermuda, especially with your mom. But if I don't or if I can't, I'm not going to lose sleep, fret, or worry. I'd be delighted to be slightly inebriated and singing "Ooh ah, ooh ah, Cantona" from the Stretford End at Old Trafford. I think it would be cool to travel by train across the northwest of North America. I'd love to watch the Boston Red Sox play the New York Yankees at their stadium in the Bronx. It would a supreme thrill to take batting practice in Fenway Park. Heck, I'd even like to try bungee-jumping. (**Dad Note:** Please don't tell your mother about the last one. I'm afraid she'd encourage it, especially if I made the leap from a tall rusty crane in a parking lot or over an active freeway.)

I would cherish those memories forever. However, I have come to the realization that the satisfaction of those thrills, chills, and spills would pale in comparison to my favorite thing in life: building and maintaining a strongly bound, lightly wound, I've-got-your-back relationship.

At a very young age I realized I favored resilient and durable relationships. Having been shy, tall, and "husky," it felt wonderful to be enveloped in fierce, wagons-circled love. I had a large extended and extendable family, especially on my mom's side. Fears subside easily in the strength large numbers provide and character is allowed to flourish within its absolute protection. My first, best friends were my brothers, sister, and my cousins. Sure, we annoyed, teased, bothered, and semi-tormented each other. I'd like to say it was all done out of love or in jest, but it's difficult to qualify each instance of the goading and badgering as love. It was standard operating procedure for a kid being a kid, especially as close as we were. But nothing—and I mean NOTHING—could tear apart our tensile but inflexible forever bond. I was loved by my parents. I was adored by my grandparents. Whichever gene pool was responsible, I grew quickly and large on my own, but I grew emotionally and spiritually with family guidance to become who I am today. I'd like to believe I offered as much to the family structure and strength as I received, but like a trick-or-treater on Halloween, I felt like I always got more than my fair share. Perhaps each of us felt that way about the ease and willingness with which our family shared its love.

Into my teen years I tested the bonds a few times. I was as loyal as ever to my family, but the devotion was slightly buried beneath teenaged angst and snarkasm. I held common adolescent notions that the world revolved around me—just like my grandparents said it did—and that my parents were not as intelligent as I thought they once were. Thankfully, I was supported by and clung to my family's resiliency and durability for love. From that foundation, I was able to seek and forge new (hopefully) lasting bonds.

In my twenties, I was as amazed as Mark Twain was how smart my parents seemed to become overnight. I finished college in a relative blaze of glory having spun through the beginning of it like a leaf in a sandstorm. It felt more like a shit storm at times from which I couldn't see daylight. As always and as ever, my parents, brothers, sister, cousins, and grandparents were the guiding beacon. There were more blips, bleeps, and blunders, but steadfastly they all remained by my side. If I've given the impression my life to this point was a complete whirlwind, it wasn't. I became a Big Brother to a wonderful kid whom I am still very close to. We met through the Big Brothers of Rhode Island. (**Dad Note:** At the national and local level, the organization has since combined and been renamed Big Brothers

Big Sisters of America. For information on how to join, go to www.bbbs. org.) In my twenties, I unexpectedly also became a father. It wasn't under perfect circumstances, but then, and especially now, I wouldn't trade it for anything. Her birth was a fount of newly discovered life-altering love I had never experienced before. I was fully motivated to provide and reciprocate love.

In my thirties, I settled down. Through my family's unwavering support and unswerving love, I found love and began to recognize the fuller responsibilities, and strengths, of love. I had a young family, people who depended on me and looked up to me. Having children is as close to unconditional love as I will ever know.

As I whipped through my forties, my life felt like it was intently affixed to a grindstone while I sprinted around and around on a hamster wheel. There were plenty of moments to reinforce what I knew about love and occasions to illuminate new ideas of its depth and permanence. Also in my forties, a bedrock-shifting event occurred: My mother passed away.

As I reside solidly in my fifties, I've learned more and experienced more. I look at things from different angles, both wider and close-up. It's not my intention to break down changes in awareness throughout my life by decades or eras. Time periods can be inefficiently segmented for conversational pieces like that, but life doesn't flow that way. I always found it rather odd that American music is categorized in that same manner, as if genre types adjusted every ten years. For example, did psychedelic rock end with the 60s or did disco really die on December 31, 1979? Of course not. Life is like that too. It's defined, or at least shifts, when moments or events redefine our outlook. Our perceptions need not amend instantly or necessarily overnight. It's full of highs and lows, randomness and predictability, risks and rewards, the intentional and the unintentional, actions and inactions, possibility and missed opportunity. The single common thread is the presentation of information. It's up to each of us to learn from it. Two significant events which altered my course and the manner I viewed relationships were my mom's death and my cousin's illness.

After my mom died, I lost faith in God. In the blinding light of hindsight, I was convinced I had lost two relationships because of her death, with her and with God. When she contracted pancreatic cancer, I prayed for her to live. When my selfish prayer was not granted, I didn't just lose faith in a higher power, I stopped believing in divine existence altogether. My mind could not comprehend why an infinitely wise and all-powerful God would not spare this amazing, selfless woman. By my calculations, it had been a very long time since the world witnessed a miracle of biblical proportions. As an act of reverence, believing in divine manifestation is a leap of faith. As an act of selfish will, challenging an almighty being to perform is not a wise idea, but letting her live would have scored huge approval ratings, in my humble opinion.

The esteem and admiration I felt for my mother was as high as it was unparalleled. My respect for her was near-reverential and in turn, I craved her approval. She was my mentor and my friend, one of my best friends. It was obvious that she was a person to emulate. In the short time you knew her you must have sensed it too. She was a beacon of goodness, the best reflection of what I thought I knew about God's love. Most people would falter under an avalanche of "highest and best" accolades, but she survived the weight in the same way a lump of coal succumbs to pressure to become a diamond. And the very best part was she lived up to her own standards while at the same time admitting and embracing her own frailties and faults.

While you may have sensed her comportment and retain slivers of fond memories about her from your youth, you probably don't remember her well. Further, I am especially convinced, and eternally grateful, that you don't remember the day she was diagnosed with pancreatic cancer. It was a foundation-shaking, root-withering, all-the-kings-horses-and-all-the-kings-men-couldn't-put-my-heart-back-together-again day. My life was altered and knocked off course for a while.

Not to relive any pain I experienced or share an agony, I'd like to provide a frame of reference about how quickly a globe on a fixed axis can have its wheels come off their axles. We were visiting Rebe and Papa in

Florida. Our plan was to drive with them to Disney World and spend four days there—every grandparent's dream and nightmare rolled into one. Minutes before we left, my mom described to me a nagging side pain she had been experiencing. She thought I might be able to assess it because of all the muscle-related sports injuries I had suffered. I told her unless it involves ice, heat, and "rubbing magic dirt" on an afflicted area I was useless. I advised her to see a doctor. Surprisingly and without hesitation, she and my dad headed to a nearby medical center for a quick exam. I was slightly shocked. I thought to myself, *Since when had my mom ever visited a doctor unless it was by appointment?* I came to the innocuous conclusion that she and my dad had contracted an acute case of "grandparent-itis." One symptom is a sudden self-realization of having committed to a three-hour ride in a medium-sized but comfy car with medium-sized but noisy kids followed by forty-eight hours of OMG-it's-a-really-freakin'-small-world-when-you-cram-so-many-kids-into-a-theme-park immersion. Half believing I had diagnosed my parents' situation correctly, I made her pinky swear they would leave for Disney World right after the check-up. I figured they would be about sixty minutes behind us. Minutes turned into hours waiting for an update. Finally, my parents called with knock-you-to-your-praying-knees news: My mom had cancer. I spent the next few days driving back and forth between their home to be with them and Disney World to be with you. I was in emotional, despondent pain with them, but feigned a painted-on smile when I came back to you. I felt like a naturally jovial actor playing the most melancholy role of his life.

My life changed after that. Everything was different, like being flung from a merry-go-round. It felt like the world flung me from its playground and traded its sensitive, beautiful colors for a harsh black and white landscape of reality. Hope and courage were waged as battle cries, but less than two years later they were overtaken. Cancer had won the war and my panorama of optimism, my encouraging spirit, and my belief in God were taken as prisoners. An intimate relationship was severed and removed permanently from my life.

I wallowed in the depths of despair for a while. With the love and support of your mom, I rebounded to a height where I could see the colors of life again, just not the vibrant ones I witnessed before. I experienced joy and happiness. I celebrated being part of your lives and grateful you were part of mine. I enjoyed my friendships and passions. But all of them were just a little less than they were previously, kinda like really good imitations and distractions. Believe me, I appreciated what I had, but I had no one to thank for any goodness returning to my life other than your mom. I still believed there was no God. There was no comfort for my soul. So, at age forty-seven, when my cousin Natalie became ill with amyotrophic lateral sclerosis (ALS), I was sad beyond belief, but I wasn't angry. There was no God to blame. There was no higher power to beg, question, or ask, "Why her!?!" I offered no prayers, I asked for no guidance. I was sad because in my very jaded, color-faded, my-soul-is-gated world, I had to prepare for the loss of another intimate relationship I valued and treasured. Another best friend and confidant would leave me. ALS, commonly referred to as Lou Gehrig's disease, is a nervous system disease that weakens the muscles. It affects the physical activity of the human body and may also degenerate cognitive functions. It is a nasty, wasty skunk of a condition. My mom's death because of pancreatic cancer and now this affliction on my dear and good cousin was nearly too much to bear. Natalie and her husband, Neil, were raising six young and wonderful children. She had just started nursing school. I imagine their life together wasn't perfect with six hungry mouths to feed, clothe, and educate, but if it wasn't, I never saw the lemons, only the lemonade.

At the outset of her diagnosis, I was doubly convinced God was nothing to me. Further, and triply convinced, He existed only as an idea constructed by church leaders to market fear, grab your pocket change, and sell you guilt to keep you coming back for more. I would still be a good person, but more cynical about religion, especially organized ones. Preachy agnosticism aside, I spent every Tuesday with Natalie. I know she was surrounded by a dedicated and loving family, but I wanted, actually, unbeknownst to me at the time, I needed to be with her.

Surprisingly, thankfully, and mercifully, my strong and ever-growing relationship with Natalie changed me once again. Natalie helped me to re-establish a spiritual connection with an almighty entity, but she also altered my narrow and selfish perception of relationships. I finally understood they don't exist solely for mutual benefit or as a vibrant entity or even as a fond memory, they are alive and can have a far-reaching effect.

In My Humble Opinion

As I mentioned before, life is a series of events; the length is unknown, but the depth is up to you. It's a commonplace, pithy, two-dimensional mantra I have believed my entire life. I am still certain of its significance, but I have come to realize it encompasses more than length and depth. It embodies the connections formed with the world around you, your relationships with all things, carbon-based or not. And more significantly, I learned relationships, especially through impact, are dynamic, long-lasting, and far-reaching. They are multi-faceted, multi-dimensional and achieve animation through their energy and commitment.

I had been given a foundation for what a relationship is. I had the greatest of good fortune to receive love, counsel, and support from my most treasured ones. I then learned how to develop my own relationships, not only to know how important it was to trust and depend, but also to be trusted and depended on. But with my mom's and especially Natalie's passing, I witnessed the emergence of a newfound recognition of the lifelong impact of a deep, personal connection. The benefits of a solid relationship are not flat, stagnant, or inactive. The bond doesn't end with cessation or even death. There is gained and shared strength. There is support in the form of a shoulder to lean on, a hand to hold, and a size 14 shoe to (gently) prod you to live a well-lived life. In a relationship there is hope, goodness, and kindness. I am confident that whatever you gain from solid personal connections will extend, increase, and expand past the mortal, past the memory, and into everlasting achievement, an endless monument to the goodness of the human spirit. There is worthy, impactful value to be acquired and absorbed from close association. By linking positively with others, you perpetuate its legacy, you show the world, or at least your corner of it, that the relationship mattered and is everlastingly relevant.

To re-paraphrase a well-known intentionally misdirected quote from the fount of observational social malapropism, Yogi Berra, "It ain't over 'til it's over and even then, it ain't over."

BONUS MATERIAL

Here is the levity I promised. The following are a few of the many stories I posted on my cousin Natalie's social media page on Facebook. I wrote them every Tuesday when I visited with her and delivered the meal your mom had made for her family. I have included some of the actual remarks from the readers. The last story I include below was my favorite. It generated the most interest, most likes, most phone calls, and incited emotions ranging from amused to angry. When I posted the original story, I added a photo to "authenticate" the fiction. It was even shared by others on their own Facebook pages as a cautionary tale about health care risks. Man, a lot of people were not happy with me when they found out I had made up the whole story!

They were composed to appear as if Natalie had written them with only my help in typing because she could not move her arms or her fingers because of ALS. I intended for them to seem playfully legitimate, as if the reader would ask, "Natalie wrote it, but did that *really* happen?" It took a while for most people to realize it was believable nonsense. Some suspected early on, others trusted my balderdash until the final post. Hopefully though, all were entertained. I certainly enjoyed my D-list celebrity from our followers, the hundreds of likes, but especially relished spending every Tuesday with Natalie. It is my goal to compile them into a book to not only raise awareness of ALS as a dreadful disease, but to raise money, like the Ice Bucket Challenge before it, to fund research for an eventual cure.

It's Tuesday and, as you know, my cousin Anthony visits with me. Today, he was playing music videos on YouTube of songs I like. I think we hit every 70s pop song, every Barry Manilow song, and the entire "Grease" album—I loved it. I was singing while he was dancing and singing. I guess he thought he was John Travolta in *Saturday Night Fever*.

I was having so much fun and nearly peed my pants when Anthony started. He didn't seem to remember any of the words to any of the songs, but he was convinced the lyrics he sang were correct. During his "performance," he sang "Rocket Man" by Elton John. "Rocket man burning up his shoes with aerosol." "I'm a Believer" by The Monkees. "Then I saw her face, now I'm gonna leave her." "Aquarius" by The 5th Dimension. "This is the dawning of the age of asparagus, asparagus." And lastly, and I am nearly in tears, "Dancing Queen" by Abba. "See that girl, watch her scream, kicking the dancing queen."

Oh boy, did we have fun today! Do any of you remember when you finally learned the actual lyrics to songs you thought you were singing correctly?

A few of the comments:

- "I love 'Anthony Tuesdays.' The funniest thing is that this could actually be true."
- "I could lend you my Barry Manilow *Greatest Hits* cd if you want. Lol!"
- "I always thought it was 'a cheeseburger and a pair of dice' for Cheeseburger in Paradise."
- "Oh my god, I am dying laughing, because I am singing these songs and seeing the lyrics he sang is hysterical. I was famous for singing the wrong words to songs. Thanks for the laugh."

- "This is the best Tuesday story yet! I would have loved it too AND I'm sure we all have a few guessed lyrics, lol."

Great News! They loved our idea!

For the past week, my cousin Anthony and I have been meeting with the producers of the TV show *Shark Tank*. First, we had a pre-interview in Florida to see if not only our invention was a good fit for the investors on the show, but also to see if our presentation skills would appear appealing enough for television viewers. Well, that went well enough that not only were we asked to meet with executives from the network, but also from the US Department of Transportation!

You're probably wondering what idea I am talking about. Well, I can share it with you now. It's called (drum roll please!) ... The Accident Blanket. It is similar to a giant stage curtain which would be set up to cover any major traffic accident. It will hide the wreckage from onlookers so there would be no reason to slow down and stare. It will allow the police and rescue units to more easily perform their duties as they would be shielded under the giant neon canvas we designed. It may reduce other accidents occurring near the scene. And one final benefit, it will make us rich!

A few of the comments:

- "Sounds like a great idea to me!"
- "Have they given you a date for when the episode will film and air?"
- "'Let us know when you will be on. Couldn't happen to nicer people. Hope you hit a home run with it."
- "Natalie, I no longer believe anything Anthony posts. BTW ... it would've been a good idea."

- "OMG! My mom and I love that show! Good luck!!"
- "What an ingenious idea, you will make a fortune!!!!! I can't wait to see that show."
- "Is any part of this true????"
- "OMG! Natalie, I have had this same idea for years! No one really took me seriously! I think it will be a hit!!! You go girl!! Let us know when you will be on *Shark Tank*."

Sorry I've been silent these last couple of weeks, but I've been on the road for nearly ten days AND I am unbelievably overjoyed to tell you that Nathan (Natalie's sixteen-year-old son) is home safe and sound.

For those of you who didn't know, Nathan ran away to a seminary to become a priest. He has done this before, but each time we tracked him via his smartphone. We were always able to meet with him and convince him to wait until he was older. Well, this time we tracked him to Saint Jacques Chelac Seminary on the outskirts of Montreal in Canada.

Since we were in another country, the rules for retrieving a minor child are different and more difficult than here in the US. Nathan used this to his advantage, at first denying that I was his parent (three times he did this!), then refusing to submit to a blood test, and finally, purposefully failing a lie detector test just so we couldn't take him home.

At nearly my wit's end, I called my cousin Anthony to help. Since he still has a number of relatives in Montreal and speaks fluent French, he was able to convince the monsignor in charge to release Nathan to our custody but only if we promised a small honorarium to the monastery and helped with their marketing efforts for their bingo/casino night.

A few of the comments:

-   "Gosh Natalie, what an ordeal! Thanking God he is okay. I will pray extra hard for your family."
-   "Anthony, you really should write a book. You have quite the imagination."
-   "Wishing you an UNEVENTFUL holiday and New Year!! Glad it worked out. Sorry you had to go through that!"
-   "I'm sitting here cracking up! Love it!"
-   "What would Tuesdays be without a Natalie and Anthony story!"
-   "You had me until you said Anthony was fluent in French!"
-   "HA!!! Now that's funny!! You guys are great!!"
-   "It was a life-changing experience." (**Dad Note:** This was Nathan's actual reply on the post. He received nine likes for his comment.)
-   "Glad you are back, Nathan, I missed you so much, xo."
-   "Just read this post and all the comments and can't make up my mind if it's a windup or a true story. Please confirm."
-   "These stories are hysterical! However, I am getting wise to you! I'm looking forward to the next one!"

I went with my cousin, Anthony, to visit my mom in the hospital after she had replacement surgery for a new left hip. My father couldn't be there, and I didn't want her waking up alone. I waited for over an hour until she finally woke up. Groggy and a little teary-eyed, she was very happy to see me.

Ten minutes later her doctor came to check on her initial progress after the procedure. "Everything went well in surgery and your right hip will heal as planned," he said.

"Um, did you say right hip?" I asked the doctor. "My mom came in to have her left hip done."

The doctor was stunned. Ever the trooper, my mom told him it was okay; she was planning to have the other hip done anyway next year.

A few of the comments:

- "Mrs. B is looking great! And I hope you are joking about the wrong hip!!"
- "Oh my goodness! Aww, I hope she feels better. Yikes on that mistake, that's a biggie!! Your mom is so sweet!"
- "Hi Natalie—please tell your mom we hope to see her feeling better soon."
- "Are you serious!?! Boy, they are lucky she is a sweetie!! I will be praying for her speedy recovery big time!! Love her so much … give her a hug for me!!"
- "My God! That's why I try to stay away from hospitals as much as I can!"
- "Are you kidding??? They did the wrong hip?? What hospital and doctor, Natalie? So not cool. I was wondering why your mom wasn't in church this am. Please give her my best."
- "Unbelievable! The next hip should be free."
- "You tell her to get a lawyer."
- "I just called Priscilla (**Dad Note:** Natalie's mother) to find out how she is doing. She is doing great, and the doctor did NOT operate on the wrong hip."

Section 3

MY BEST GUESSES

I love the way my brain works. It sometimes shocks, frightens, and amazes me, but generally I am pleased with the functionality. My eyes observe a lot, but my brain decides which information needs to be stored and which needs not be bound; it's a strange game of tag and release. Your mom wishes my brain wasn't so indiscriminate or seemingly arbitrary. She would prefer it if my brain acted more meticulously like a fastidious file clerk and not like some oddball angler who keeps the guppies he catches and sets free the trophy fish. For some odd reason she thinks I am in control of my brain's fishing tackle.

Once the knowledge is stored, some of it sits close to the surface to be restated quickly in the form of poor jokes, useless data, and movie quotes like from a Pez dispenser. Other stuff sits there like Emily Post's book on etiquette in a high school library. My brain does perform maintenance checks on all of the information stored there. Though it isn't routine maintenance and sometimes what comes out of my mouth or typed into a Word doc sounds as if an off-balance tailor looked under the hood instead of a certified mechanic.

I promise I try to assess and process from what I learn and from what I witness. Some of it is understood easily and is pondered more rigorously. In this manner, my opinions and ideas seem reasoned, thoughtful, and conclusive; I share those nuggets of wisdom with you next in "Section 4: My Best Advice." Before that, I would like to relay my lesser shaped thoughts here in "Section 3: My Best Guesses." Since I never use the oven, these are not half-baked ideas. I prefer the stovetop to cook. I like to see what I am making, adding and mixing constantly until it is ready to serve. Section 3 contains the never-tastes-the-same-way-twice evolving and possibly more creative life recipes. They are my debatably-educated-but-constantly-ruminated guesses.

SPEAK YOUR MIND OR HOLD YOUR TONGUE?

I am awestruck by word choice and usage by Americans. For instance, we'll insert adjectives like "bad" or "sick" to indicate the exact opposite if something or someone is good or nice. "Dad, when you dance to your 80s New Wave music, those moves are sick! You really are a baaad dancer." (**Dad Note:** Since this is my book, I'll interpret your mischievous/malicious intent any way I want!) Americans interchange "hot" and "cool" to signify the same value or equal effect. "That is so cool!" is equivalent to saying, "That's hot!" We'll say, "What's up?" as a greeting and if we are "down" with something, it means we understand. And don't get me started how when we attach the word "ass" as a suffix to a myriad of different adjectives like "dumbass" and "smartass" to change the connotation entirely. In Rhode Island we take word choice/usage a step further by adding the adjective "wicked" in sentence or speech. We use it as an adverb to imply that something or someone is extra, particularly or especially. "Dad, you are wicked awesome and so wicked funny!" (**Dad Note:** It's still my book—if you don't like my jokes, write your own book.)

I'll "let the cat out of the bag," I am even more fascinated by American-English phraseology—I wicked enjoy descriptive and quirky sayings. There's "no beating about the bush," our way of saying things is peppered with abstract imagery and symbolic, nonliteral statements. And "at the drop of a hat," I enjoy "burning the midnight oil" to research our countless and distinct colloquial expressions. I am "head over heels" in love with our odd phrases and strange idioms. Other cultures have quirky language articulation as well, but we seem to "have the market cornered" on weird-angled, specifically mangled, often wrangled, new-fangled, and star-spangled "mother tongue" ways of speaking here in the USA. I can't imagine a more "uphill climb" than studying American English as a second language. It certainly is "no piece of cake." And good luck to any brave student wishing to master more than the basics because I guarantee "they are biting off more than they can chew." No "corners can be cut" learning "the whole ball of wax." Our terminology, phraseology, and syntax are definitely "crazier than a soup sandwich." Ultimately, it is not an impossible "can of worms" to eventually capture the essence of our language, so I guess "every cloud has a silver lining."

My favorite American-made idiom was invented by your mom. Presently, she is the only one who uses it, but it may catch on someday with your help. On chilly days, especially during winter, she uses a benchmark indicator to gauge how cold it is outside. If I ask her the temperature outside, she checks the outdoor thermometer (OT) and relays the number in "X degrees above snow," but not the actual reading. (**Dad Note:** X is always a calculated number. The formula is X = OT-32). The figure represents the total temperature degrees above thirty-two degrees Fahrenheit, i.e., when water freezes. Her logic is that any precipitation can/will/would/should turn to snow at that temperature. So, if it is 39 degrees outside, she refers to it as "seven degrees above snow." If you start to use her methodology, others may follow. With your assistance, it may transform the way we speak about weather AND (for my specific enjoyment) add another idiom to our language. So, come on! Help out your meteorologically rebellious mom!

When you read the title of this chapter, "Speak Your Mind or Hold Your Tongue," no special explanation or extra details were required to convey my thoughts. You had no problems with the sentence structure, meaning, or imagery. For example, you didn't read "hold your tongue" as a command to speak while pinching your tongue between two fingers. The combined idioms in the question are obvious. They easily translate as: *Is it advantageous and/or wiser to provide additional verbal input or is it smarter to say nothing?* Speak your mind to voice what you are thinking. Hold your tongue to not say what you are thinking.

As a subjective choice it is easily understood, but it is difficult to properly respond because no standard or baseline exists as to when you should speak up or when you should shut up. Generally, if you are asked a question, you answer it. Unless the question is one of those tricky mom/wife inventions known as a "rhetorical question." For example, and a bit of husband/fatherly advice, never respond when the first part of the discourse begins with your partner asking, "How stupid do you think I am?" or some other quicksand-like sounding question, especially if you sense a few exclamation points' worth of antagonism in their voice.

It is a personal decision to interject, reply, or hold back. Usually it isn't a slippery slope, however, I have developed an only-a-fool-such-as-I nearly foolproof system. It is my private subjective litmus test. I call it my TMI Assessment. (**Dad Note:** To me, TMI stands for "transform, maintain, improve," and is not the common acronym for "too much information" or "Tennessee Military Institute" or the more appropriately ascribed for me, "too many idiots.") I use it for business purposes and proposals. I use it for personal planning and setting goals. Simply, I ponder what I am about to say or do and consider if my actions or words will transform, maintain, or improve the situation. Factored into my decision process are two questions.

- Will I add value to the conversation, issue, or topic?
- Is it fairer or more advantageous to say nothing?

It is a reasonable and humble test for my grumbly brain. The analysis simmers like a sorcerer's brew inside my cauldron of a head. The two questions help me decide whether thoughts should remain as ideas in my gray matter potion or become words and zoom out of my mouth like a witch on a broomstick on Halloween night. The modest assessment is not fool proof though; there is a wart on the tip of its nose and a scar on its cheek.

1) The wart on the nose flaw is that personal emotions may influence the decision to speak your mind or hold your tongue. Those feelings may coerce you to say something or to not say something. Often and in hindsight, regret settles in. The overriding consensus of an emotionally guided decision is "it seemed like a good idea at the time."

2) The scar on the cheek blemish is a rash I suffer persistently. It's a non-life-threatening disorder called "blessingandacurse-itis." It's pretty similar to Foot-in-Mouth disease and IHaveNoFilter syndrome. My itchiness comes from my belief I know the thoughts of a group. The blessing part is, either telepathically or intuitively, I divine what others are reasoning. The curse function is that I sometimes blurt it out.

To speak your mind or hold your tongue is a personal decision. Based on my simple TMI (transform, maintain, improve) test, decide if what you are about to say will inspire, instruct, defend/correct, or advocate. If you are adding input or answering a question, be confident in your facts/statements/opinions. You are smart and you are passionate. As a health benefit, speaking your mind may reduce levels of stress and help you avoid regret.

Holding your tongue may be an effective choice, especially if you think what you are about to say might be misinterpreted as mean-spirited—teasing and bullying dance a narrow, subjective line. You may want to withhold your facts/statements/opinions if it will be received as overload in excess of what is required or necessary, i.e., the "other" TMI (too much information). After reflection and deliberation, you may decide to suppress participating if the reason is not only to make yourself feel better, but also to make someone else feel worse, i.e., your pursuit of happiness should not come from an "I-told-you-so!" moment. And sometimes, there is a lot to be gained by just shutting up, i.e., listening is becoming an extinct virtue.

Speak Your Mind

Translates as, "to verbalize your opinions, educated or not, formed from contemplation, consideration and possibly experience, concerning the subject or situation." In the format of a command, input is requested. The answer may be used for the purposes of securing a confirming opinion or providing a dissenting one. For example, a parent might ask a child, "Tell me what you learned in school today," or a prospective employer could ask, "Give me three good reasons why I should hire you?" or as your dad I might even ask, "Enlighten me with what you love about me?" Sometimes the request may be genuine or disingenuous, so be careful.

If you choose to speak your mind in the format of an idea, a proactive and unsolicited announcement is made. Instead of silence, discourse is provided to stimulate or concur with an existing conclusion.

Speak Your Mind to Inspire

Back in college, I had the same professor for a few math classes. She was a good instructor who knew her stuff and how to teach mathematics to a dummy like me. She kept the rules and calculations at an understandable level. Coincidently, she was the wife of one of my high school math teachers. I doubt they compared notes on how little I seemed to grasp math concepts. During my senior year in college, I had one final math course with her called Financial Analysis and I did pretty well. I don't remember that her methods improved or that I paid more attention, but my GPA rallied with this subject. I had a 90+ average through the middle of the semester. After receiving an A grade on the mid-term exam, she congratulated me on my effort and comprehension of the topic. I told her I wasn't trying any harder than I had previously, but things seemed to click for me. I'll never forget what she said. "You really seem to understand numbers when there are dollar signs in front of them." It may have sounded a bit patronizing, but it wasn't meant as an insult and I didn't take it that way since she is a very nice person. She was gently and slyly teasing me about the limits and depth of my math knowledge. I took it as a compliment. It resonated quickly with me and sorted out a bunch of things in the barely used, rarely analytical without my trusty financial calculator left side of my brain. I comprehend amounts and quantities related to money. I appreciated her honesty and her comment. Other teachers may not have spoken their minds and kept their comments to themselves. I was glad she said this. It inspired confidence in me. There was something out there that made "cents" to me. I had to go find it. (**Dad Note:** Sorry for the lousy "sense/cents" pun. You could have bet a dollar I would make a currency joke. I'll never "change!")

Speak Your Mind to Instruct

The theme of this section is about when and why speaking your mind can have a positive impact. This segment should have a caveat: Sometimes, to speak your mind is as simple as getting involved with the best intentions to lead and educate. Not necessarily as an expert, but as a willing, passionate mentor/instructor. There are numerous opportunities to engage by offering to share your own expertise and enthusiasm through teaching, training, and coaching. Perhaps speaking your mind in the form of instruction is less flashy than the others I indicate here in this chapter, but the teaching element of speaking up offers a mutually beneficial shared experience for the tutor/coach/teacher and the student/learner. Getting involved is the first step.

Coaching sports is one of my passions. I have logged hundreds (probably thousands) of miles driving to games and I have charted hundreds (probably thousands) of Xs and Os on a dry-erase board. From managing your youth baseball and basketball teams to coaching high school football, basketball, and baseball, I can honestly say I have loved every minute of it. (Well, at least most of the minutes!)

My "coaching career" had a very humble beginning. One summer a long, long time ago, when I was even younger than you are now, I was a playground supervisor for Hope Villa, a neighborhood park in my hometown of Bristol, Rhode Island. Each morning I had to organize on-campus activities like Nok Hockey, tetherball, and volleyball which had become very popular because of the 1984 Summer Olympics. After a morning's worth of sweating, running, and jumping, we would board school buses for a variety of afternoon activities and competitions at the town beach. The rivalries between the five parks were friendly but fierce; every kid was proud of their own neighborhood and delighted to represent its playground. One of my duties included coaching our park's boys' soccer teams. Back then I knew very little about coaching and even less about soccer and my strategy was simple. With the younger kids my objective was to keep the kids involved, active, AND moving in the same direction. They usually resembled the nomadic rumbling game pieces on one of those old Tudor Electric Football games. With the older kids my aim was to teach fair play, basic athletic skills, and to respect their opponent as well as the officials. There were some pretty good players and I ran some drills, but I knew I didn't know enough about soccer to make them better technically. My instructions to the teams were even simpler than my training routine: "Go score more goals than the other team." It must have worked. Our teams won the town championship. We celebrated in the style of a Michael Jackson song: "Hope Villa is a Thrilla'!"

My training methods and preparation techniques did evolve eventually as I stayed involved with coaching. I improved by becoming myself a better student of each sport I taught and a better leader of the kids I coached. Some basic tenets never changed, like my insistence for respecting the game, an opponent, an official, and yourself. I required my teams to bond together towards a common goal, to play hard for each other, and not try to impress me. Along the way, I've upped my Xs and Os, my motivational techniques, and at some juncture in my coaching career I told a kid (probably you) to "rub some dirt on it and get back in the game." It was my first dad/coach-ism point.

I managed a few championship winning teams of yours and even coached an undefeated junior varsity high school basketball team. (**Dad Note:** If this ever gets published as a book, I offer a special shout out to James, Pat, Marc, Felix, Paul, Jamal, et al. for that special season!) I have also coached a few teams whose winning was measured by participation replete with the awarding of yellow "thank-you-for-showing-up-on-time" ribbons. My coaching improved because my enthusiasm never waned. I wasn't fixated on a final score. I was motivated and satisfied to teach life lessons through sports. It was my ambition to gain common ground with players through hard work and instruction towards a common goal.

I realized at a young age that passion is part of who I am. For mostly better and occasionally worse, it factors into the decisions I make. To instruct is to teach. Learning doesn't have to be done with passion, but it is an everyday, all-the-time-super-duper important part of life. It's my lowly opinion, but teaching cannot and should not be done without it.

Speak Your Mind to Defend/Correct

In the early 1990s, I was working for a defense contractor as a financial analyst. The national and local economies had soured, and I was laid off. Since I couldn't find a relatable job in Rhode Island, I moved to Michigan to work at a mortgage bank. My brother, your Uncle Bob, was a vice president there and arranged an interview for me with the president/owner of the bank. The conversation went very well. Immediately I was offered and accepted a position to learn mortgage banking by working in various departments. It was comparable to an informal executive training program.

I still like to think I was garrulously impressive and extraordinarily loquacious, but it didn't hurt my chances that the gentleman whom I interviewed with was also Uncle Bob's father-in-law. Once the euphoria of a new job waned, I was nervous because I would be moving my entire life 750 miles from my comfort zone and my family minus my beloved stereo, my even more beloved 1965 Ford Mustang convertible, and my most beloved nieces. On the plus side, I had a new job with dollar signs in front of numbers again and Midwesterners were purported to be very friendly. I was looking forward to the challenge.

After shedding a few tears driving away from everything I be-loved, I settled in quickly and nicely to my new environment. I loved my move to Michigan, except for the quirky vehicle pattern of turning right to go left at many intersections—appropriately called a "Michigan Left"—and trying to figure out what "pop" was. (**Dad Note:** Pronounced "pahp." In Rhode Island, "pahp" is pronounced "soda.") I made great new friends and was learning as much as I could about the mortgage business. My new life exceeded my expectations and broadened my perspectives. There was but a lone downside: money. My income unfortunately hadn't exceeded my expectations or stretched my wallet. Between rent, groceries, and other expenses I wasn't able to save much money for entertainment or travel. It's a common tale of twenty-something-year-olds throughout history— chock-a-block full of willingness and ambition, but unmatched and empty pockets. As a single guy with limited funds who drove a four-cylinder "grocery-getter" station wagon, my social prospects were constrained; my "wicked charming" Northeast sarcasm, accent, and personality were imperfect in their appeal. (**Dad Note:** It's pronounced as "wikked chahming Nawhtheast sahkasm." By the way, I don't think I have an accent, but my Michigan friends often said that I did in fact "heeyav an ehccent.")

Fortunately for your impoverished dad, I stumbled upon a tacit perk offered through the bank which exponentially increased my potential—season tickets to area sports venues. Detroit is known as "Hockey Town" and Red Wings tickets were the hottest of commodities. In the late 1980s Detroit was infatuated with its professional basketball team, the Pistons. "The Bad Boys" were a top draw, but this was the early/mid 1990s and interest had waned enough for me to be offered the bank's four tickets as long as no senior employee wanted to attend. Surprisingly, being the four-hundredth of four-hundred employees was not a disadvantage. I proudly admit my support for the Boston Celtics never wavered, but I did enjoy being six rows behind the bench in a reserved section watching the Detroit Pistons play. Often I would invite new acquaintances I had met from where I lived or from work in order to gain friends and increase my social circle. One time I went with a very attractive woman whom I was interested in dating. She also worked at the bank. She had a beautiful smile, was very pretty, and wasn't terribly offended by my sense of humor, accent, or that my transportation was a "grocery getter." Being on my best behavior has never been my strong suit, but I would try because I liked her. At the very least she might be impressed by the seats and think I had spent a lot of money on her, so I had that going for me. During the car ride to the game, we found we didn't have a lot in common and many of our interests weren't aligned. However, we found the challenge to be an attraction in learning about each other and we both liked to laugh. Once there, we continued our conversation. It was problematic at times because of the cheering for the home team who was winning. From my perspective—and I think/hope from hers as well (and not just because she was a Pistons fan)—our date was going well.

The mood changed when a man behind us about eight rows started shouting insults at the visiting team. It was intermittent at first but grew louder and more frequent, as if he suddenly, perhaps drunkenly, assumed the audience of 20,000 was there to see him perform and not for a basketball game. His bellowing wasn't positive or supportive—or funny. (**Dad Note:** Despite what you think, I know funny because I am funny.) I have been to numerous professional athletic contests and witnessed plenty of derisive shouting at opposing players and it's never bothered me unless it was offensive. I am kind of sensitive and I have a low threshold for what's offensive, but if a fan pays for a ticket and wants to be negative, who am I to judge how they "cheer?" But this man was loud. His shouts and taunts weren't racist or bigoted, just distracting, boorish, and making others around him uncomfortable. Nothing I cared for, but nothing I would do anything about because his only serious misconduct was being an idiot. I am sure he thought he was amusing; I am equally confident he didn't think he'd had too much to drink.

He continued to be very annoying and made it difficult to be attentive to my date. (**Dad Note:** I agree with what you are thinking right now. *My dad knows annoying because he is annoying.* Kindly also note I guessed you were thinking annoying. I added zero descriptive adjectives to your thoughts like extremely, most, or unbelievably annoying.) Even though I wasn't paying any attention to the game, my ears were radar-like, picking up obnoxious mouthy blips from the obnoxious mouthy guy behind us. I was distracted and had to redouble my efforts to lengthen my continuously short attention span. I was doing okay until the blowhard repeatedly shouted very insensitive remarks at the visiting teams' African American head coach who had battled drug addiction while he had played in the league. After the fourth stupid comment which now included some racial references, I couldn't take it. I apologized to my date for what might happen next. I stood up, turned around, and barked at the guy, "Hey, stupid! Shut the hell up!" Truth be told, I may not have used the word "hell," but I assure you it only had four letters. He screamed back, telling me to shut up and told me if I didn't, he would make me. I laughed when I heard this. I am a large human. Short of turning green, sometimes, if you make me angry, I can become a large, enraged human. I figured I didn't look too indomitable from eight rows below so I decided to walk up a couple of steps to give him a view of what might be coming his way. His obscene bellowing waned only slightly. I walked up another two steps. He continued. I took steps five and six towards him. From my perch, I reiterated that not only should he shut up, but also apologize to everyone around him for being such an idiot. Before he could respond and before I ascended to his row, I was stunned by what happened next. Fans around him started applauding me and joined me in defense of a coach none of us knew. No one appreciated what that rude man was saying, but no one tried to stop him until someone led them.

I let my emotions get the better of me and I am glad I did. It doesn't always work out well, but I can't sit idly even to minor injustices. It is important to speak your mind against unfairness, prejudice, and inequality. If one person spews hate from a pulpit unchecked, the message appears acceptable and grows as the number of followers swells. Stirring up hatred or inciting to discriminate is like playing with matches in a dry forest—it is difficult to extinguish a fire when it is raging. (**Dad Note and Date Epilogue:** We went out a few more times, but the relationship eventually ended. You are correct to assume it was probably because of something I said!)

Speak Your Mind to Advocate

Passion resides in each of us, bridled slightly unnervingly between love and hate among our emotions. Passion is the thing that spurs either of those feelings into action ready to sacrifice for a cause or a person.

Except for my love for you and my intense dislike for the New York Yankees and Liverpool Football Club, I am not extremely passionate. My emotions tend to lie on my sleeve, but fortunately I often wear a sweatshirt and they're mostly kept under control. I love my family and my country. I support efforts to save the environment, feed the hungry, and shelter the poor. I believe it is a personal responsibility to improve a community through coaching, teaching, mentoring, and advocacy—all of which I have done and will continue to do. I am not entirely zealous to join charitable organizations as I prefer to do what I can on my own terms. Though I feel a bit guilty, I am not a bad person; I regret slightly, but I don't chastise myself. I wish I was more passionate about other things, but I am not. I care a great deal, but unless it is for you or to a slightly lesser degree, my country, I am not compelled to act.

My mom was a different kind of emotional animal. Her passions hotly radiated from the inside and burst past her sleeves as words and actions. She championed many causes, but none was dearer to her than the Right to Life. She especially believed every baby had a right to be born. Without debating the ethics or principles of her conviction, I want you to know I always admired her for her certainty.

She donated and joined in many causes, supported political candidates, attended rallies for the underprivileged, participated in local marches and even in demonstrations in Washington, DC. The key components to her principles were her unwavering faith in God and the idea that **voiceless individuals need an advocate**. I was always proud of her for her passion for what she believed. As uncertainty continues to proliferate, the world needs more people like she was.

It is important to speak your mind for those who are unable or forcibly unwilling. I am proud of the times I have spoken or acted on behalf of those who can't. I do not sit idly. It will forever be my goal to be a part of a solution through advocacy, aid, and awareness rather than a cause or furtherance of a problem. I trust you will surpass me in terms of passion to defend, to support, and to produce positive results to make this a better world. I pray for and dream that you will equal or outshine my mom, your grandmother.

Speak Your Mind to Avoid Stress

I come from a large family—a mom, a dad, two brothers, one sister, grandparents, aunts, uncles, and a billion or so cousins who either are or aren't related to me. Our members include tall ones, smart ones, nice ones, good cooks, gossips, etc., and ad infinitum. In the entire assemblage, no one has ever been described as "the quiet one" or even "a quiet one." When we got together at a planned family reunion, Sunday afternoon spaghetti dinner or social gathering for a holiday, the noise could drown out a jet airplane landing or a thunderous and large marching band practicing next door. Even if the numbers were reduced, fewer seemed to be louder, as if the fewer were required to compensate for a smaller group. My family is a special group, but we are not immune to the tensions, anxieties, and strains of everyday life. However, of all who have passed away, I am 100% certain that stress produced by withholding what was on their mind was NOT the cause of death.

Holding your tongue is a good practice sometimes, but deeply burying pent up negative feelings is never ideal. If the stress of bottling certain emotions causes anxiety, they should be discussed. (**Dad Note:** I am already aware of the apprehension and unease I have caused you throughout your lives. If you haven't already unloaded on me, sorry but the statute of limitations has expired. However, I continue to be the same person I always was, so a new window of opportunity to let loose may be around the corner.)

If you want something, ask for it. Don't amass regret for unfulfilled aspirations or matters you wished you had addressed. Be a squeaky wheel if you need some grease; don't wait around like a tin man praying Dorothy wanders by with an oil can. When speaking your mind to avoid stress, don't be condescending, and if you can help it, don't be overly pushy or aggressive. Be forthright, intrepid, and firm. Too often opinions are withheld or requests are concealed for fear of offending. Many times, I have noticed the other person appreciated that I voiced my appeal.

I have jokingly referred to an informal yet very probable distinction I held in my twenties—the world record for most girls having declined a date with me. My memory may be fuzzy and my math incorrect, but I recall thousands of responses that sounded like this: "Umm … no. But that's really so nice of you to ask. Thank you. Umm, but I have to _____ (fill in the blank) so I can't." Even though it was personal, I never let it affect my personality or change who I am. (**Dad Note:** Dating websites and smartphone apps may alleviate the personal interaction, but left or right swiping still produces angst. You'll never know unless you ask.)

Speak Your Mind to Avoid Regret

More math for you. Superstar hockey legend Wayne Gretzky is famous for the aphorism, "You miss 100% of the shots you don't take." The logic is succinct, poignant, and mind-numbingly simple. I've always thought, *Why does a famous guy who's got the world at his skates conceive such a slick line? Why didn't I or some other regular guy originate that phrase?* I think it's because I don't play hockey, but more likely I was an unenlightened, unsophisticated eighteen-year-old kid when he said it.

Regret is the feeling you get when you sense a missed opportunity. It is a heavy basket filled with weighty phrases like "I wished I had" or "If only I had" and encumbering words like "would have" and "could have" and "should have." My high school football coach added a whole quote's worth to the bin: "If 'ifs,' 'ands' and 'buts' were candy and nuts, we'd all have a helluva Christmas!" He may not have been the first to say it, but he said it so often and so uniquely he gets my vote for the credit.

To be fair, it is near impossible to live life without regret to some degree. Chances, occasions, and prospects present themselves endlessly; you can't act on every opening. But if you lead a good life and know what is important, speak up when the time is right.

Hold Your Tongue

Translates as the opposite of speaking your mind. As a request or demand, you are being asked to keep your opinions to yourself. As a conscious decision, you decide not to add discourse. Literally, holding your tongue with your fingers is quite an image. It definitely prohibits you from revealing your position, at least coherently.

Hold Your Tongue If You Can't Say Something Nice, Idiot!

The first "real" job I ever had was the one I mentioned I was laid off from before I went into the mortgage business. I was a financial analyst for a defense contractor managing multi-million-dollar budgets for international contracts in their submarine signal division. It sounds high profile and exciting; it wasn't. But it was important enough for me to wear a sports jacket, tie, and a low-clearance level government badge. Except for sporting my maroon L.L. Bean backpack I used in college, I was quite the young suburban professional. I was proudly indistinguishable from the other fifty bean-counter specialists carrying briefcases not backpacks. Settled into life in a cubicle, I had a company health plan, a 401K savings account, and I worked with numbers with dollar signs in front of them. Life was pretty good.

I was being trained by a woman about ten years older than I was. She was a nice person and knowledgeable analyst. We didn't have much in common and our personalities didn't mesh perfectly, but we developed a friendly-enough work relationship. A few months after I started, she went on maternity leave. On her final day, there was a party for her. We congregated into one of the larger cubicles. She was gracious as she opened presents, cards, and thanked everyone. I was one of her final goodbyes. After a big hug, she joked in front of the few remaining guests about how much I would miss her. Teasingly, I replied that I wasn't going to miss her too much. She continued and again stated how much I would miss her. Playfully, I said, "The only way I'll miss you is if I swing a dead cat at you in the dark." I thought it was lighthearted and clever. Apparently, I was the only one pleased with my jesting remark. She left in a hurry soon afterwards. I didn't see or talk to her until she returned to work a few months later. I had hoped she had forgotten my stupid clowning comment, but I sensed she hadn't. Our interactions were icy and awkward. I felt bad because speaking my mind was the cause. I thought I was being funny. I wished I had held my tongue.

I am quick-witted. It is the double-whammy curse and benefit of my brain. I wish sometimes the trap between my brain and my mouth was made out of steel and not out of straw. Since my unintended but hurtful comment to that woman, I learned that sometimes it is best to shut up and interject nothing. I would love to tell you I learned something from that experience (**Dad Note:** I did.) and tell you I never did it again (**Dad Note:** I can't.). With the benefit of experience and maturity I have improved, but it is a constant struggle. I try to evaluate my comments before I deliver them. I assess my audience and identify if they are empathetic. Sometimes, I shut up and say nothing. Sometimes I don't. And sometimes I can't.

Hold Your Tongue - TMI (Too Much Information)

At some point in life, everyone has been guilty of offering too much information. No one is immune—you have either heard it, said it, written it, or read it. With no filter and only straw to prevent mistakes out of my mouth, I have slipped up too. I have considered you might think this book is evidence beyond reasonable doubt I often offer too much information and quite possibly file it in your personal library under "TMI."

Unfortunately, I have no perfect plan to eliminate this error in judgment. It relies on many factors of objectivity and subjectivity before it can be classified as a miscalculation. As a rule, if what you are about to say or write may cause embarrassment for you or the recipient, consider this: You rarely get the chance to take it back and with social media displaying personal opinion/information at the speed of light, be extra careful.

Hold Your Tongue - "I Told You So!"

IMHO, "ITYS" is a RDTTS. DGT! DYJHIW sm1 does that? TIFM, TISL. NGWCOI. IDKWW: NIFOC or saying, "ITYS?" DDT b/c CBAK@U. So, B4 U HTB or say "FML," TAA: Is this NYC or NIYBI? If you say it, u will DARFC. IYAM, WOT. 1FT: WWJD or even WWJJD? TWIWI? LMAO! TTFN! DFTBA!

Translation:

In my humble opinion, "I told you so" is a really dumb thing to say. Don't go there! Don't you just hate it when someone does that? Take it from me, this is so lame. No good will come of it. I don't know what's worse: Sitting nude in front of computer or saying, "I told you so." Don't do this because it always comes back at you. So, before you hang the bastards or say "f*ck my life," think again and again: Is this not your concern or not in your best interest. Say it and you will have to duck and run for cover. If you ask me, it's a waste of time. One final thought: Ask yourself, "What would Jesus or even Joan Jett do?"

That was interesting, wasn't it? I'm laughing my ass off! Ta ta for now! Don't forget to be awesome!

Hold Your Tongue to Gain Something

After two years on my first job, the company downsized me. As a large person, I am offended by that word. I prefer the British version: made redundant. It's more polite. It was the early 1990s, the economic pace of the country had slowed, and the federal government wasn't re-committing the same levels of funding to defense projects. As a financial analyst for a defense contractor, I didn't need dollar signs in front of the numbers I saw written for my future. I was the fifty-third hired into a department of fifty-three. The big boss had wanted to keep me around because I was good at my job. I made it especially difficult for him because he was also the manager of the corporate basketball and softball teams I played on. I helped him win a couple of championships in the industrial league, but not enough to save me from being "made redundant." I couldn't complain. I made some friends, acquired some business knowledge, and learned I didn't like working in a "big box" business structure where I didn't matter.

Next stop was the Midwest mortgage bank in Michigan. I fumbled and floundered at first because everything—the area, the people, the industry, even the cubicle arrangement—was new to me. I eventually got the hang of it. The same dollar signs I was used to just a different composition of the numbers. I passed through many departments and learned a lot about how homes are financed. My last stop was as a mortgage consultant in the sales department, technically called a "loan officer" at the bank. It was awesome. I was on the frontline meeting with customers offering awesome low loan rates and awesomely great service. I visited professional offices to convince them to refer clients to me because I was so awesome. I answered an awesome number of rate calls. I attended seminars, workshops and expos—anywhere I could tell potential customers how awesome I was. After a few months of the non-stop awesomeness tour, my bank account showed a less than awesome balance of below zero where the dollar sign doesn't even register.

One day, I was in the office and a senior loan officer asked if I was okay because I seemed subdued. I told him I liked the job a lot but was having a difficult time and was thinking about quitting. He asked me if I liked the mortgage business and I told him I did. He cheered me up by telling me there's a learning curve in a new business and don't become too overwhelmed. He noticed I was good at some things, and he admired my enthusiasm. He also noted there was one thing I was doing wrong and offered advice on how I could improve. With three digits below zero in my checkbook and not feeling entirely awesome, I was open to new ideas. He told me, "Sometimes you have to know when to shut up." I think he sensed being quiet was not my strong suit. He explained that you have to allow the customer time to ask questions to find comfort and to engage to build confidence. You must let them tell you why they need this loan, not just the dollar amount. You must let them talk to build a bridge from the other side. If you can shut up and listen, the person shifts slightly from potential one-time customer to potential client for life.

It was great advice. I employed it immediately and positive results soon followed. Holding my tongue allowed me to uncover customer needs in order to match them to my and my company's benefits. In a few months the bankbook numbers and dollar signs were no longer in the red and I was in the pink.

In My Humble Opinion

To speak your mind or hold your tongue is a difficult personal decision. To speak your mind may reveal a brilliant side and garner positive attention for you. To speak your mind may also put you under the glare of a bright light you would rather avoid. To hold your tongue has its own high peaks and low valleys. To help you decide the best course of action, start asking yourself, "Does it add value?" Use my nearly idiot-proof cognitive TMI test: Speak if you can transform, must maintain, or be able to improve the conversation, issue, or situation. It is nearly idiot-proof because the decision involves not only what you think, but what you feel.

Passion is my blessing and my curse. It affects whether I speak my mind or hold my tongue. Simultaneously my passion can be the monkey wrench to fix a situation and the spanner thrown into the works. Enthusiasm interferes with my thought process. I don't always know what to say or if I should say anything at all. For proof, below are three examples.

1) When my eldest daughter was a newly minted, acerbic teenager, she revealed something no conservative, God-fearing father wants to hear. "Dad, I'm a New York Yankees fan." I was in shock. *How could this happen? Wasn't she raised with good New England patriotic values? Where in the name of Ted Williams did I go wrong? Why couldn't she just tell me she was pregnant or something easier to hear?* The traitorous words pierced worse than the scorpion sting of Bucky Dent's homerun in 1978 or Aaron Boone's snakebite in 2003. I was hurt, worried, and nervous. *Would Red Sox Nation revoke my membership?* I carried the original Red Sox sin of the Bambino's Curse. I served my penance in 1975, 1978, 1986, and 2003. I was born again and finally cleansed in 2004. I revered Yastrzemski and Evans while I denounced Steinbrenner, Dent, and Boone. Each summer I worship at the altar that is Fenway Park. I wear the hats. I buy the shirts. For goodness' sake, I tried harder than most fans to support Carl Everett and Pablo Sandoval! Surely my blindly unyielding patronage should count for something, right? So, how did a kid of mine end up on the A-Rod dark side in the evil empire?

   It took every ounce of my willpower to override my Beantown-centric passion. I calmed my liver. (**Dad Note:** "Calm your liver"—pronounced "livah" in New England—is a slang expression to tell an agitated person to calm down.) I did not lament; I did not scold her. I was betting this was part of a teen rebellious phase to torment me like a Tim Wakefield knuckleball. I would hold my tongue and be as patient as Kevin Youkilis waiting on a 3-1 pitch. Fast forward fifteen years and four World Series wins. My gamble paid off. She lives in Boston and will soon marry a man who is as nearly as devoted to our Pats, Cs, Bs, and Sox as he is to her. (**Dad Note:** It's the main reason I gave him my blessing to marry my daughter. Now if he would just post a photo on social media of her in a Red Sox ball cap, my liver would be sufficiently calmed about their upcoming marriage.)

Moral of the Story: Passion nearly got in the way. I kept my mouth shut and everything turned out okay.

2) For the record, I wouldn't have held my tongue if one of my other three children proclaimed such blasphemy. I smartened up and indoctrinated you earlier in your lives about my fierce loyalty to Boston teams. When you were toddlers, I taught you the "Red Sox Rule!" rule. You are allowed to support only two Major League Baseball teams—the Red Sox and whoever plays the Yankees. If you challenge this rule, you will not live in my house. (**Dad Note:** I thought it was fairer they know very early the level of unwavering behavior I expected regarding my favored sports teams.) While you have tested my patience and pushed the boundaries on other edicts, so far none of you has challenged the "Red Sox Rule!" household rule. For this reason alone, you are always welcome in our house, your home base.

Moral of the Story: Slightly dictatorially, I spoke my mind, but it paid off.

3) However, I am a bit nervous that two of you live in New York and date Yankees fans. I am uneasy that your relationships progress in that big rotten forbidden apple and your careers keep you away from our Eden called Fenway Park. Would you forget your Royal Rooters roots? Would you forget the words to "Tessie" or "Sweet Caroline?" Worse, I have a recently recurring nightmare that my future grandchildren begin life wearing pinstriped onesies. (Breathe, Anthony. Breathe.)

Moral of the Impending Untold Story: Do I say something? Should I keep quiet? I guess I will pray to the almighty Dennis Eckersley and the RemDawg that my children will do what's right when the time comes.

Besides confirming your fears that I am a bit nutty, I hope you learned from this three-part mini-story that I don't always know when to speak my mind or hold my tongue. Passion is part of my makeup, but I try like heck not to let my emotion dictate every choice. Armed with no greater wisdom than any other dad, I make decisions based in reason and on past experiences. Left to my own wits and observations, sometimes I get it right and sometimes I don't. Fortunately and proudly, all of you are much smarter than I am and will learn more quickly than I did when to speak your mind or hold your tongue.

Speak your mind when you know your words add value, enhance, or defend. Hold your tongue if they do not. Remember, your voice, words, and actions have the power to improve or injure, but so does your silence.

BOYS ARE STUPID. GIRLS ARE ...

Dad Disclaimer

Before you skip this chapter, or worse, wish to seek vengeance for a perceived slight against your particular gender, below are my twenty provisos/conditions that apply directly to support my claim that "Boys are stupid. Girls are ..."

1) I refer to "boys" and "girls" as representative of a self-identified gender, i.e., boys = males and girls = females. I will not debate the multitude of acronyms or classifications. If someone wants recognition aligned with a different gender than the one they/he/she/it/them are born with, so be it. This chapter is meant to GENERALLY inform and HOPEFULLY entertain based on my observations and experiences.

2) In the supposition that "girls are ..." the three dots (...) represent a single word which has hitherto not been created. The yet to be designed word will be defined as "behavior which simultaneously manifests as random and deliberate, erratic and consistent, changeable and rigid, impulsive and cautious, fickle and reliable, and capricious and foreseeable." The closest I have come to inventing the demonstrative turn of speech is by

compounding two seemingly conflicting words of "predictably" and "unpredictable" to form the term "predictablyunpredictable." Hey, if "ginormous" can become part of our vernacular, why not my word? (**Dad Note:** As of today, I have not submitted the word for approval to the dictionary management commission.)

3) Not all boys/men/males are stupid. (**Dad Note:** If my computer allowed for an emoji, I would have placed the "smirking, disbelieving smiley face" one with a raised eyebrow here instead of this Dad Note.)

4) Not all girls/women/females are … (**Dad Note:** But they are.)

5) The statement is sexist and biased.

6) The statement is open-ended, unfair on numerous levels, and borders on stereotypical. It identifies as an unqualified and no-chance-in-hell fully quantifiable hypothesis.

7) The statement is a generalization. It is impudent, impious, and licentious.

8) I remind you this chapter appears in my "Best Guesses" section. Cut me some slack.

9-20) All boys are stupid.

"Boys are stupid. Girls are dot dot dot" is one of the tenets of my parenting repertoire. It is a phrase you have heard me say at least a million times. For the record, I repeated it or thought of it at least a million more times silently. If you ever saw me close my eyes and shake my head, that's what I was thinking. And for full disclosure, it outpaced my daily Serenity Prayer at least 10:1 when you were teenagers. Saying it or thinking it, answered, and continues to answer, every gender-associated question I had/have. It satisfactorily explained/explains every doubt, every issue, and every uncertainty I had about raising children.

Most people are skeptical of statements I make and have difficulty with how to respond. For instance, I have said:

"I once ate a four-pound cheeseburger … with fries!"

"I once ate nine lobsters and two steaks ... with a salad!"

"Back in '82, I used to be able to throw a pigskin a quarter-mile."

With the exception of the third statement as a nod to Uncle Rico from *Napoleon Dynamite* and eating the salad, I can honestly state those as facts. People are usually dumbfounded by things I say and usually have no reply. "Because boys are stupid" is a spot-on reaction. Still uncertain of the prowess of "Boys are stupid. Girls are ... ?" Here are questions I was asked either about you or to you. My answer to myself in each instance was, *Because boys are stupid,* or *Because girls are ... well, I don't know. Do you know?* Apply my response to any of the following scenarios.

"Yes, I know, but why is she dating *him?*"

"My God! What were you thinking?"

"On what planet is that behavior acceptable?"

"You did WHAT!?!"

It was my instinctual response to something I saw you do, heard you did, or knew you were about to do. If you want hard facts about why boys are stupid, I can only offer opinions. If you want empirical evidence why girls are ... , I have none. For answers, it would be wiser and smarter to ask a wiser and smarter person than I am. My theory is based on observation and my microscopically limited knowledge of psychology, sociology, chemistry, and a bunch of other fields of study concerning the human condition. Not only am I short on proof and evidence, but I am also probably insulting your level of intelligence with my broad sweeping generalization. For that, I apologize. Everyone knows I don't like to generalize. Oops, I did it again.

Muddying any attempt to qualify my theory that boys are stupid and girls are... is that I am an impudent member of the imprudent; I am a male human. According to current social and economic opinion, my gender is responsible for the declined present status and diminished future expectations of the human condition. We are war. We are heat. We are hunters and risk takers. We are a terminal and perpetual self-fulfilling adverse prophecy. We are the trigger and the explosive. Further mucking up the challenge to explain the second part of my theory why girls are … is that I am not female. How can I gauge a secret society in which I am not included? Can I judge the same sisterhood alliance I prevented from voting until the 19th Amendment? What right do I have to critique a group solely obliged to bear children? Not being a woman doesn't entirely prevent me from assessing a gender, but it would probably help. (**Dad Note:** I am old, but not even close to old enough to have voted against the 19th Amendment. And for the record, if I had been old enough I would have been actively suffrage-ing along with you, my sisters!)

So, there is my quandary. I am male and not to be trusted with truth AND I am not a fully-responsible-for-maintaining-the-human-race female. Fifty percent of my attempt is to admit idiocy and the other 50% of my attempt will lack subjective insight. So, why should you believe me? Answer: Since I am your idiot dad making the bold statements and I have your attention, let me defend myself. First, I would like to indicate my qualifications to assess gender issues regarding human thought/feeling, its manifestation through interaction, and probable outcomes. My four key points/aptitudes are:

1) **Cogito, ergo sum.**
   Translation: I think, therefore I am. Honestly, my brain does work!

   I am an abductive theorist. The self-designation is not on any business card I carry. I hold no college degree in it. It's a title I have given myself and it sounds like I am either smart or that I take hostages; neither is true. I observe things and try to make sense of what I observe. I look for the simplest and most likely explanation.

   For the record, the process isn't as easy as it appears, but there is method to my dad-ness madness. I gather information, question everything until I understand it, and then I spew information as if I should be trusted. I receive and examine feedback and throw it into the hopper for more dad-ness madness scrutiny. It is a challenging routine and unfortunately doesn't mean my conclusions are true, factual, and/or accurate. It just means that I comprehend them to the point of true, factual, and/or accurate to me. I subscribe to the theory "If it looks like a duck, swims like a duck, and quacks like a duck, then, the boys are stupid and girls are …" Like Sherlock Holmes, I eliminate the impossible and whatever conclusion remains, no matter how improbable or wingless, it is a duck. I postulate based on intuition and gut instinct. Remember, I am your dad and I have a big gut, so I go with my big instincts.

2) **Arma virumque cano.**
Translation: I sing of arms and the man. I know what I'm talking about, usually.

Personal Statement: "I do not own a chainsaw." This statement neither proves nor disproves that I am stupid.

As a Personal Declaration (and don't tell your mother I said this): "I do not own a chainsaw, but I'd like one." (Seriously, do not tell her.)

(**Dad Note:** Substitute any dangerous, fast, or loud object for the word chainsaw and the [il]logical conclusion remains intact.)

3) **Forsan et haec olim meminisse iuvabit.**
Translation: Someday we'll look back on this and it will all seem funny. Okay, it isn't the literal translation, but it's a line from a favorite Bruce Springsteen song, "Rosalita," and it converts nearly the same. To support this claim, please read the three lines below and I guarantee I know your reactions without seeing your faces.

1) "If you can hear me, if it got into your brain somehow … that I spread my buttcheeks as Mike Honcho."
2) "He said 'fart!'"

3) Michael Scott's Dunder Mifflin Scranton Meredith Palmer Memorial Celebrity Rabies Awareness Pro-Am Fun Run Race For The Cure

I have four children, two boys and two girls. My two sons are grinning. Both of them are recalling the "Fun Run" episodes from the television show *The Office* while simultaneously recalling other funny lines from the movie *Talladega Nights: The Ballad of Ricky Bobby* and laughing because their dad wrote the word "fart."

My daughters rolled their eyes and thought, *Why am I still reading this nonsense? My dad is SO not funny and boys are SO stupid.* (**Footnote:** One of my daughters was tempted to laugh then changed her mind.)

4) **Hic est fabula a pulchra domina.**
Translation: Here's the story of a lovely lady.

Okay, so I'm not funny, but the following is a true story. (**Dad Note:** This chapter was written before my cousin Natalie's passing. The excellence of her life and impact of this segment is unaffected by relaying the message in the present tense. For readability and uniformity, I know I should probably review this entire text for timeline inconsistencies, but for me, it shows I didn't need 20/20 hindsight to know how special she was.)

Every Tuesday I visit my cousin Natalie to deliver a meal Mom makes for her family. While I am sure Natalie's kids love your mom's cooking, they'd be happier if their mom was able to stand and cook for them. Because of her condition associated with ALS, she can't. We spend hours together. First, I tell her the farfetched story I am about to post on her Facebook page. Next, we either listen to music or I will read to her parts of this book; she is a wise friend, a sort of pre-editor confidant for me to present my obtuse opinions of the world as I see it. We spend the day together talking and laughing. Everyone knows that Tuesday is "Favorite Cousin Anthony's" day. I am protective and jealous of my time with her. She inspires me, supports me, and challenges me. Her spirit has not withered like her body has. ALS does not define her. The word "indomitable" was probably invented for her.

One recent Tuesday, I arrived to see extra cars in the driveway. I was a bit wary and harrumphed all the way to the door carrying Mom's meal. I was mildly perturbed to find four of Natalie's girl-friends from college sitting at the kitchen table with her. They were there to have lunch. I was slightly, but silently, resentful; my brown eyes turned green with envy. Natalie is so inviting and so very special that I shouldn't begrudge anyone wanting to be with her. Honestly, it is wonderful to watch her in the presence of others. I witness the positive effect she has. I thought, *Well, if her friends made the effort to arrange this, park your butt and your guarded envy in a chair.* I sat at the end of the table and listened while they chatted and laughed about children, husbands, and past experiences from their younger days. After some time, one of her friends noticed I wasn't participating in the conversation and tried to include me. I told her I was content to sit and listen; they were enjoying themselves and didn't need my input. Natalie's friend persisted, and to draw me into the dialogue asked for a sneak peek at the tall tale I would be posting on Natalie's Facebook page later. Surprisingly, all attention diverted to me. Apparently, each of them had been following my just-north-of-funny-but-well-south-of-truthful "Favorite Cousin Anthony" stories. I felt like a (very) minor celebrity knowing that these women were entertained by my Facebook fibs. Then I felt apologetic; I hadn't yet conceived the yarn I would be spinning. I had nothing to share. Natalie noticed my vacant stare, (**Dad Note:** It's the look I display before I dive into my brain's playground to create a story.) and she quickly pulled me from the fabrication sandbox in my head and told them I was writing a book in the for-mat of a letter to my children. Their attention was diverted from the unwritten Facebook post to my still-under-construction book. She then asked me to share a recent topic. It was this chapter.

Before I revealed, I set some ground rules. I told them the chapter is "under construction" as I was still writing it. It contains some paragraphs, but it is mostly scribbled ideas and notes at this point. I asked that they listen and then provide input —positive or negative. Usually, Natalie and I discuss my ideas and I read the sections as I form them, but today I had a larger audience to garner some feedback. They were happy to oblige. I didn't get past telling them the title "Boys Are Stupid. Girls Are…" when the friend who dragged me into the conversation interrupted immediately.

She was mildly indignant and before I spoke the first word after the title, she asked where I found the evidence to support my statement. I promised her I would get to that, but just let me read what I had written. My request wasn't satisfactory to her. Again she interrupted before I read the first word. She first wanted to know my thought process. She said it would help her know what to expect. *Okay*, I thought, *we're skipping the reading and going straight to the Q & A session.* I began with how boys never really grow up and repeat patterned behaviors. Her face snarled past mildly indignant. She insisted that her sons were smart (she has four of them) and all of her brothers were also smart and respectable men (five of them). She said my title was sexist and added that girls can be equally inept and possibly more naïve. I shifted gears slightly trying to lighten the mood and joked that having four sons, five brothers, and one husband should be enough evidence to prove that boys are stupid. (**Dad Note:** Perhaps your mom is correct; I am not as funny as I think I am.) The other women and Natalie were mute and uncomfortable. Even the crickets in the garden below her kitchen window went silent. I asked her to share a funny story about raising boys or growing up around so many. But she didn't follow my shiny lead and held course: Boys are no less intelligent than girls. All eyes were on me like heat lamps. I don't remember sweating, but

I probably did. I felt like a lone Spartan warrior at Thermopylae who showed up on the wrong day to encounter the entire Persian army wearing a "Kick Me!" sign. How would I defend myself and my statement? If the chapter title was correct, then I would have to admit I am stupid, ergo, not to be believed. If it was incorrect, as she proposed, that boys are not mentally inferior, then I would have no reason to write this chapter. She seemed pleased to have maneuvered me into a Socratic cave/corner, but it wasn't quite check and mate. I reiterated that I am a male/boy and that all males/boys are stupid. (**Dad Note:** No groundswell of support was gained, crickets were still silent, but Natalie's dog appeared to feel sympathy for me.) To prove my point, I asked them to close their eyes and listen to a brief anecdote.

"Imagine a distracted child runs into a kitchen holding scissors and heads straight to an electrical outlet. The kid becomes fixated on a grand idea—to stick the sharp end of the scissors into the socket."

I asked the women to open their eyes. I asked them if the child they envisioned was a boy or a girl. Before anyone answered, I told them I hadn't revealed the gender in my scenario. Each of them, including my cousin who has four sons of her own, admitted it was a little boy they had visualized. Further, two of the women sheepishly confessed they pictured Natalie's youngest son, Matthew, running with the scissors. (**Dad Note:** Everyone was aware that Matthew had swallowed a AAA battery when he was two years old. He was the likeliest candidate to conjure up.)

It was a minimal test about preconceptions. The women confirmed what I assume as a truth: Boys are stupid. The answer would have been the same if I asked a group of men or even a mixed audience to identify the gender of the child running with scissors. Thousands of years have predisposed us to see a boy in the story. And if it looks like a duck, swims like a duck, and quacks like a duck, then it must be Matthew.

Qualifications Accepted?!? Yes? Then Let's Move On. (Fart)

The four points do not precisely define or necessarily prove my theory that boys are stupid and girls are … BUT, I take (sort of) educated guesses based on what I experience and witness, that I am a man, that I have intimate knowledge of the minds of men, and that I realize countless experiences must count for something. The preceding paragraphs don't prove boys are stupid and that girls are … Further, I cannot share from a female perspective and have not offered any indication I understand the decision-making process of women. My four claims provide a decent foundation based on personal observation and thousands of years of male evolution. "Male evolution" outperforms any oxymoron like "jumbo shrimp," "liquid gas," and "honest politician"—we put the "moron" in oxymoron.

I'll speak on behalf of my entire gender and reveal a section of the "Man Code." We don't really evolve. We are hardwired as hunters, have fight-or-flight instincts coded into our DNA, and are hopped up on passion-igniting testosterone most of our lives. Males are predictable and imitate past behavior; even if it is incorrect, it is highly probable the actions repeat. The best we/you/the world can hope for is that we make better decisions the next time we run with scissors because we always head towards the electrical outlet. While I'm confessing, I'll let you in on an open secret—men tend to act naturally and are clearly confused. I'll let you in on another secret—I just used two more oxymorons in one sentence. I am seriously funny! (**Moron Dad Note:** "Seriously funny" was another one!)

Boys Are Stupid
In the Beginning: Testosterone, Hunting, and Risk-Favored Bungee Jumping

If human existence began with Adam and Eve, I have no quarrel. In the beginning, Adam and Eve had children. The first two were boys, Cain and Abel. One day, Cain's schoolboy jealousy drives him to kill his own brother.

Think about it—these two morons comprised the second generation of humans on the planet. One murders the other, his best friend and playmate. They weren't blessed with a great male role model as Adam started the family rap sheet by lying to God and blaming Eve. This family was ticking off boxes on the list of the Seven Deadly Sins at an alarming pace. I'm surprised they never had a reality TV show.

If you believe our genesis was when a primate walked upright, noticed he had opposable thumbs, and thought, *I stink therefore I am*, I have no problem with that either. In the beginning, there was a cosmic collision. Substances on our planet reacted to form primordial slop. The goo formed amino acids, the building blocks of proteins responsible for species. Eventually, plants and animals sprung from the sticky stuff. Much later, humans evolved from early primate animals. Testosterone was already in the sludgy gene pool. The rest is history.

Both beginnings include the naturally occurring human hormone, testosterone, and lend credence to my dim view of dim males. Whichever evolutionary path, testosterone was present, driving competition for food, shelter, mates, and prestige. It was there, influencing sexual behavior, desire, and initiating the human male instinct to hunt and take risks.

Testosterone is a chemical produced by the body. At conception, it is responsible for gender assignment (i.e., whether a penis is present at birth). Later, it is responsible for muscle mass, fat distribution, increased bone density, maturation of sex organs, facial and other hair. Testosterone factors in intensity of sex drive and other desires to produce cravings, yearnings, and aspirations. For males, the level is about eight times the amount produced by females, which equates to an 800% increased chance to affect the decision-making process of running with scissors.

Whether hunting prey or a dollar, human males are coded to provide sustenance, comfort, and protection. (**Dad Note/Reminder:** This is a generalization. There are numerous instances in the animal kingdom where the female is the lead hunter, like in a pride of lions. Female humans have this trait as well, BUT generally it is an inherent male protein-sequenced role. For the record and since I don't own a gun, bow, or arrow, I would probably trust Mom to hunt for the family—I faint at the sight of blood.) Male DNA pushes to hunt, but there is no gene-coded map that tells you how to do it. Initially, man was motivated by the preservation of his primary social unit. Instinctually, he was driven to provide for and protect those closest to him. Nothing has changed, but his desires have increased. He wants more. He seeks better and wider grounds for hunting. He requires better accommodations for himself and his family. The problem is, so do his neighbors.

Humans are driven to endure. Basic needs and primal urges request attention. Testosterone-initiated character traits force males to hunt and compete. Competition produces contest. Contest produces challenges. Challenges produce risk. Risk presents a higher possible return, but also a higher chance for males to make mistakes. Males tend to thrive on even the simplest of competitions, i.e., we are willing to risk more—real or imagined—for a greater potential reward. The problem is we do not always learn from our mistakes. We repeat actions through risky testosterone fueled ambition. The dangerous pattern is innate behavior. (**Dad Note:** Just so we are clear, I am still generalizing. Men have contributed positively and intelligently to humanity despite, and sometimes because of, mistakes. For example, Christopher Columbus sailed the ocean blue in 1492. He didn't find a passage to India but discovered the Caribbean. His mistake led to further exploration in the Western Hemisphere which eventually included the eastern coast of what is now known as the United States of America. Another example of a mistake by a male which ultimately changed modern life was an accidental discovery. In 1945, an engineer at Raytheon noticed a candy bar in his pocket had melted while working with microwaves. His mishap eventually led to the invention of the microwave oven. The presence of testosterone did not necessarily lead to these errors. I am emphasizing that not everything a man does is bad, and every once in a while, an advancement or improvement can be the result of a mistake.)

It would be incorrect to assume that every decision a man makes is motivated by our loins; we do, in fact, AND on purpose, use the cranial lump resting on our shoulders. Logic chafes for exercise against our seething, bridling emotions in the decision-making process. Male reasoning is sort of like the little engine that could—it competes with other powerful motivations to influence critical thinking while it proclaims, "I think I can, I think I can, I think … I wanna watch sports."

Testosterone sways and interferes. It drives human males to participate, contend, and look at a final score. It pushes us to fear complacency and dread diminished pride. It knows which drawer the scissors are in and where the nearest electrical outlet is. Is it really a mystery why we live in a less than peaceful world?

Ergo, boys are stupid.

Fight or Flight

"Fight or Flight" is a physiological response to a perceived threat. The reaction is common among all living things. In humans, it is more dominant in males. Instinctually, men act more aggressively when confronted with danger.

When you were young, each of you asked me the same question: "Dad, how did you get that scar?" I never liked to answer and always switched the subject. I haven't changed my mind. I am not going to answer the question except to admit most are sports related injuries and that the fight or flight instinct was present in nearly every scar-resulting encounter. I will further concede there were times I wished I had chosen flight more often. With the exception of a deep, two-inch, seven-stitched gash on my head, flight would be my hindsight-is-20/20 preference. My slight reveal is not intended as bragging, quite the opposite. I made choices when I perceived a threat, real or imagined. Psychologically or with a pound of flesh, I paid a price each time. In retrospect and honestly, there is a racy, ambiguous feeling associated with each instance agitating between pride and shame. Sometimes I wish I had used better judgment in my youth.

Ergo, boys are stupid.

As your dad, aggressive instincts remain strong, but my focus has shifted from my pursuits of desires to support and defend yours. Like an older male lion, I accept whatever comes my way unless it is harm in your or your mom's direction. Threats to your well-being acutely trigger my fight or flight instincts. I suspect it's a common theme among dads like me—we'd much rather be snoring on a couch than roaring in a bar, but we remain keenly lion-hearted and crazy to protect our own with all our capability.

Men Are Sooo Predictable

Due to decision-influencing hormones, human males are guided by instinct more than females. Women are more likely to use reason in an evaluation process. (**Dad Note:** For the millionth time, I am generalizing. Human males, including your dear old dad, analyze and employ logic before a decision. However, human males are instinctually prompted towards a more aggressive initial response.)

It is said that the definition of insanity is "doing the same thing, again and again, while expecting a different result." This maxim is part of the human male credo. We are driven by impulse to choose patterned reactions as a result of stimuli, opportunity, and experience; we are Pavlov's salivating dog.

Whether to fight, flee, or take risks, men are subject to reflex disposition. Choices may appear random and haphazard, but they are not. Chance is random, risk is not. Every day we face uncertainty and select a course of action even when the outcome is predictable. Males tend to satisfy initial challenges by design. It is when pushed to higher limits of personal risk primal urges take effect.

It is why I swing a bat as hard as I can at a pitched ball whether the team needs the runs or not. It is why it is painful to choose to bunt to advance the runner as the better part of a strategy. And unless the weight of the result outweighs the adverse action, boys and metal objects will always find electricity. There is hope. We do learn from our experiences of "at-the-time-it-made-perfect-sense" determinations, but sometimes it feels like we are floating above bodies watching ourselves juggle chainsaws.

Ergo, boys are stupid.

Girls Are ...

According to relationship counselor and author John Gray, women are from Venus and value different customs than we males adhere to on Jupiter. (**Dad Note:** Men are not from Mars as Gray has stated. We are from Jupiter. According to every grade school girl whoever rode a yellow school bus, "Boys go to Jupiter to get more stupider.") Females are biased by emotion more than males are. Women are predisposed to gather and to nurture. Feelings fuel protective instincts to defend family and principles. Feelings AND reason guide decisions and propel engagement. Since the female spirit is not limited by a Y chromosome or burdened with as much lothario-like testosterone, it is less extreme, less patterned, and exhibits as not specifically predictable; females possess an x-factor of "je ne sais quoi" proportions.

Emotional Rescue

I know it is sexist to state, but it is the mom's responsibility to provide comfort after the breakup of a relationship and especially one of the teenage romance variety. I could provide guidance but offering solace and supportive reassurance is not in my repertoire. I am sensitive to the pain caused by heartbreak, but I want to fix/correct the issue and not discuss it until you feel better. (**Dad Note:** I am too occupied suppressing the rage to *Hulk Smash!* whoever hurt you.) As luck would have it so that no good dad deed goes unpunished, I was forced into a nurturing role after one of my daughters endured the anguish of a "first love" high school breakup.

I heard semi-muffled sobs from her room. As immeasurably as I wanted to quickly walk past to do anything else but go in there or to believe I hadn't heard her weeping, I had. She was crying the kind of tears that can't be faked; it was startling and sobering for a dad to hear. I took a deep breath—semi-cursed your mother for not being home—and then went in. She hid her face when I asked what was wrong, but she couldn't conceal the tearful noise. I performed a mental checklist of what could be the cause. *Was it the car? Was it school? Was it a boy? Was it sports?* (**Dad Note:** I crossed my fingers and prayed it wasn't a boy problem, but a sports-related issue. I thought, *I'm the go-to guy for a minor injury remedy. I sure hope she just sprained something or pulled a muscle because I am ready with my 'rub some dirt on it' speech.*) Since man plans, God laughs, and no good dad deed goes unpunished, her grief was caused by heartbreak. I sat next to her and did my admirable best to comfort her, but honestly, I felt less uneasy at my first prostate exam. I sat and listened. I stroked her hair and gave her reassuring hugs. Eventually, the tears subsided, and I think she felt better. I quietly retreated from her room still wanting to *Hulk Smash!* and now wondering what kind of idiot wouldn't want to be with her? Weirdly, and in hindsight, I'm glad I was there for her and I would do it again if she ever needed me, but I'd still prefer mending a broken arm than a broken heart.

I would be overstepping scientific bounds to declare that the human female is more compassionate. Despite the countless supportive hugs from Mom, there is no evidence to support this. A human brain senses compassion without reserve. Feelings of sympathy, empathy, or concern are not restricted to a specific gender. However, through instinct and nurturing, GENERALLY the difference manifests in the method of expression. Women are not more sensitive than men, but they tend to display it more readily. And since the hug, kiss, or just talking is the therapy, no game plan is prescribed to fix or cure or eliminate the next time this happens. When feelings and emotions are challenged, jostled, or hurt, an outcome is rarely predictable.

Ergo, girls are … unpredictable.

Women as Gatherers

(**Dad Note:** I have literally walked on thin ice. I have never fallen through, but one of your uncles has. He and our cousin had ambled about a half mile from shore on a frozen bay. Ever the intrepid lads—read "intrepid" as "stupid"—they ventured farther even as the ice cracked beneath their feet. I don't recall if they both fell through the ice, but my cousin is the uncle of scissors-running, battery-swallowing Matthew.

Throughout my life, I have made statements north of provocative, south of incendiary, west of fiery, and not quite east of seditious. My moral compass guides me; sometimes it's through demagogic straits, but mainly I travel supportive, calming routes. As I write this seemingly polarizing chapter, it might appear I'm throwing lighter fluid on a gender debate, especially regarding male/female predisposition, historical roles of women and men, and societal expectations of them. I feel like I am further than trying to walk across "thin ice" and am attempting to promenade across a lake full of slush. Try as I might—and thinking all the positive thoughts I can—I know I will be sinking with my first step.

Do not be insulted if I write something you do not agree with. None of my words in this section are meant as slings and/or arrows. I am not offended if you question my logic, my facts, or my statements. A curious mind is the best kind to have.)

Thousands of years ago, the roles of men and women were more clearly defined by the division of labor. Because of instinct and strength, men hunted for food. I think I would have been a good hunter except for the tracking, killing, blood, and skinning. I would have been better suited as a classic Neanderthal knuckle dragger dragging heavy things. Women were responsible for birthing newborns and caring for progeny. The duties prompted women to remain in close proximity to the home, leading to primary care of the fire, the hearth, cooking, and clothesmaking. Because of the central proximity of these obligations rudimentary farming was discovered. It may be why Mom is adamant about maintaining our small herb garden and my aunt continues her large garden; they're genetically coded to cultivate. Learning to grow food was equal to the high value of cooking it and added value to the human omnivore diet.

Ergo, girls ... were/are the chief cooks and bottle washers. (**Dad Note:** No ambiguity here to lend credence to the predictably unpredictable female composition. Perhaps a nod to current blurred lines of formerly assumed gender duties.)

Women as Nurturers

I love watching series or films about nature. The documentaries about oceans and animals are my favorites. It is utterly fascinating to see rarely explored or newly discovered oddities; there is so much we still don't understand about our own planet. (Did you know fewer than two hundred Devils Hole Pupfish remain?) I am even more mesmerized by the similarities animals display that mimic our own culture roles, especially regarding the care and responsibility of developing offspring. Even though it's only on a television screen, watching elephants and whales tend to and protect their young is awe-inspiring. But not all animals raise their own young. For instance, leatherback mama sea turtles rely on natal homing to travel hundreds of miles home to lay eggs in a sand beach near or at where they themselves were hatched, then disappear. In fewer than three months, the two-ounce hatchlings emerge to fend for themselves armed only with DNA-coded instincts and their ultimate cuteness.

Human females are tasked with childbearing and (GENERALLY) child-rearing. They provide an immediate source of food and instruction. Because of this natural arrangement of closeness, a personal bond initiates more quickly and possibly more strongly for life with a mother. (**Dad Note:** I have no preference for family design. Whether opposite genders, single-gender, or same gender, I subscribe to the theory it takes a village to raise a child or an idiot. If leader[s] of a family promote, provide, and demonstrate love and support, you have my love and support. Presently, there are so many internal and external pressures on the sustainability of the family model. For a family unit to function properly there must be structure, rules, respect, and tolerance. It is necessary to foster learning and growth from within. Further, it must be an obvious source of strength and security, a place to feel protected, while acting as a springboard to accept challenges and exhibit behavior. I encourage any format of a family, with love present, as the new standard, the new "traditional." However, I believe positive input from either specific gender is important and invaluable. It has nothing to do with assumed roles, but an affirming male influence is as constructive as supportive female guidance is for teaching how to live a well-lived life.)

Ergo, girls are … bottle washers and archetype emotion teachers.

Women as Defenders of the Galaxy and Principles

I grew up in Bristol, Rhode Island, but I went to grade/primary school at Saint Philomena School with my brothers, sister, and cousins. The school was in Portsmouth on Aquidneck Island, the nearest town to the south of Bristol, but separated by Mount Hope Bay. There are eight of us related as the grandchildren of our mom's and their mom's parents. Our family, their family, and our grandparents were inseparably close, separated only by a sixteen-minute walk or nine-minute bike ride, add four minutes to get to our grandparents' house, three if you were hungry.

Some years we carpooled with our cousins when there wasn't enough interest from other families who sent their kids to the same school. Until now, I never thought about the moving violations our parents committed cramming eight of us into a station wagon equipped with at most six safety belts. Back then, the driver (my mom or my aunt) didn't wear a seat belt either. Times were different, and besides, the statute of limitations to charge them has probably passed. Most years, we rode on a big yellow bus to school along with about half of the Irish American Catholic kids from our town. I don't remember much specifically about the ride to school other than we played ball games until the bus arrived, made the driver wait if the score was tied, boarded, zig-zagged around town picking up the other kids, crossed the bridge, and then arrived slightly disheveled from the seatbelt-less drive. It was pretty standard fare and probably mirrored any other bus ride to school in the country: Girls clapped to "Miss Mary Mack," talked about boys, and sang pop songs with other girls; the boys talked to boys about sports, TV sitcoms, and more sports. Like I said, standard operating yellow bus procedure.

However, I do recall one un-standard, very eventful scene to support my claim of a woman's hyper-heightened sense of defense. Though only ten years old, I witnessed my cousin, Julie, raging in unbridled, protective anger that would have scared the tattered pants off the Incredible Hulk. One of the other kids on the bus had insulted and pushed one of our family members. Julie isn't the oldest or largest in our group, but she has the persona of a frenzied, shielding alpha female elephant. Truth be told, I have lived my life trying never to make her too angry. Her rage was a blur of loud shouts, crashing noises, pile-driving fists, cement-cracking kicks, and then, eerie silence. Ten-year-old Julie had defended reflexively and without maternal instinct; she was compelled to guard and protect as if she had no choice or chance to overwrite her coded DNA.

I have seen this characteristic in other females also. Despite the odds and risk of personal harm, women adopt a kick-ass-first-ask-questions-later mentality if family, close friends, or causes they champion are under severe attack. As a very large anger-tinctured human male, I find the inclination to shield and assault statistically and comically bewildering.

Ergo, girls are … don't-make-me angry-you-wouldn't-like-me-when-I'm-angry *Hulk Smash!* scary.

Tend and Befriend

In an article published in *Psychological Review* in 2000, Dr. Shelley Taylor proposed the tend and befriend theory as the common female reaction to stress including worry, strain, tension, anxiety, and shock. The immediate response of the female is to protect and calm the family unit. Then depending on the size and level of threat, she will/may summon the accumulated support group consisting of (usually) other females. The model and theory has a basis in biology and psychology, surprisingly two science subjects I wasn't terrible at. But with pint-sized comprehension and tablespoon-ed retention, the article was well above my brain grade. However little I understand, it does make sense to me that women exhibit a patterned but contrary behavior to men in a stressful situation. It isn't actually the opposite of the male fight or flight inborn credo. When threatened, a female may fight, but only after immediately managing the concerns of those under her care. Retaliation may even be delayed until after a consult with her show-of-force girl posse.

It was amazing how much this made sense to me as I reviewed instances from my youth of my mom, my aunt, and my grandmother. Your mom mirrored their traits when you were young; she still exhibits the same characteristics under her older, seemingly calmer "tend and befriend" self. Instinctually, the women I knew/know and the ones you know were supportive and protective, but ready for DEFCON 1 if required. (**Dad Note:** Heaven help the person who would challenge the order of their familial units because they would likely end up in a larger world of hurt than I end up in when I say stupid things.)

Ergo, girls are … keen to supervise their own flock, willing to assist, but tougher than Captain America's pure vibranium shield. The scary part is they are willing to protect against any enemy armed only with Steve Roger's original steel triangular shield.

Less Extreme

You may have taken exception, perhaps even eyebrow-raising umbrage, to each characterization I have made regarding gender pre-programming. I can almost feel the dagger-darting, furrowed-brow angry stares from your mom if I ever revealed any of my chromosomally challenged/enhanced views. She may not even be first in a possibly long line of people who would question my theories. I might not argue if confronted. These are my opinions; they do contain factual evidence, but perhaps not enough to withstand repeated-knee-to-the-groin defiance. This chapter has required specific, focused thought of which I am rarely capable of achieving. I questioned my interpretations. I doubted my assessments. I re-questioned and re-doubted. Then I remembered what I learned about the female praying mantis and female black widow spider. I felt boldness return to my spine. I went back to my tuffet, resumed typing and eating my curds and whey.

The female praying mantis and female black widow spider belong to a number of species where the male is killed, by his mate, after sex. This is the most prime example of why boys are stupid and girls are … Without contemplation, the male is driven to mate. Without remorse, the female is compelled to murder. You would think that after millions of years of evolution these poor bugs would have learned a defensive trick or how to communicate, "Not tonight, dear." Guys, fake an injury or mutate a body part for protection. You would also hope these fatal femme fetales could find nourishment elsewhere or just nod off to sleep after sex. Gratefully and most appreciatively, human females don't imitate this deadly mating ritual. However, there are other behaviors I question. (**Dad Note:** There is evidence to support my claim, but fearing for my personal safety, I will refrain from noting specific examples of conduct.)

The actions and reactions of women are GENERALLY less extreme AT LOWER STRESS LEVELS because of their intuitive biological and psychological predisposition. The problem is that stress is a personal assessment. There is no standard level of anxiety/fear/tension. It is simultaneously evaluated unevenly with and without passion. For human males our motivations are clear: hunt, mate, talk about sports, sleep, repeat process daily. In the animal kingdom, some are even willing to literally risk their necks because of impulse. For women, the reasons are unencumbered and transparent: protect, serve, protect, gather, protect, make online purchases, protect. Men sally forth instinctually. Sally, on the other hand, may kiss or kill depending on individual sensitivity to peril.

Ergo, girls are_____. (Fill in the blank yourself. I've disappeared like "Where's Waldo?")

In My Humble Opinion

I have stated a million times throughout my lifetime that boys are stupid. I'm living proof and (sort of) proud of it. While I am ultimately responsible for all of my actions, I feel at ease knowing some of my conduct is instinctual. Human males act and react to avoid complacency and boredom. We are ruled by instinct. Our incentives are obvious. We limit outward signs of vulnerability. We are happiest and most productive when we compete; if we fear competition, we really fear our abilities to succeed.

Boys are stupid. We run with scissors. We run fast with scissors. Be honest, daughters: Do you think we ever really grow up?

Girls are ... predictably unpredictable. Human females, like their XY counterparts, are also influenced by genetic coding. Though males seem to be governed linearly and emphatically, females operate, barraged by sensory input from emotions, and evaluate/react at heterogeneous levels. This is not to say women are more emotional than men are, just that emotions punch a bigger ticket on their judgment card. PLUS, as formerly traditional gender roles have become indistinct at home and at work, there are newer pressures interfering/influencing the decision process for women as well. Personal and societal expectations are being reevaluated constantly.

So, yeah, I think girls are "dot dot dot." And sometimes even an extra "dot" if stupid boys are involved. Simultaneously I thank God and curse the devil for how little I understand the female mind.

WHAT THE WORLD NEEDS NOW IS LISTENING, SWEET LISTENING

(**Dad Note:** If you think this title is corny, foolish, nonsensical, inane ... full disclosure, I don't really like it either. But bear with me; this is actually one of my better "Best Guesses." 😊 If I ever undertake a project like this again, I'll ask for your help naming the chapters because I know you deem me and everything I say corny, foolish, nonsensical, inane ...)

Cellar Door

Father Ambrose Wolverton, OSB, taught English and Christian Doctrine at my high school. Far exceeding his Benedictine vows, he had the unenviable task of teaching English to me. A sacred oath of stability, fidelity to the monastic way of life, and obedience are one thing, but instructing me on how to write must have challenged his faith. If he were still alive, and though it's *possible*, I doubt he would have classified teaching me as a notable achievement. More like an additional pledge of patience, sacred burden, or proof that God does actually exist and has a tremendous sense of humor. It's even quite *possibler* Father Ambrose may not have remembered me. But if he did remember and he were alive today to read the ramblings in my book, it's most *possiblest* he would have refuted my claim that I was ever his pupil. If pressed for confirmation, he might deny even knowing me if asked ten times; it's an even-money, safe bet that Jesus had better odds of Peter acknowledging knowing him after the Last Supper.

Of course, I am kidding. Father Ambrose was the embodiment of his oath to God and to his fellow man, and then some. He was conspicuously gracious, soft-spoken, intelligent, and inconspicuously modest. I am forever indebted for his strict but tolerant tutelage. Besides his remarkable tenure as a teacher, he was a very accomplished pianist. I attended a few concerts when he performed on campus. I am no critic and know very little about classical music, but his gift opened my eyes and ears to new and wonderful sounds from a piano. Though I remained true to Springsteen, The Clash and New Wave, he inspired me to widen my music appreciation to include classical, jazz. and other genres. (**Dad Note:** Yes, I typed the word "classical." I enjoy classical music and sometimes, not often, but sometimes I listen to my classical playlists. However, I avoid compositions with a harpsichord; it sounds like what my stomach feels like if I was forced to eat liver for dinner.) Anyway, I am grateful Father Ambrose taught me how to write. He displayed unique tolerance/leniency/mercy towards me and my fellow imprudent, impudent imps. And I am also thankful he unlocked an interest in types of music I had not previously enjoyed.

Father Ambrose's message on how to write: Keep the structure limited to a beginning, a middle, and an end. An end is not necessarily a conclusion, but a place where the reader is satisfied. Support your ideas. Write easily understood words in a simple format, i.e., write short sentences. I think he wanted to exclaim, especially to me, "Keep it simple, stupid!" and God bless him he never uttered those words (at least not to my face) and God bless him for his unflappability in the face of my overwhelming underwhelmed-ness. Though I continually violate his lessons to write more goodlier, to avoid weird(er) use of words/phrases, and to avert tangentially trapped thoughts, I will forever appreciate his solemn desire to instill good writing habits in me. (**Dad Note:** Lest I forget another overdue mea culpa, if any former English teacher of mine reads this book, I apologize for the claptrap crap I wrote before the eleventh grade. It was horrible and inconsistent. I thank you also for your patience.)

One other significant habit Father Ambrose asked me to develop in order to improve my writing was to sense the sound of a word or phrase in my head before I commit it/them to paper through pen. Now, minus my old-school school writing instruments, I sit at a keyboard watching words populate a screen in front of me as my mouth moves in sync while I type. The first time I remember doing this, he asked me to consider and repeat the words "cellar door." As he spoke them, they sounded gracefully paired together. He challenged me to think of words in a rhythmic context as I write them. Since then, and even though it seems like most words just fly out of my mouth without a filter, I contemplate the composition of words before I write or speak. I choose words by an expressive, flowing standard. To this day, I repeatedly, but not always privately, speak aloud lyrical, poetic-sounding words. Two of my favorites are "alliterative" and "envelop." I enjoy onomatopoeic words like "crackle," "sizzle." and "hiss." I adore the swishing quirkiness of "triskaidekaphobia" and "transmogrification." I admire inventive descriptive words like "ginormous" or original creations like "squozen" made up by your mom, and like "itchkaditch," a word frequently used by your Grammie to describe a restless person, i.e., your Grampie.

Long ago I saw the phrase "meticulous, kindhearted, and attentive." I don't remember where I first viewed it, but I doubt it was on my own school report card. Perhaps I saw it on a classmate's or maybe on a television program. The grouped words are affirming and encouraging, but as positively as they were applied, they sounded stilted and harsh to me. In my head and out of my mouth, I heard the stiffness as "meh-tick-cue-lus," "kined-hart-ed," and "uh-ten-tiv." I challenged myself to create a similar phrase from a combination of three poetic-sounding words. I came up with "considerate, thoughtful, and attentive listening." Yes, I recycled "attentive," but I preferred my less artificial-sounding locution. I liked it so

I added it in my *Favorite Quotes* speckled notebook. Short of hailing it as a line from an epic poem or charming Haiku, I think Father Ambrose would have relished my lyrical grouping.

"Thoughtful" and "attentive" sound a bit wooden, but "considerate" and "listening" are softer and complement unassumingly. I really like the word "listening." It comes to the edge of sounding rigid but recedes gracefully and melodically. "Listening" is a powerful yet unpretentious word. It doesn't sound threatening or commanding. It is universal in that everyone knows what it means. As an ability, it is common; almost anyone with the slightest capacity to reason can do it with their ears or even their eyes. As a skill, it is formidable and should be afforded considerable significance; its proficiency is as necessary as the honeybee is to human survival. It is powerful yet overlooked. It is handy, yet underutilized. It is essential, yet everyone has forgotten its importance.

Listening, like hearing, is an anticipatory action, i.e., a word must be spoken or a sound must be made before listening/hearing can happen. I guess you could add that listening can occur through contemplation, i.e., heeding the thoughts in your own head. I do this often, but I hardly consider my own head's voice as being expert or proficient. I want to focus on listening as it pertains to human interaction, i.e., hearing then processing all the Is and the Es and the ones after Cs you receive. (**Dad Note:** Or is it "recieve?" 😊)

If Father Ambrose's spirit will ignore a few final assaults on our precious language as I circumvent everything he taught me, permit me my demi-deranged, wide-ranging hyperbole. Listening is off-the-rails important. It is 8.6-on-the-Richter-scale powerful in its silence. It is as overlooked as a skill as Boxer was in *Animal Farm*, but just like the discreet beast it accomplishes more than anyone acknowledges. Listening is a soundless force. It can give new hope to building personal and professional connections, or it can be the obstructive phantom menace causing more relationships to die than any lightsaber-wielding Sith lord. (**Dad Note:** At least I made a reference to George Orwell's book from my assigned summer reading list in high school.)

Hear vs. Listen

The words "hear" and "listen" seem synonymous, but they are not. They're like fraternal twins, not identical ones. To hear is to sense sound in your ears and recognize it as input available for your brain. The act of hearing is innate. (**Dad Note:** It is an ability 99.8% of humans are born with.) It is participatory in that noise is detected, but non-contributory. It is an important social exercise, but it burns zero calories. If you want to get in shape, jump on your bike or take a walk.

To listen is different from to hear. It is harder. However, there is no added burden, no additional physical exertion, and it expends no extra calories. It requires the same auditory stimulus and only one further procedure: to process what is heard. It is to participate in speech, song, or conversation, not only to receive entertainment or information but also to administer and manage it. I guess there is an added burden—you gotta use your brain to complete the task.

As an example of the difference between hearing and listening, imagine a scene you have witnessed a million times before. I am in a room talking about sports or music with your mother. Your mom hears every excited word I speak to/at her about Manchester United, the Boston Red Sox, or some rare trivia leaking from my brain's Nonsense and Other Trifles files. She sees my mouth moving and detects noise emanating from it, but she looks like a wearied teacher at the end of a raucous school day. She does hear me. But, I often/always/continually wonder, *Is she listening to me?* Rhetorically and literally, the answer is firmly/emphatically/decisively/thoroughly "NO!" I am resigned that I am proverbial white noise to her. I am her classic conundrum of the if-a-tree-falls-in the-woods-and-no-one-listens-to-him-talk-about-sports-do-I-have-to-respond-to-him? debate. (**Dad Note:** That is unless the conversation steers towards Mom's beloved New England Patriots.)

Inspiration From Perspiration

I have tried many times not only to contemplate ideas for this book, but also to write them whenever we are on vacation. It rarely, if ever, happens. Mostly I spend time correcting my non-goodly grammar, proofreading recent sentence structure, or improving an anecdote to support a story line. I have learned the hard way it is impossible to create or reinforce a thought on a vacation. The pressure ratchets upwards to generate meaningful words like a thermometer in the tropics. I prefer the comfortable your-dad-is-an-island isolation in my small home office. I need to be alone there with both the dissolute and righteous noises in my head. Solitude is essential to cultivate my thoughts into words. My contemplations are nurtured like mushrooms in darkened recesses; they grow wildly in my brain. My observations grow in the sunnier patches of my mind as well, not everything is dark or dingy. The more flowery thoughts blossom in the lighter, brighter sections of my mind. But honestly, either process is best promoted when I am alone in my office. I tend my own garden of Eden/evil. I enjoy the sowing; I appreciate the harvest.

On vacation, the incentive to be inventive surrounds me and the motivation to write should be as easy as finding snow on our driveway in winter. But it's not. I cannot produce genuine, reflective writing during a holiday. Inspiration dissipates in the distraction of the dawn 'til dusk distractions. Ideas are drowned out by happiness and sunshine. Inventiveness gets in a car or on a bus or on a boat. My ingenuity swims on a beach, skis down a mountain, goes snorkeling, or putters around in a town I will probably never visit again. My thoughts are interrupted by ever-present laughter, non-stop food and drink, and paradise in abundance.

A vacation is a wonderfully weary and marvelously manufactured experience. It's supposed to be maximum capacity for enjoyment at minimum effort. It's full-on family fun, especially the full-on, all-in, extended family versions. Contrived to be pleasurable, they can become strained by inclement, forceful storms, and I ain't talking 'bout the weather. This is not meant as an insult. The destinations have been splendid and worth the panic attacks I suffer to fly across large bodies of water to get there. I am grateful for the gatherings, and I am especially pleased to see you interact with your cousins. For better or for worse, the family dynamic is what it is. Words and drinks get mixed and mashed while smiles, hugs, and great memories are generated. Family closeness is tested like a beach-goer risking a painful sunburn on a cloudless afternoon without sunblock. Everyone laughs. Everyone enjoys. They laugh and enjoy until the first reddened back is slapped or someone's loose lips sink the social ship. After the egos and sunburns have been massaged with kind words and aloe vera, and I am safely kissing continental U.S. soil again, the memories of the happy, precious moments burst to the surface as the bad ones fade into our plane's contrail.

For these reasons of stifled creativity, I am presently smirking at my computer screen. I furiously tap, tap, tap the letters on my keyboard against a setting sun here in hot Jamaica.

For the record, I had nearly completed this chapter before we left for vacation. In theory, I planned to return to my desk, obsess on my notes, and fixate on the unfinished progress. I would hammer out a cohesive, thoughtful chapter on the importance of listening. In reality, I moderately dreaded revisiting the chapter; it felt inadequate and insufficient when I stopped typing in my office and started hyperventilating about getting on a plane. The paused product was not of poor quality or incoherent, but slightly jumbled and lacked specific clarity. I was hesitant to abandon it in a fragmented state for three reasons.

1) The swirling words in my head hadn't translated into text to explain the differences between listening and hearing.

2) By experience, I was convinced no cleverness would arise on a vacation of ranting and roaring like British sailors on shore leave in Kingston.

3) I knew it would be impossible to type with a bottomless rum drink in one hand and an ever-present premium cigar I purchased in Kingston in the other.

Surprisingly and supercalifragilistically, my hesitations disappeared like umbrellaed Mary Poppins at the end of the movie. I came to understand the value of listening versus hearing. The clarity hit me like two statistically improbable, expialidociously figurative bolts of lightning. The first insight flashed like a gentle intuitive jolt at your Grampie's "Jolly Holiday" birthday celebration. The other one struck like a lightning bolt to my heart during a nearly no-holds barred, I-should-have-used-a-spoonful-of-sugar unfortunate argument with my son. With these two events, however garnered, I identified chim-chim-cheree simplicity, clearness and precision for this chapter on than substantive value of listening.

In Jamaica, your grandfather turned eighty. The significance was reveled in family style and tradition: lots of beaming smiles, more raucous laughter, and most imperfect, off-key singing. The highlight was when I witnessed Grampie's "gift" from his grandchildren. You and your cousins serenaded him with your grandmother's special song for him, "My Special Angel." (**Dad Note:** A personal note to the estate of Bobby Helms. You needn't worry that my children, nieces, and nephews will ever displace his version on the pop charts as I don't think it was recorded. But if it were and you heard it, you would grin as widely as I did when I saw how entertained my father-in-law was with this spectacularly discordant yet loving version.)

Immediately after dinner but before the cousin crooning, your mom, aunt, and uncles each made a short speech. Each professed why their father was so exceptional. His children indicated through spoken word, and thankfully not through song, that their dad was not only Grammie's special angel but theirs as well. They told him how important he was to them and how grateful they are to be his kids. A few tears were shed or choked back recounting his significant impact on their lives, then and now. Honestly, it was very touching. It was/is/will be my greatest hope that I have had as great a positive influence on you. (**Dad Note:** If I have, don't wait until I turn eighty to tell me, okay?)

The first thing to open my eyes about opening your ears was when your Uncle Ralph spoke. He mentioned the attribute he most admired about his dad. He valued how great a listener your grandfather is. The sentimental passion struck me as if I were an emotional metal rod in a lightning storm. His words immediately cleared up overcast thoughts I had about the different kinds of listening and their important functions. Though my body was still in attendance, smiling and watching, I retreated unobtrusively into the library in my head. I wished I was in front of my computer or at least had a pen and dry napkin to write on. In my mind I began to reminisce about my relationship with my own parents. My dad is a good listener; he listens and then tries to resolve the issue. I find myself doing this too. I read somewhere it is a predominantly male characteristic, but my mom was good at it too. She'd listen and often offer a solution. However, sometimes, and to her greatest credit, she would just listen without a reply, an answer, or a verdict. As thoughts pinged around my brain, I discovered that listening is not simply a singular purpose attribute and has many forms. I also realized that anyone who possessed a superior listening trait to mine was older than I am. Perhaps it is a skill acquired through wisdom after many, many trips around the sun or, just plainly, through a well-lived life. I needed to pong those ideas for a while.

The second reason I changed course on what I had written about the importance of listening was the inopportune time I chose to quarrel with my son. Immediately following our vociferous run-in, I learned just how important it is to be a better listener than a talker. I also learned that I can and should improve my interpersonal skills by leading with my listening and not a verbal jab. (**Dad Note for My Son:** I know you are reading this. I want to apologize. Not specifically for what I said or the message I was trying to deliver, but for my manner. Though you were young, you were nearly an adult, old enough to serve your country and to vote. I often forget that you are closer to your first job, first apartment and (first?) marriage than to the boy I see sometimes when I look at you. I made a mistake, please accept my apology. Even past age 50, I still don't possess perfected listening skills, but I have improved. I TRY to focus on what is being said. I TRY to avoid indifference towards topics I don't enjoy. I TRY to respect that a conversation should never be one-sided. Like human existence, I am an evolution in progress. Further, please accept my apology in blanket past/

present/future format. It is highly probable that I may still lapse, blunder, and misspeak, but the good news is I will definitely show more respect to the person you are becoming.)

On one of our last nights in Jamaica, long after the reverie of laughter, the heartfelt speeches, and awful singing finally went to bed, I sat on the terrace by myself. My eyes traced moonbeams back to the heavens as they shimmered off the faraway ocean. My ears exulted in the silence. My fingers wanted to clack away on my keyboard and wished, along with my big butt, I was home plopped in my comfy office chair. My brain had a mind of its own and churned with what I learned about listening. Actually, only 25% of my brain churned. Another 25% nervously anticipated the imminent return flight over a large chunk of the Atlantic Ocean. And the remaining 25% of my brain power was spent wondering how I would finish this chapter when/if I got home. Before the mouse on the wheel in my head ran out of churning power, I set aside negative thoughts and contemplated a hypothesis about the different types of listening.

I found the last three napkins not soaked by rum or humidity. I found a pen tucked in a crossword puzzle someone had left on a table near the pool. (**Dad Note to the Puzzle Book Abandoner:** 46 across was "chassis" not "classic." You're welcome.) With the borrowed ballpoint, I wrote a goal-oriented, personal mission statement:

> "For a society to deem itself worthy and valuable, it must interact effectively. For a society to propagate and continue, it must communicate ideas and be receptive to change and criticism. And for a society to improve and justify its existence, it must listen more than it speaks."

However, I have determined that if a society is to be effective, respectful, and willing to develop, then at least one person is required to be listening. Whether to nature or to each other, it is imperative to await answers/clues/signals for personal and societal improvement.

AND while the ability to listen has not diminished, the aptitude for it has declined severely.

My questions: What can I do to reverse the trend? How can I become more proficient and skillful at listening to help others?

(**Dad Note:** If you were adding up my percentages above, your math is correct. My cognitive functions were disclosed at 75% capacity. Twenty-five percent of my brain was churning, 25% was worrying/obsessing, and 25% of my brain was formulating a theory to rewrite some of this chapter when I got home. The final 25% continually exhausts itself in an infinite loop retrieving movie quotes and song lyrics.)

In the semi-dark light on that full sticky night, I concluded that there are six modes of listening. Scientifically, I freely admit, there may be more or there may be fewer; I was never good in any of my high school scientific classes. I also noted, like certain educational disciplines, that I am good at some and need to improve at others. To carry the school analogy further, here is the list on how I graded myself. (**Dad Note:** Believe it or not, these are appropriately appropriated comments from some of my actual report cards and tests during high school.) The different types of listening according to your gentlemanly scholar of a dad are:

- Listening to learn. ("Very good effort but needs to focus.")
- Listening to solve. ("Fair effort, but there is room for improvement.")
- Listening to be entertained. ("High aptitude for this subject.")
- Listening to help. ("Spirited endeavor!")
- Listening to talk. ("Attempts to mitigate this behavior should be undertaken.")
- Listening to listen. ("Requires much, much more determination.")

I identified each by examining my own personal deficiencies/inefficiencies of my listening proficiency, i.e., items I could/should change to improve my listening aptitude. I performed this task with tunnel vision clarity, focused on one prize: my grandchildren singing for me. If I can decipher the different types of listening, it is my my-eyes-are-closed-tightly-as-I-blow-out-candles-on-my-birthday-cake-and-wish-upon-a-shooting-star wish that you, my children, will "encourage" (**Dad Note:** If required, substitute "coerce" for "encourage.") my grandchildren to sing me one of my favorite songs on a birthday TBD. My fingers are crossed and with no pressure on you, I hope that it will be sung more harmoniously, less tunelessly, and equally lovingly as you did for your Grampie. On the plus side for my melody-challenged, ballad-impaired, harmony-defiant offspring, my favorite songs require loud, boisterous singing, a trait my grandchildren are guaranteed to inherit from you.

Below are six listening formats. These are your-dad-only verified. There may be/probably are others I have overlooked. If you discover additional arrangements, let me know. I would love to LISTEN to what you find. (**Dad Note:** See what I did there? I capitalized the word "listen" in a chapter about listening. Clever, huh? Okay, I'll shut up now ...) In the truest spirit of shutting up now, I will list them minus my usual long-winded, circuitous anecdotes. Well, I fully intend to write them in that manner ... no promises. Forgive me once again, Father Ambrose ...

Listening to Learn

Listening to learn seems obvious. Humans are equipped with ears to sense sound. Ears are highly prominent in the process of gathering information for the brain to consider. Once it is accumulated and ruminated, a course of action is decided. Sometimes, the strategy is to hold onto the data because it is interesting, necessary, or required. My brain categorizes movie quotes, song lyrics, and odd details/facts as important; discourteously, but semi-justifiably, your mother refers to it as "the crap taking up too much storage space in my head." Someday, I hope, I will be vindicated if ever I am a contestant on a trivia game show or at least the phone-a-friend lifeline option if you're ever on one.

Other examples of listening to learn are heeding an instructor, a teacher, a mentor, or a coach. This mode demonstrates instances of compulsory/important types of listening. As your current dad and former coach, remember how much you learned from me about sports and life when you did pay attention. I preached the importance of teamwork, self-sacrifice, self-confidence, and the high personal value of getting up one more time than you were knocked down. Despite your mother's opinion of my mental acuity, not everything in my brain is useless.

I enjoy listening to learn. My ongoing challenge is to focus on necessary and essential elements to improve the quality of my relationships and my own life. I would like to add that listening to learn encompasses more and goes past the singular form of just listening to be informed. It requires multiple sources of input to consider, to validate, to cross-reference, and to deliberate. Listening to learn is comprehensive. It obliges, compels, and ultimately reveals life-long interests.

Listening to Solve

If listening to solve were limited to responses solely based on comprehension, then I could/would/might/may (probably) be an expert. Listening to solve has a foundation of responding to questions or deciphering equations. Answers are provided from retained or learned knowledge. Even I can unravel the mystery of X if $2X+3X=10$. Even I can reply correctly if asked, "Which is the only Caribbean island completely surrounded by the Caribbean Sea?"

The type of listening to solve I identify is more than offering regurgitated information. It is more than just solving for X. It is based on prior experience, involvement, and occurrence; it is about delivering proficient wisdom constructed from knowledge and familiarity.

Forgive my condescension, but maturity is a key component of listening to solve and you, my dear children, do not possess it … yet. To become skillful at it, it is imperative to gain experience. This happens only from the frequency of occurrence. This is not to say that a) it is impossible to acquire it during youth, and b) that numerous years do not necessarily make you a proper source of prudence. But they do provide a foundation to build upon.

When your Uncle Ralph spoke about his father's gift of listening, my guess is that he admires your Grampie's advanced skill at listening to solve. Your grandfather fits the profile. He is old and has learned from experience. He is very attentive when asked a question. He gives it thoughtful consideration before answering. (**Dad Note:** I debated for nearly ten minutes whether I should write "He is old." After all, he is my father-in-law and he's always been respectful and kindhearted to me, but I couldn't furnish a more creative, less insulting-sounding, or apt phrase. There is no way around it—in human years, he is old. I will add, if only to preserve my standing as one of his top two sons-in-law and your mother's inheritance, in mind, body, and spirit he is young. He impresses me with his considerable determination, vast knowledge, and velvety low-key disposition. Age is just a number. He is youthful in his desire to help, to learn, and to share. I hold him in the highest regard and value my relationship with him.)

My mom was another person who was good at listening to solve. Plus, she had an uncanny ability to produce an answer or option I had not previously considered. She was an out-of-the-box thinker and reflected on all angles of a problem. It is ironic that she always said she did her best thinking in the shower which is technically a glass box. Therefore, she did her best, abstract out-of-the-box thinking inside an actual, tangible glass box. (**Dad Note:** Okay, so I am the only one who thinks that was funny.)

A simple go-forward mental exercise. Think about how you respond to a request to solve a problem. Do you carefully consider it? Do you react quickly? Do you hesitate? My advice is to draw from what you know and offer an educated guess for the rest of the solution. Be confident, practical, and reasonable. Your ability to solve is burgeoning. Learn from your experiences and your mistakes; it will serve you well for your entire life as others depend on you for sound guidance.

Listening to Be Entertained

Your mom and I danced to two special songs at our wedding: "December 1963 (Oh, What a Night)" by Frankie Valli and The Four Seasons, and "Love Shack" by the B-52s. Our guests kindly viewed our choices as eclectic and fun. Privately, close friends and family quietly questioned our selections more than they questioned her sanity for saying "I do" to me hours earlier. They feared Mom was not allowed input for the songs. If that were true, it could have been worse. I could have subjected everyone to tango around the dance floor to my favorites from Rage Against The Machine or the Beastie Boys. The gospel truth is the songs are very dear to Mom and me. They represent special meaning to us and our relationship.

There are a million more anecdotes I can/could provide to illustrate how important music is to me, but I promised I wouldn't. My stories, though unique to me, would not be much different than your own in terms of impact. You don't need much input from me to understand what "listening to be entertained" means. But consider that this type of listening also includes what is sensed from movies, television, speeches, or conversations: the wit and sparkle of a comedy, the intrigue of serious dialogue, the joy of hearing cleverness. In the future, I ask that you consider adding more formats to your inventory of entertainment. It's the way I learned to appreciate classical music, Delta blues, and country music. It's also the way I learned I don't like operas, a harpsichord, or the Broadway show *Cats*.

Listening to Help

A few years ago, I called your cousin, Alden, to help me move some office furniture I was donating to our church. My request was specific: I needed his young, strong muscles to load and unload a truck I had borrowed from a friend's company. The task would take about two hours to complete. With very minor complications, mission accomplished. In the end, as I rubbed the stress from my arms and back, I knew I would be sore for days from all of the lifting. I watched Alden bound happily back to his pickup truck, none the worse for wear.

Listening to help seems the most obvious form of listening and often it is. I asked my nephew for assistance then he agreed to lend a hand, biceps, and legs. Surprisingly, this can be the most convoluted and controversial form of listening. It is more than it appears. It incorporates listening for clues, undertones, and non-specific verbal signs. Worse, you must prepare that the reply may not be favorable.

The ways and manners of human speech are relentlessly ambiguous. The address is sometimes indistinct because of sincerity of purpose or feelings of pride. I try to be direct when asking for help. I try to make it easy to understand my request. I am prepared for a "yes" or a "no." But, asking for help and listening to help are like life itself—it is never as simple as it appears. Be alert for signs of indifference. Be wary of feigned commitment. Listen to the words but be vigilant for accompanying nuance.

Listening to Talk

I have/had a friend who would attempt to trump any story in any conversation. If I climbed part of a mountain, he made the full ascent on a larger one. If I hit a ball a "country mile," he had hit one farther, and by his accounts, out of the actual country. If I caught a large fish, then the one he caught was a mid-story, conversation-stopping trophy fish. I will cede the advantage here since, as you know, I am not much of an angler and I've never caught a large enough fish to brag about.

I have/had another friend who seems to reply with a dissenting or opposite opinion every time we talk/talked. In the extreme and in the least, if I say one thing, I can hear his voice 180 degrees the other way. Politics, best color, favorite sports team, his answers mirror mine but only in reverse. I feel like one of us has gone down a rabbit hole and busted through Alice's looking glass. One time, to test my theory and to trick him, I espoused a contradictory opinion I had previously supported about politics. Without skipping a beat or taking a breath, he railed on how mistaken I was. Yes, it is surprising I have any friends.

Have you ever had a conversation where the other person seemed to idle at a high rate just waiting for you to pause, to finish a thought, or to take a breath? Before your eyes, his/her attention dissolves to zero interest in what you have to say. Their own thoughts rev and churn, waiting impatiently to dominate the conversation like the leading race car on its final lap with the checkered flag yet to validate the win only because you are still talking.

Most people have mastered the ability to listen only in order to talk. It takes no talent and there is no real aptitude other than indifference, disinterest, or apathy. It is the lowest hanging fruit of an interpersonal skill—waiting to talk just to hear yourself talk. Actually, no reach is required; the fruit has fallen to the ground. It is as easy as bending over and picking it up.

At times, each of us is guilty of this offense. For instance, I might not concentrate because I will forget an idea or theme of my response. I might listen to less than a completed discourse before the mouse jumps on the treadmill of thoughts in my head. Listening for the sole purpose of providing input without bearing is insulting and lessens social interaction. To my credit and I want to thank you, I became a better listener when I became a dad. You each were so very special. I quickly discovered the depths of my own insignificance and fathomed that my opinions, ideas, and thoughts had better improve. I'm still working on it.

Listening to Listen

During the summer before my sophomore year in high school, a full year before I learned how to write, my mom found me crying in our garage. When I noticed her looking at me, I wiped away all the tears she could see on my face and tried to choke back the sadness welling up as new tears gathered in my eyes. When she asked what was wrong, I answered, "Nothing is wrong." Ever the detective, she pressed me further. After a few rounds of "What's the matter? Nothing's the matter," I cracked. Before I invoked my Fifth Amendment privileges and just after she read me the rights for being her son, I revealed I was unhappy because I missed my friends from school. With the kindest look on her face, she sat and listened while I grumbled and complained. I lamented the lack of friends I had at home. I admitted I felt silly for being so emotional. Eventually my blubbering subsided and she spoke. She didn't say much except something like, "Things will get better, you'll see." She hugged me and left me alone again in the garage. My sorrow had disappeared, and I felt better. Years later, the memory popped up in my mind. I reflected on how my mom was able to make me feel better. The more I thought about it, I realized something. She didn't offer a solution to solve my problem, distract, or entertain me. My mom hadn't done anything special except to listen to me and let me talk. She was a student of human nature and understood as Henry Wadsworth Longfellow surmised, "The best thing one can do when it's raining is to let it rain."

Listening for the sole purpose of listening is perplexing to me. I am hardwired to resolve and disentangle. If asked for help, advice, an answer, or an opinion, I struggle to remain silent. If someone vents frustration, I want to correct the situation. Listening to listen is a remarkable skill. I admit I am a work in progress and am still learning when to just shut up and listen.

In My Humble Opinion

The ability to listen is under attack much like the European honeybee is. It is dying out because of a man-made problem. Humans have become self-centered, apathetic, and indifferent because of technology. Honeybees have been losing flowering plant food sources caused by human destruction/encroachment. They are also under pressure by aggressive bees accidently released in South America over fifty years ago. Efforts to curtail the advancement of the hostile swarms, and to protect the honeybee, are in place. If scientific correctional endeavors fail, the existence of mankind will be tested.

Listening, as a skill and as a form of interaction, is under siege as well, and no one seems to care. Talking is being replaced by texting. Conversations are deemed wasteful and threaten the new world order of communication via social media. Worse is the social convolution we've been thrown into because of the COVID pandemic.

I do not have any/all the answers, but like a long journey begins with a single step, so must our ability to interact effectively begin with an initial desire to connect to the new and reconnect with what seemed lost. Henry Wadsworth Longfellow poetically theorized that, "A single conversation with a wise man is better than ten years' study of books and that the social exchange of information through dialogue remains superior to surfing the internet and relying solely on mercenary websites as primary sources for information." (**Dad Note:** Professor Longfellow's quote is verbatim, but please cross-check my reference for accuracy.)

I love honey. I pray for the survival of the honeybee. Since I am not a scientist, the best I can do is pray and follow modest, impactful steps to preserve their habitats. I love a good conversation and it is as beleaguered and threatened as the honeybee. It is being bulldozed into silent submission by eliminating the need to listen. Still not a scientist, but your human dad, I must do what I can to steer listening away from the precipice of extinction. I yearn for the reduction of non-personal formats of information exchange. I ache to see two people in a discussion where only one mouth is moving.

I cannot change the world, but I can tend to my small garden to alleviate some problems. My influence may be minimal, but I have to try. Hopefully I sway your reliance away from technology. I want to make a water-rippling, domino-falling difference in your lives. Talk to each other, but more importantly, listen to each other.

Section 4

MY BEST ADVICE

For longer than twenty years, your mother and I have attended all of the touring Broadway shows at Providence Performing Arts Center, or PPAC, as it is known locally. I enjoy most of the shows except a production where each word is sung. I feel overwhelmed, bored, and lost. I want to be entertained by the pageantry, the sets, the costumes, the dancing, AND the singing. Mostly, I like to feel immersed in a setting and understand perspective and message from the performance.

One show I have always enjoyed is *Fiddler on the Roof*. I have probably seen it on stage seven times, the first time was with my mom at the PPAC theater when I was about ten years old. I was too young to understand the politics and history of ethnic persecution. Even as a young boy I sensed sadness and foreboding, but I also detected the shared joy of a close family connected to its community. My mom loved the music and wanted to share her enjoyment with us. I became a fan too. Years later and a long time after I left the theater singing along with my mom in the car, I recall the first theme I understood in that play: tradition.

Tradition is a matter of perspective. It's an acceptably innocent and unexamined answer for why we do things. (Because that's the way it's always been done.) "My Best Advice" should be viewed in the same manner. Not because of custom, ritual, or convention, and not even because I say so, but my best advice to you is regarded from my perspective. It may or may not be valuable to you now. It may not be in line with your points of view at this stage of your lives. But it is the manner I view things presently after late-night, solitary deliberation. I consider. I ponder. I implement. Right, wrong, true, or factual, these are my views from my not-so-lofty perch.

Good advice is easy to find and easy to dispense, but it isn't always easy to take. Further, sometimes its straightforwardness is not always straight or forward, if you know what I mean. "Eat your vegetables" is a perfect example. Questions could arise from the uncomplicated statement. Do I eat just the vegetables I like? Can I eat just one type? Why are foods that are supposed to be good for me taste so bad? Like this book and this section will imply, I don't have all the answers. I have some. I'm working on others. I wish I had the confidence to say to you what my mother always said to her children: "I'm not always right, but I'm never wrong." Accept my advice lovingly and respectfully. If I'm wrong about something, tell me. I can handle it. My Best Advice is generated from experience, from living through good times and bad times. If any of it is misleading or incorrect, it won't be the first or last time this happens. By the way, one of my daughters should note that you are not allergic to peas; they are not toxic. You should feel safe telling your children to eat them and the rest of the vegetables on their plate.

SELL YOURSELF!

I realize the title "Sell Yourself!" drips with hyperbole and that this chapter seems foreign, impractical, and like I'm teaching a course for which you receive no credit. Worse, it looks like it doesn't relate to you and/or you feel no connection to it. Worser, if you skimmed ahead, your geeky dad itemizes sales strategies and a method to answer personal questions and/or present yourself called STAR. I can literally imagine your lips pursing and brows furrowing as you contemplate whether to get in touch with your mom because your (mostly) dear and (very) OLD dad has finally lost it. Before you text or call her to inform her of my diminished mental capacity AND before you skim or skip this chapter, pretend you hear a drum roll as you contemplate this: **Being able to "sell yourself" may have the most impact on your personal and professional lives**. If it incentivizes you to read on, I'll use fewer Dad Notes in this chapter. (**Dad Note:** However, I will probably end up highlighting in bold more often the things I think are important. Not off to a great start, am I?)

I understand your hesitancy; a chapter titled "Sell Yourself!" replete with an exclamation point for enhanced effect, looks like a cheerleading, power of positive thinking/attitude article I stole from a trade magazine on how to increase sales. I agree—it does seem like a "Rah! Rah!" piece I could have lifted from a retailing training manual, but I didn't, I swear on my "Siss! Boom! Bah!" Despite the amount of time I spend in my office writing, vacuuming, using my smoker, doing yard work, or drinking beer with my softball buddies, I have actually spent most of my life in sales. Through osmosis and example, I have observed the business of transactional selling. My parents were in sales; they owned rental properties, a real estate company, a mortgage company, a title company, and even at one point, a laundromat—though I am stumped about how to relate clean clothes and sales. My dad's parents were kind of in sales having owned a convenience store and my mom's parents were definitely in sales having owned a factory that made ladies' dresses. Selling, vending, and dealing is in my blood, I guess. Of the many things I learned from my family, the most beneficial is that **no one buys a product or service unless needs have been met, value is perceived, and most importantly, a high level of trust has been reached with the representative presenting it to them**. Whether in my DNA or nurtured, I strive to exhibit that I am consultative, trustworthy, reliable, honorable, and an expert—all extremely valuable for closing a sale or gaining confidence. And these character traits align perfectly with my personality attributes of being personable, passionate, and persistent. This is why and how understanding the mindset of selling benefits you.

Selling yourself is a dynamic and self-motivated process. It involves taking inventory of personal assets, the self-examination of figuring out who you are. It is an ongoing assessment of goals and what you will do to achieve them. It asks, "Am I the person I want to be?" **Selling yourself is accomplished by knowing how best to present yourself, how to highlight evaluated positives, and how to mesh/meet/exceed the expectations of another person, group, or business organization.**

What Is Selling?

Selling is the exchange of goods or provided services for money or some other commodity. For more than twenty years, I was in the mortgage industry. I will not bore you with technical jargon on how the mortgage business works; I know if you didn't pay attention then, I am sure to lose you now. Suffice it to say, we arranged financing from a lender for a borrower who would pledge real estate as collateral for the loan. For our efforts, we were paid a transactional fee when the loan settled. We provided a service and were compensated for it. (**Dad Note:** See that wasn't so difficult?)

Selling is transactional, like buying a bike. It is the release of a good or service for a return, payment, or benefit. Selling is also persuasion, like convincing a voter to endorse a candidate—it is getting someone to agree to a position for approval or support. Selling can be performed personally or presented through marketing efforts advertised through various media.

But What Is Selling, Really?

Before I get into selling yourself, I would like to eliminate a couple of notions you may have about what selling is with two anecdotes. First and very often, whenever your mom and I go on vacation, we engage in a time-honored method of killing time—we shop in local gift and specialty stores. Well, she shops. I'm the bored gentleman transforming into a petulant man-child who looks like he was dragged into the store kicking and screaming. Countless times we have walked in—in my case, yanked in—to a store and are approached politely by an attendant or the owner. Without fail, we will be asked, "Can I help you?" Just as often and because I'm acting like a two-year old, Mom will quickly reply, "No thanks, I'm just looking." Sometimes our retail escort will add, "I'm here if you need help finding anything." Most often, the person will retreat to watch us shop from a short, pretending-to-be-disinterested distance. While he or she semi-hovers, I am positive they empathize with Mom being stuck with me, her anti-shopping, grouchy, hasn't-had-a-banana-in-weeks gorilla baby. Most people consider the role of this attendant as a "salesperson." Remember, for this to be selling, there must an exchange of goods/services for money/other commodity. There was no exchange except for pleasantries and pity for Mom. The person who approached us was willing to present, thus performing only part of the process required to close a sale in the same uncommitted, not fully engaged manner a clerk at a drive-thru asks, "May I take your order?"

Another example of what selling is not, is when your mom and I went new car shopping for my first VW Bug, a 2000 Volkswagen New Beetle. It wasn't a convertible like I drive now, but a red one with a sunroof, 5-speed manual transmission, and a rear spoiler that engaged if the car passed 80 miles per hour, though I don't remember breaking that speed barrier. There was chrome lettering on the rear stating "Turbo," which seemed more wishful thinking rather than an actual giddyup-and-go turbocharged engine. The New Beetle paid homage to a tie-dyed generation with a standard-issue fake ornamental flower in a clear plastic vase inserted in the dashboard. It wasn't even an option; the mini faux floral arrangement came with the car!

Mom and I arrived at the dealership. She was carrying her purse which had the checkbook in it. I was carrying a portable baby car seat which might seem odd, but fortunately we had a baby in it. Though I had wanted a convertible, Volkswagen wouldn't be building them for another two years. I had done my research and knew the alternative I wanted. I was kind of excited; at age thirty-five it was only my second new car purchase. Within thirty seconds of looking at the first vehicle, we were quickly met by a friendly yet slightly over-eager salesperson. He was on us like a lemon shark sensing two drops of blood in the shallow end of a swimming pool. He greeted/attacked us with a great white smile and a gas tank full of enthusiasm. He first noticed and remarked about the portable car seat. I think he was content it contained no harpoon but carried a baby within it. He assessed the situation, and his battle plan was to list all of the wonderful safety features, to demonstrate how easily a car seat fit in, and to highlight the cute, distinctive options the VW New Beetle had. He was highlighting everything for Mom's benefit. He assumed she would be the primary driver. He never looked at me as he prattled on. When he was finished, I politely interjected that while I really, really liked the flower in the vase, I would be driving the car, not Mom. His stunned reaction was priceless as he fumbled through a reconsidered sales pitch while tripping over his toothy jaw which had hit the ground. I wish I was clever enough with words to recount the contortions of his body language and grimaces of his face as his brain short-circuited searching for clues on how to save this sale. Perhaps he was new to his position. Maybe this was the first time a man had inquired about the New Beetle. (**Dad Note:** In a non-sexist, non-judgmental, hooray-more-for-me! observation, after twenty-plus years of driving three successive VW Bugs, I don't remember seeing five other males driving the car.) Whatever the reason(s) for his mistake, he committed two errors a knowledgeable salesperson would not make— **understand your target audience and never discuss benefits until need has been established**.

Though you gleaned from both anecdotes that you feel sorry that Mom has to put up with me, there are other lessons. The first situation illustrated that offering to help or presenting information is not sales. The second event identified an inability to discern the ultimate buyer; the presentation was wasted and no deal would be closed. Neither represent what selling is; there was no intent on getting us to sign on a dotted line. A friend and colleague had a slightly crude motto to explain closing the deal: "He who gets the ink, gets the stink." Sure, in both instances there was hope we would purchase something but offering assistance and presenting information is not selling. Those are just part of the process, but the full spectrum from sales alpha to sales omega is getting someone to commit so that you get compensated.

Selling Yourself

Selling yourself incorporates methods similar to selling a service or product. Think of yourself as a commodity. In a business situation, you want your services to be engaged by the highest bidder offering maximum satisfaction. In a social setting, you want to form a synergistic relationship with a most agreeable partner or receive validation from a community.

There are pluses and minuses to personality composition. No person is one-size-fits-all. It has been relayed to me numerous times I am not "everyone's cup of tea" or cup of any liquid, gas, or solid. I take no offense. My character profile includes flaws and traits that don't play well with others in a sandbox of feelings. However, I have presented myself often enough as honorable, reliable, and knowledgeable that there are many who trust me, respect my opinion, seek my advice, and value my input. To many, I am a valuable resource.

To properly sell yourself is to present your eligibility and/or your intellectual process as advantageously as possible for the purpose of understanding, engagement, or commitment. Selling yourself for any other reason, especially for money, is illegal in most states. Kidding aside, it is imperative to:

- Prior to presentation, assess key components of your personality, acquire knowledge, seek people or organizations which match your passion, and have a desire to improve.
- At presentation, discover synergy, reveal knowledge, display passion and self-awareness. Show desire by offering willingness to transform, maintain, or improve. Sell yourself as proficiently and positively as possible; try using an interviewing tool called the STAR Method.
- Post presentation, whether you are newly engaged in a friendship or business relationship, deliver as promised and retain the principles you deem most dear to you. Continually assess that those values are aligned.

I have faith in your intelligence and enthusiasm but understand that just because you want something doesn't mean you'll get it. Even if all indications are positive, disappointment could still result. To correctly pursue a goal is its own satisfaction. The bottom line, in sales vernacular, is to get someone to sign on the bottom line which is dotted. I am 105% positive this will happen to and for you.

PRIOR TO PRESENTATION:

Gather information. Review strengths/weaknesses for the intended relationship. Ask yourself, "Do I have passion for it?"

- **Inventory Of Personal Assets**
  To properly market and receive commitment, you must know yourself. To achieve anticipated results, there are three key components:

1) *How well do you know yourself?*
   Self-examination should be a continual process throughout a lifetime. I cannot propose the frequency to do this, but definitely well above the level of "I never gave it a second thought," and a few clicks south of the agonizing level of "I've reviewed it a few times but let me re-examine it just a little bit longer." *Look*—I have an opinion about you. Others have opinions about you. You have opinions about you. Choose which ones feel and fit best to retain, to develop, and to project as your personality. These are your passions.

2) *Do you believe in your own effectiveness?*
   "I always give 110%," is a favored response of employment candidates to express how willing they are to contribute. I have heard it many times during interviews before I hired someone. I understood the person intended to deliver a high level of effort. I nodded my head to indicate I appreciated their enthusiasm, but internally my brain was laughing a smirky laugh and thinking, *One hundred and ten percent? Come on, people! Use a calculator! Do the math!* (**Dad Note:** Surprisingly, I have spent middle-of-the-night hours contemplating whether it is possible to exert at a rate in excess of 100% of a standard. If yield is constant at the highest level of output, doesn't that prove that 110% is actually 100%? In other words, if maximum effort is

the ceiling, and if that threshold is exceeded, then a new point becomes full capacity. Hmm, what do I know? I'm a conceptual thinker with a finance calculator.) Anyway, this is about believing in your own effectiveness. A success is presumed to be measured in a manner that both parties receive the best value and benefit from the interaction.

3) *Will you meet or exceed expectations?*
The most successful way to manage for a positive outcome is to always give at least 105%. (**Dad Note:** I know. I think I am clever. You do not.)

- **Acquire Knowledge**
Without getting entirely philosophical about obtaining knowledge or increasing wisdom, gather information from multiple sources including internet searches, people who have awareness/intimacy of your target and personal references, i.e., go beyond first page results of an online inquiry.

- **Are Outlooks Similar With Or Favorable To Yours?**
Determine if what you have learned aligns with your personal goals and personality traits. Establish if what you have absorbed will challenge your intelligence and matches/supports your level of ethical and social responsibility.

AT PRESENTATION:

This is the "meet and greet" segment to develop a relationship. For most people, the encounter can be overwhelming. Too often a person feels inadequate, nervous, and unprepared. However, if you follow a few sensible steps the anxiety to present yourself dissolves like salt in a pot of boiling water.

- **Discover Synergy**

  Primarily, attending an interview or meeting is to share information, interact personally, and evaluate a potential relationship. A decision to proceed could be made at this point without further interaction. For example, I could decide to change banks because another one offers a more attractive interest rate for a savings account or has favorable lending products. My criteria are important, but I could easily switch again if I discovered a different bank with better financial terms.

  However, if I want to know if a relationship will initiate auspiciously and continue with benefit for each/all parties, especially for me, I must uncover synergistic motives. That is, will the affiliation be interactive, collaborative, and agreeable?

- **Reveal Knowledge, Display Passion, Exhibit Self-Awareness**

  In the context of "selling yourself" to establish a relationship, disclosing personal information and exposing character traits are obvious necessities. But a profound question arises: "How much should I reveal?" To answer, view this task as a presentation and examine what you will divulge from the perspective of your target audience to make a decision. If you'll allow me a little latitude, perform it tactically in the framework of a stratagem disclosed by Sun Tzu in *The Art of War*. That is, "To know your Enemy, you must become your Enemy." Not actually as a tactical conflict, but as an opportunity to make an informed evaluation. While revealing knowledge, displaying passion, and exhibiting self-awareness, gauge the levels of your target's ability and willingness to accept what you propose to make a choice. Measure the ebb and flow of the interaction; attentiveness, cognizance, and effort should be from both sides.

- **TMI**

  At a point where you know yourself well and believe in your effectiveness to offer the best solution to meet a demand or requirement, what else are you willing to do to secure the transaction? I propose my routine: TMI. TMI is accepted as an abbreviation for "too much information" and you might reason I rename this chapter, heck, even this book, with that acronym. TMI stands for "transform, maintain, improve." In excess of meeting the expected or ordinary, always be in a position to employ best methods; those which you could renovate, those you would sustain, and those you would enhance by your involvement in the relationship. It is crucial to have confidence in your abilities. Young and inexperienced or old and qualified, doesn't matter; trust your instincts and value your perspective. You will find others will as well.

- **Proficient and Positive: The STAR Method**
  Most often, I relay anecdotal evidence to support my opinions. On a day I will never forget, one of you remarked that you enjoy my narratives even if they are often non-linear. You told me, "I don't know how you get there, but you always come back around to support your position." I suppose that was your nice way of saying I am old and forgetful, or I deviate from my targeted conclusion. Admittedly, my logic is sometimes puzzling and tangential, even to me. (**Dad Note to Self:** Ask my son what he meant. Was he being polite or slyly expressing his boredom with my opinions?) Okay, sometimes my stories stray. BUT this time, and fortunately for you, I have an effective method for you to sell yourself: the STAR method. I didn't devise it in case that adds to your level of confidence using this approach.

  STAR stands for situation, task, action, result. Interviewers attempt to gather information. Replying with the STAR method satisfies the query and provides insight into personality, assessment capabilities, commitment, results-oriented critical thinking, and possible outcome; and if valuable knowledge was discovered, the probability for future encounters. In a casual setting like meeting someone, the method proves valuable as well. It doesn't fit perfectly but offers a way to connect by submitting evidence of commonality.

When asked about a topic or situation, relay or explain your answer in this manner:

Situation: Offer a situation in which you were challenged. If possible, present a recent test or set of circumstances.

Task: Provide information on what you were trying to achieve from the assignment. Instead of the word "task," "target" can be used as a substitute in the acronym.

Action: Explain what you did to correct or improve the situation.

Result: Give an account of not only the outcome but also what was learned from the achievement.

During a conversational evaluation, the STAR method is easily utilized to reply to any behavioral question. For example, I was asked, "Did you ever have to work on an assignment with someone you didn't get along with?" I answered, "I worked as a financial analyst for a large defense contractor. Though I was still new, management asked me and two other associates to provide strategic input for a project. Though the objectives seemed clear, for whatever reason one of my co-workers and I had difficulty seeing eye to eye on certain issues of the mission. Rather than argue and delay our efforts, I suggested since the goal of the team was provided by our superiors, we should agree on that as our vision. It would be wise to assess our individual strengths and provide input based on our plan. We all agreed. I was in charge of financial impact while the others worked on marketing and regulatory concerns. It worked out well because our plan involved specific business acumen each of us could provide. We were able to complete the task ahead of time and I learned a lot from the others whose insights differed from mine. The information proved valuable to management as our plan was made part of the company's ongoing business model."

I realize the scenario may have been a little boring to read especially since it was a specific anecdote from my oh-so-exciting business life, but it was a sample of how to employ a tried, true, and tested method to answer a question. It has significant value if you apply it.

- **Ask Questions!**

I have talked to a lot of people in my lifetime. I may have a few phobias, but I do not fear asking questions or engaging a person in a conversation. I wasn't always so willing to speak. When I was very young, I kept quiet because I was afraid to embarrass myself. I was saddled with a self-designated, self-diagnosed malady—I called it What If syndrome. The symptoms are common. They manifest as doubt of your own intelligence, uncertainty of self-worth, or disbelief in personal value. It is a widespread affliction. You know you have it if you constantly either think or say to yourself something like this: "What if they think it's a stupid question?" or "What if they think I'm stupid?" or "What if I'm wrong?" What if … what if … what if …

Fortunately I shed the condition in high school, even before my skin was free from adolescent acne. The fear of embarrassment of "what if …" was overridden by my zeal to learn why, who, where, and especially the suffix-less what. Since then, I've asked nearly a million questions, and I continue to ask until I understand, or the other person runs out of patience. To your mother's semi-vexation, I think she would have liked to have known the quieter, more reserved version of me. I ask a lot of questions. Whether for business or personal reasons, I am willing to commit to learn something from someone and allow them to learn something about me.

One day, during a professional seminar, the instructor shared his conversational method for a successful interaction. Most of the class seemed unimpressed, as if they had heard it all before. To be honest, I had attended a lot of similarly styled seminars and thought I had heard it all before as well. Most times, the phrases are recycled or condensed versions of someone else's recycled or condensed version of a You Can Do It If You Want It Bad Enough! speech. His was different though and reached me on a new level. I remember afterward wishing I had heard it earlier in my lifetime.

It pinpointed a key, yet at that time, still growing tenet of my belief for fruitful engagement—confidence in my own self-worth. I already possessed confidence, I am not reluctant to speak with, to, or in front of others, but this was clear, concise, and inspiring without the "Rah! Rah! Siss! Boom! Bah!"

After the class, I told him how thoughtful and insightful his message was. We talked for a while, and I asked if I could share what he had said. Apprehensively, he asked whom I would be sharing it with. I told him, "One day, I am going to give this message to my children as a gift." He was honored, but I sensed his disbelief. With minor changes, here it is, disclosed as a personal mantra.

- I must see the world as plentiful and abundant. If I believe anything other than this, I am limiting my wants and desires.
- I must be a steward of all I see, properly caring for what surrounds me.
- I must be a student of right thinking, allowing others to share my vision.
- I must be a champion of giving; humble enough to receive all that my giving has prepared.
- I must do things I have never done before to get results I have never accomplished before.
- I have value. I am talented. I am successful. I am creative. I am passionate. I am strong.

I am still fascinated by his statement. It communicates explicit action to take immediately, implies that I am responsible for more than my own actions, and dares me to draw from my own inner qualities to accept challenges. More succinctly, it implores me, "Anthony, if you want to sell yourself, you must believe in yourself." Confidence in my own thoughts and abilities inspires me to learn and share my ideas.

POST PRESENTATION:

Selling yourself doesn't end with the presentation. It continues further than commitment, when an accord has been reached, a desired role is obtained, or a sought-after position has been secured. It is revealed throughout participation and/or involvement in the new relationship. Selling yourself is constant, and for lack of a better-hijacked idiom, "YOU are the gift which keeps on giving." Before you think I am advising you to incessantly demonstrate and showcase your capabilities, I am instructing that the competence and potential you offered must now be demonstrated as ability and proficiency. Again at a loss for a better saying, "It's time to put your money where your mouth is." Involvement is the time to show you are willing to participate to transform, maintain, or improve your relationship and yourself. It is the most important part of the selling yourself process for two reasons:

1) Appointment/Engagement is the time to deliver what was promised.
2) It is appropriate to frequently assess that benefits are maximized for both/all parties.

In My Humble Opinion

Since I've already twice wandered down the rabbit hole of pithy sayings, I owe you a couple with real inspiration. (**Dad Note to Self:** Time to up your game, old man. Find less trite, newer material. Put away your speckled notebook of dusty old sayings even if "quality never goes out of style.")

Thomas Edison said (and take this advice sans a grain of salt because it is extremely valuable), "Many of life's failures are people who did not realize how close they were to success when they gave up." Obviously, and I apologize again for a pedestrian truism, it ties into a when-the-going-gets-tough-the-tough-get-going mentality. But I visualize it more at its roots; that is, before I get going, I need to believe in my ideas, my own substantial value, and myself. My dearest children, fear less about failing than you presently do. Know your strengths, face your fears and overcome obstacles. Become acutely aware of what/where you want to be because you are worthy of your own and others' praise.

Albert Einstein said, "If you want to live a happy life, tie it to a goal, not to people or things." I have no idea why E=MC^2, but I recognize Einstein's theory of satisfaction: A goal is within my personal realm of management. I must visualize the result and make plans to achieve it. For the purpose of living a good and well-lived life, my pursuit of happiness is paramount and should not solely be reliant on others or other things. Ask yourself, "Am I the person I want to be?" You should know yourself better than anyone, therefore you should know what makes you the happiest. Your ability to sell yourself will be easy; your passion through joy will be apparent.

It may sound derivative and pretentious, but I believe **life is all about selling, not just presenting, but closing as well. It is everywhere**. It is not an exaggeration; don't kid yourselves. It exists in every social and business relationship, and that's a good thing. It lets you know ahead of time what to do and what to expect from an interaction. The only time selling yourself doesn't and shouldn't matter is within a spiritual relationship. For instance, if you believe in a higher power, it is impossible to market yourself; no amount of political spin changes the verdict. And if you do not believe in God, it is equally unreasonable you could lie to yourself. Surprisingly, however, a key component of your divine relationship or moral integrity is valid: faith. Not about believing in a higher power but knowing and having faith in yourself and expressing it to the best of your ability.

My dear children, I am your dad and I believe in you. I think you're great and smart and handsome/beautiful. You have so much to offer and anyone who doesn't hire you or want to be your best friend is an idiot. Okay, sometimes, perhaps, it is possible I get stuck in a "dad proprietary hyperbole mode." You are mine and I think the world of you. I perceive positives in you that you have yet to recognize or attain. I MAY be prone to exaggerate but being able to sell yourself will influence others when they meet you, foster continuing confidence in those who know you, AND allow you to control your imprint on social and business situations.

Selling yourself is important because you are asked to do it all the time, either explicitly through a formal interview or in a situation where it is necessary to present yourself or your ideas as a best option. Remember those days when I would drive you to middle school? As you shudder recalling those felt-like-an-hour five-minute rides, you are thinking about how I used to force you to talk to me AND if you didn't, I would blast alternative music at a deafening level. I was pressing you to engage, to involve yourself, and to participate in an exchange of thoughts. It may have seemed excessive, but I was teaching you the significance of self-confidence, your examined ideas, and how best to offer them. (**Dad Note:** Regarding those short drives to school, I loved them. Often, I wanted to drive past and spend the day with you. I knew I'd have to answer to your mother and to the administration for your truancy. I regret that I didn't do it on occasion. It would have been worth it.)

I believe in you because I know how intelligent each of you is. Sometimes life gets a little confusing and overwhelming. If you take the time to learn about you, both the weaknesses you can improve and the strengths you already possess, you will feel empowered knowing you have value and will want to share it. Be considerate and persuasive. Look your audience in the eye. Deliver your message with passion.

YOU DIDN'T ASK

Okay kids, here's an easy personal quiz about our relationship. Which one of these questions have you never asked me?

A) "Dad, will you drive me to my friend's house?"
B) "Dad, TURN DOWN YOUR MUSIC!"
C) "Dad, why are you SO annoying?"
D) "Dad, you're sooo NOT funny!"
E) "Dad, what is the meaning of life?"
F) "Dad, are we there yet? Are we there yet?"

The correct answer is E. You have never requested my insight concerning the meaning of life. You do receive bonus points for noticing B and D were not questions. However, I rescind the bonus points on the grounds that in question A you rarely said "please," for statement B each of you has shouted at me too often to lower the volume of MY music, and for statement D you have all shouted too often and too emphatically that you don't think I am funny.

By the way, my responses to your other questions:

- to A was always "Yes." (**Dad Note:** "Yes," but with added riled muttering under my breath.)

- to C was, "I know you are, but what am I?" (**Dad Note:** Or other equally annoying reply.)
- to F was, "Stop asking me! We'll be there when we get there!"

(**Dad Disclaimer:** So that we understand each other, until the day I leave this Earth I will always listen to MY music loudly and my trademark humor will not cease.)

Chatting With My Children

I am as much a sucker for a dumb joke as I am for my children. Did you hear the one about the dumb dad who was asked during an interview, "If you could have a conversation with any person, alive or dead, whom would it be?" The dumb dad thought about it for a moment and replied, "I'd choose the live one."

A conversation with all of my children together is a dream I dearly hold, perhaps even too dearly. Our interaction is limited to an occasional phone call, two-way texts, or three or more group messaging chats. We share updates, good news, photos, and banal comments; though I admit the banal-est are usually from me. I fully understand the been-there-done-that stresses of your lives: pushed and pulled, pulling and pushing back, struggling to climb ladders as you attempt to plant roots. My family room fantasy remains unasked, thus unanswered. With you all in different places, at different heights, and with different concerns, I feel uncomfortable summoning you home for a chat. If I put too much mental effort into the logistics, my vision comes to semi-nightmarish fruition because our gathering is usually instigated by a tragedy like a death in the family. So as not to distress you, I guess I would rather clutch the dream closely rather than grasp at what might never be. If I am allowed to pursue my fantasy, I have imagined all of us seated together in our den having a conversation. I admit we have convened on couches or in the kitchen occasionally, but this time there are no distractions; and if you want an "adult beverage" while we converse, there is a two-drink limit. The television is off and cannot be turned on because I have hidden the remote controls and you have no idea how to turn on a TV manually. There is no reception because the Wi-Fi has been "conveniently" disconnected which doesn't actually matter because I have kidnapped your smartphones and/or other devices which would divert your attention from me. You, my children, are eager for answers. You look at me adoringly and deferentially like you did when you were young; that same hungry look when Mom serves homemade eggplant, or we sit down for Thanksgiving dinner. You brim with questions, and I am stoically prepared to bestow insightful answers like a scholarly meat grinder full of tasty wisdom. (**Dad Note:** Okay, I see it now. Eww.)

One on One Time

Please note that I am grateful for the one-on-one time we have spent chatting over the years, but I wish we had talked more frequently, sharing ideas, thoughts, and dreams. I am happy to have helped when I could whether in my role of dad, coach, instructor, semi-expert, or now, friend. I just wish you had asked me more "life" questions along the way. It was not necessary for my ego, but I would have enjoyed sharing what I had learned up to that point.

I would have loved to have addressed your concerns and answered some meaningful questions. I don't know why it didn't happen. I just know it didn't. At least, not close enough to the level I would have wanted. Looking back, family life seems like a blurred posterboard with photos of all kinds of memories thumbtacked to it. I cannot pinpoint a time on my imagined placard when I could have or should have had more input if you had asked. Your life whipped along right in front of me. One day, you're in kindergarten (*click, click, click*), the next you're in high school (*click, click, click*), and the next you're graduating college (*click, click*), followed by your first job, first apartment (*click*), first house (*click*), and first (and hopefully only) marriage (*click, click, click*). Seem silly? Just wait. You'll understand when you have your own children and look at the photo albums on the shelf and the ones stored as memories in your head.

I will take the blame. Perhaps I should have been more approachable, more amenable, and more inviting of a conversation. I thought I was. I should have been more adamant about you sharing time with me. It may sound meaningless, but I appreciated those few minutes when it was my turn to drive one of you to school. It is a cherished memory for me. (**Dad Note:** The OMG-and-FML-dad's-driving-me-to-school memory is not sugar-coated. Of course I remember forcing you to turn off your phone and talk to me for the short ride. The deal was talk to me or I would deafen you with loud music right up to the curb at the main building and in front of all of your friends. Heck, I even provided conversation starters so it would never have to be an OMG or FML moment. Only once did one of you call my bluff figuring I would never embarrass you with my ear melting option. In hindsight, I feel a bit ashamed, but you basically "double-dog dared" me. Funny, I even recall the song: "Bullet with Butterfly Wings" by The Smashing Pumpkins. Funnier still, you ACTUALLY thought I would lower the volume when we approached the drop-off spot. How I wish I had a camera that day! [*Click, click, click, click!*] Mea culpa it was a bit heavy handed, but nothing ever again interrupted our precious gone-in-a-few-minutes moments.)

Perhaps, at times, I seemed unapproachable or distracted and you didn't want to interrupt. Perhaps, at times, I should have appeared more interested in the things you said and did. Honestly, I was and still am. Usually I backed off for fear of intruding. I don't know what I was afraid of. Maybe I assumed you would think I had nothing of value to offer or that I was out of context in your world and that I wouldn't understand. For whatever reason or reasons, I shoulder the blame. It is my wish that our interactions were more frequent, and our personal conversations were more poignant.

This book represents lessons, points, and opinions I have shared with you. It also includes those missed opportunities when I should have said something but I didn't. This book is also a testimony to signify I haven't figured out all of life's mysteries. I have theorized and guessed. I have learned from my mistakes (okay, mostly learned from them) and my positive experiences. I know a little about a lot concerning the micro and macro of living. As Papa would say about himself and I think it applies to me somewhat, "I'm a jack-of-all-trades and master of none."

On With the Show

In my mind, we are sitting in our comfy den in comfy clothes. The internet is down, the TV is off, and your smartphones are nowhere to be found (hehe). It's an overcast, late afternoon which offers no better alternative than our family room, but it's early enough not to interfere with your nightly plans. You sip your expensive, store-bought coffee or a glass of wine while I gulp my economical, homemade iced tea or the first of my self-imposed two drink max IPAs. We are happy to be together. There is no place we'd rather be. You are bursting with questions for me. This is my fantasy. It is a great day. (**Dad Note:** The great part about writing this is that I can present ideas to you without interruption and/or without argument, otherwise known as "Any Dad's Nirvana" which is equivalent to a dad retrieving his golf ball out of the cup after a hole-in-one and also finding the deed to a micro-brewery, 1,000 one-hundred-year-old IBM stock certificates, and the holy grail of baseball cards, a mint condition Honus Wagner resting in the legendary Holy Grail chalice. An uninterrupted nap would be nice too.)

"Dad, what is the best quality to possess?"

That is a great first question! Persistence would be my answer. **To be successful, you must be persistent, not only in business or sports but in learning**. When I moved to Michigan to work for a mortgage bank, I wanted to differentiate myself from other loan officers. Since I did not grow up there, had not previously lived there, had no friends initially and only one family member, I was nervous about how I would establish myself professionally. I came up with a few plans to generate business. I worked with clients who needed help with credit repair, I visited potential referral sources like real estate offices and attorneys, I attended home shows, and a few other ideas that some of the more senior consultants were doing. I realized these required a lot of effort and persistence. Since I was young and had very little money, I was willing to pound the pavement. It worked well, but I realized I was doing the same things others were doing. I wanted to separate myself from the pack. I decided to learn more about a relatively new loan product that no one seemed to be using. Asking around, I found one guy who arranged these loans for customers and was willing to teach me about them. He worked for another company, but he was a friend of my brother. He offered to meet with me. We actually met a few times. I think he needed a break from all the questions I asked the first time, figuring no one could be as dumb as I was. Bless his heart, he taught me until I understood the loan product, its benefits, and who my target audience would be. I became kind of an expert and included it in every presentation I made to clients and referral sources. Within a few months I was able to buy a used car and two new business suits. (Yay me!) Needless to say, had I not been persistent in learning something new, I would have been doing the same thing as every other broker.

Have a vision, make a plan, and be determined until you get there. Keep asking questions until you understand. Keep striving to meet your goals. And if you really want something, get up one more time than you are knocked down.

"Dad, then what is the second-best quality to possess?"

It is difficult to say since there are so, so many excellent replies to the question. Since I am a product of nature, nurture, and personal 'nvention, allow me a bit of leeway. I would like to respond in three ways: on behalf of my dad (Papa), on behalf of my mom (Rebe), and as myself.

If you asked Papa, he would say **a sense of humor is a best quality** and I couldn't disagree. From him, I learned the importance of having a light-hearted demeanor and not taking life too seriously. Since I am often misinterpreted, please don't misunderstand my assessment of your grandfather as care-free, negligent, or unconcerned. My father was a hard-working man. He was dedicated to his family. He pursued business opportunities and personal improvement with gusto. He challenged himself daily and set long-term goals. However, he approached his passions without severity, without ruthlessness, and without sternness. He has a sense of self and of humor. Papa possesses a gift: He has the ability to sense difficulty and interject appropriate levity, i.e., to lighten a mood. He is a very optimistic and positive person. In my estimation, he understands you get a single ticket to ride planet Earth. If you are solely focused on only the brass ring while you gallop around an axis, you've missed wonderful sights and delicious sounds. Papa would tell you to enjoy some cotton candy and laugh with the clowns before the carnival moves on to another town.

If you asked Rebe, she would say **having faith is the finest personal decision** and I would agree with her too. My mom and I aligned on many levels and issues, but our views and depth of faith differed. She had the ability to yield absolute confidence in someone or something, especially God. I admired her complete trust in the unknown. She believed in the goodness of mankind, confident her fellow man would (eventually) do the right thing. She believed in a higher power, a judgment, and an afterlife. She also believed in herself, which I admired most. For example, during any disagreement, she often announced, "I'm not always right, but I'm never wrong." Whenever she said this, and no matter how intelligent or reasonable the salient points of your argument may be, you began to experience a kind of seasickness as your boatload of rational logic and other judicious cargo was being cast adrift towards Unusable Island. It was always the 'Uh oh!' portion of any disagreement with her.

Rebe could be pragmatic, sensible, and forthright, but never all at once. She understood that life, relationships, and business can be cold and cruel. But the unpleasantness was a choice, not a result of human nature. She reasoned it is a choice because anyone can choose to be unkind or nasty just like they can choose to have faith. However, she was certain that the capacity to believe profoundly was not entirely a gift either, reserved for a select few, because anyone can commit and show loyalty and dedication.

Once, during a late-night discussion with her when I was in my early thirties, I remember telling her faith was not only a gift, but a rare one indeed. She told me I was wrong. "Hope is the gift, not faith. You have an obligation to possess faith. It's all around you in what you see and what you don't. If you can trust and have faith in yourself, in things you understand, and even in things you don't understand, your reward is hope; that's the greatest gift." She told me that hope is not only a result of having faith but also is intertwined—meaning you can't really have hope without faith in something or someone. Faith avoids/averts despair and allows for confident expectations. It's an idea she would have confidently supported as a sound principle for living a good life. (**Dad Note:** The quote I used is paraphrased from a memory long ago. My mom and I were alone in her kitchen talking. We were enjoying Rebe's favorite cocktail, Dewar's on the rocks. Well, she was enjoying it. I lasted two rounds before I cried "Uncail!" as the Scotch whisky blazed a lava trail down my throat. And except for a private remembrance drink I sipped on the one-year anniversary of her death, it was the last time I had Dewar's.)

Though Papa and Rebe provided great insight, I think the second-best quality to possess is to know when to shut up. It seems trite but identifying when to speak and not to is a skill. A skill many people have yet to master. Building respectful, trusting personal relationships is a foundation for enjoying life. Sometimes relationships collapse, attempts fail, negotiations stall and/or ill will spreads because one word too many was spoken or written. Think about that for a moment. Just a single, simple added word or phrase can cause an interaction to unravel. Not speaking can be as powerful a tool of communication as you can possess. Knowing when not to speak is not an easy thing to do; your mother will say I definitely have not mastered it.

"Dad, name three things you regret and tell me why."

Honestly, I don't regret much of anything. I'm not trying to be evasive. My life has progressed not exactly in the manner I had planned, but full of hope and love, and I've never had to compromise my core beliefs. Sure, there are stupid things I have done, things I could have done differently for a better result, but honestly, no one specific instance comes to mind. I sort of regret that I have never owned, or even driven, a 1965 Pontiac tri-powered GTO convertible. I experience pangs of remorse that I have never watched my beloved Manchester United play at Old Trafford because of my fear of flying across large, shark-infested, tempestuous, hurricane-wielding bodies of water. I have some shame, but those are choices I can live with.

However, I can address one specific very unhappy instance—and this is going to sound crazy—but I regret that on the weekend of Mother's Day 2015, I was not two people. Not just two people, but I regret that I actually could not be two of me. On that weekend two of my children graduated from college on the same day, one from Rollins College in Florida and one from Syracuse University in New York. In the months leading up to that weekend, I did three stupid things. First, I held out hope that a wormhole in the universe would be discovered between upstate New York and central Florida. Second, I hoped some scientist would invent a way to transport matter from one place to another. (**Dad Note:** It sounds crazy, but it looks so easy on *Star Trek!*) Third, I didn't tell your mother about my dilemma soon enough.

I realize the first two were highly improbable, maybe impossible, but stupidly, I wished anyway. The real problem as I saw it was that if a machine was created to allow for tele-transportation or a wormhole was discovered, the lines to use them would be exceptionally long—longer than the "It's a Small World" ride at Disney World during school vacation week. The third was just plain stupid, but I was truly paralyzed by fear, as torn as I had ever been in my life. I wanted to be there for both of you, but I could not. I knew I would disappoint one of you as if I had made my choice based on favoritism. I procrastinated telling your mom until just a few days before and the sparks flew. Did I say sparks? It was closer to raging wildfires. There was some shouting and silence and more shouting. In the end, we solved the issue. I learned the real problem was I didn't trust her enough to share. She was mad that I bottled up something that would have been resolved if I had talked to her. I learned another thing—your mom is my best friend, and I will never doubt that again.

"Dad, what is a skill you think a lot of people lack?"

I think there are a lot of skills people should have. Here are a few from my long "how-to" list:

- communicate properly
- being polite, how to accept a compliment
- close a sale, negotiate
- manage money
- argue respectfully

These skills are lacking by my standards, but the one that no one should be without is **the ability to write effectively**. It's a great skill because it pushes your mental boundaries to entertain, think critically, and communicate properly. It can be technical and formulaic but is always a creative process. It gives you the opportunity to express your opinion and share your thoughts with others. I consider myself above average at doing it, but I know there is still room for improvement. As old as I am, I am still learning. I cherish the challenge of finding out what else exists besides I before E except after C. I am pleased that each of you has a budding mastery of language. I would advise you to continue the pursuit and would add the caveat: Know your audience.

"Dad, what are the two best things you ever did?"

The number one best thing I ever did is easy to answer: I married my best friend because I loved her. I realize it is probable that she will read this one day. She might think I wrote that to be diplomatic for our next, inevitable disagreement. Envisioning I would use it as a reference point. "Sweetie, remember when I wrote that you are my best friend?" Whether I use it or not for my advantage, it remains true. I am married to my best friend. I would advise any long-term commitment to be with a person whom you trust and who trusts you, whom you laugh with and makes you laugh, and whom you support because that faith/support is reciprocated.

The second-best thing I ever did was be a dad. Actually, the answer is semi-complex because it was not a singular event that caused the occurrence. I say "semi-complex" for two reasons.

1) Life should be challenging, but not too complex. If it is, you're doing it wrong.
2) I have four children from a "hers, mine, and our" configuration. My first daughter was born during a relationship I had. My second eldest daughter and eldest son—technically are my stepchildren but I view as no less my own—arrived via a package deal when I married their mom. My youngest son was born during our marriage.

A singular response is not valid. My life was enriched by having a first child, and if I didn't know any better, I would have said not only enriched, but complete. Logistically, conceptually, and mathematically my answer interchanges along a timeline perspective. You are my children; there are no exceptions. I am your dad; sorry, but no exceptions there either.

"Dad, have you ever been bullied?"

I am surprised you would ask me this question. Just look at me! Have you forgotten I have names for each of my biceps and each of my fists? Don't you remember one of my primary rules of parenting? Does the phrase, "Me big. You little," sound familiar?

I am a very large human being and have always been. I have an intimidating presence especially when I don't smile. And when teenaged boys came to our house, my demeanor would go from mild-mannered suburban dad into *Hulk Smash!* overdrive. I am a charter member of D.A.D.D. (Dads Against Daughters Dating). I scared away potential suitors with a single look—not even a flex of a muscle or a grunt—just a look and adolescent voices cracked. Have you erased from your mind my weight room in the basement and my protective dad instincts? Have you also overlooked how likable I am? Seriously, who would ever mess with me?

My sideways responses should have satisfied your general curiosity, however, to specifically reply to your question, the answer is sadly and surprisingly, "Yes, I was bullied when I was young."

I wasn't trying to minimize a wretched social event with my glib answers. My rhetorical humor was to illustrate that bullying can and does happen to anyone. It is especially impactful on its largest recipients of verbal and physical abuse: children. Before age eighteen, a child's brain is not fully developed. It has developing but incomplete social mechanisms for coping with instances of bullying. 'Fight or flight' instincts contend with hormonal changes, evolving emotions, and emergent life experiences. What's worse from this adolescent stew of a perfect storm is the lasting impact. Per concise, personal online research, the statistics for school-age children who suffer mistreatment from their peers are depressing and indicate areas for social improvement through guidance, example, and teaching. Honestly, it makes me angry we so often overlook the common threads that bind us and embrace the instruments which tear us apart.

In the United States:

- 160,000 elementary and high school students stay home each day because of harassment.
- 15% of all students admit they were absent because of personal safety concerns including bullying.

- 33% of kids who are bullied say it is a gender issue AND 10% of them will remain at home four days each month rather than go to school.
- Over 80% of parents report they have talked to their children about bullying yet more than 90% of all incidences go unreported.
- Over 90% of bullying is missed by adults in a school setting.

When I was very young, I felt like I didn't fit in. Whether in grade school or on local sports teams, other kids seemed to clique and cluster around me as if they had been best friends since birth. I had trouble learning things others grasped easily. Sometimes it was difficult to pay attention and the harder I concentrated, the more frustrated I would become. I could read very well, comprehend subject matters, and memorize unique facts, but math and science concepts swirled in my head like a foreign language someone forgot to translate for me. I felt out of sorts because of my size also. I was a husky kid, taller and heavier than any of my classmates and even most of the older kids at school. I stuck out like a sore fat thumb on an angry fist when all I wanted to do was be like all of the other tight fingers curled uniformly and safely together.

Don't feel too badly for me. I had some good friends and always had my family. But I sensed exclusion from others and felt on the fringes, always looking in. In retrospect, mine was not an uncommon tale. Many kids feel differently from their peers. It is hard to imagine that no one realizes we all experience the I'm-a-square-peg-in-a-round-hole-world feeling at one time or another.

In grade school I felt excluded, rejected, and dissimilar. I felt different. Maybe I was, but those feelings were on me. I may have been too sensitive, but they were my perceptions, so they became my realities. Often it wasn't pleasant, and I retreated within myself and sought refuge at home.

I am silently, privately recalling three specific instances when I was bullied and taunted. I don't want to relay the incidences to you. Not because I am not ashamed of how I acted or because the memories are too painful. I don't want to reveal my tales because I don't want your pity; they are ones of unfortunately millions any child could retell, and you may draw the conclusion that revenge to "even the score" is the best response and be proud that I defended myself. Twice I endured the hazing mistreatment and silently suffered. The other time, I tolerated the intimidation and harassment, but retaliated when I could not stand it any longer; 'Enough is enough!' and I struck back in anger.

The pain was real all three times. The teasing and ridicule were persistent. I felt awful. I never told my parents because there was nothing I wanted them to do, I didn't want to upset them or disrupt the good feeling of being at home with them. I think about those experiences from time to time. They are part of who I am. I am a stronger person for gaining perspective from them.

Bullying persists in many forms, from physical intimidation to social discrimination to harrying mental torment. It happens to people of any age, creed, or color. It is not specific to levels of income or education. Sometimes it occurs for the most absurd reasons: jealousy, misinterpreting a word, misunderstanding a look, singling out someone for trying too hard or not trying hard enough. But I have noticed bullying is never a sole undertaking or exclusive mission. One person may initiate victimization of another person or group, but encouragement from weak or like-minded sympathizers is the fuel that stokes the evil engine. A flame needs oxygen and fuel to survive like a bully needs a crowd for support.

The teenage years seem to be the toughest. A life phase that is equally agitated and agitating. The body goes through hormonal changes. The person asserts some independence while trying to "fit in" and simultaneously worrying about details of life most others ignore. I have the utmost compassion for kids who are bullied and have no outlet to feel 'normal.' They gain zero perspective other than rage or retribution because the mistreatment is severe and/or relentless. It makes me angry that personal and relational assaults persist. Some kids don't have the family support I did. Worse, some kids can't escape it because cyberbullying follows them home and destroys the safe haven afforded to those of us before social media became an attack forum. I ask that you be vigilant of abhorrent behavior. It is never acceptable to single out and ridicule someone because they seem different than you. Never follow a pack or a leader who only puts others down so they can appear more powerful. Most importantly, stand up to those who oppress others. I know it is hard, but no one, especially a child, should ever be a target of abuse and ridicule. I realize these requests seem like platitudes, good in theory, but lacking in practicality. However, I know you will do the right thing and I trust you will teach your children, my future grandchildren, the same.

"Dad, would you rather be rich or famous?"

That's a strange question, but surprisingly—or not surprisingly—I have pondered it occasionally. I assume you are referring to having gobs of money versus having social notoriety. The model to be rich or to be famous is a goal which requires a plan to accompany the vision of either. Since no statistical position exists to indicate a point as to having "too much wealth" or "too much fame" it can be further assumed the desired result is subjective and personal.

Based on personal assessment and the context of one versus the other, I would choose to be rich.

First, because no amount of money or level of fame is designated, only being rich appears to have a fluidity of personal satisfaction. That is, at different times in my life I may need/want higher piles of cash as my requirements adjust. If I crave fame, it is garnered by popular choice, i.e., someone else's opinion of me. If my fame is derived from disrepute, it hardly ever ebbs, but only flows.

Second, being rich or being famous flirt too closely to the heat of the sins of pride, lust, gluttony, especially greed, and could cause slothful indifference. Again, I would choose rich versus famous. While I would use my popularity for good, not everyone might view it that way and say I was self-serving. If I was rich, I would be altruistic with my excesses.

The third reason I would choose to have disproportionate wealth is because I am already years into a sly plan to become famous. I am aware my present level of fame is minor at best as a neighbor, coach, and D-list celebrity on Facebook for stories and jokes I have posted. I am cognizant that no statue, building, river, or bridge currently displays my name and that the vociferous chants of "Rondeau! Rondeau!" I have heard were for Rajon Rondo when he played for the Boston Celtics. No one follows me around or on social media, unless I'm driving my 1965 Ford Mustang convertible. And when I'm gone, I'll be remembered for a little while by you, family members, friends, and others who have had the great (mis)fortune to have known me.

However, I have a single-tiered master plan in place to increase my prominence and more probably, my level of notoriety. I have undertaken an odd, unpronounced tact to acquire fame as memorable as Don Quixote's quest to revitalize gallantry. It is my mission to ensure people continue to incorrectly use the phrases "should have went," or "shoulda went," or my personal favorite, "should of went," instead of "should have gone." (**Dad Note:** As I type these misused expressions, my computer's grammar function is having a meltdown. There are so many mistakes highlighted in green and red my screen looks like a Christmas tree!)

Either in conversation or print, my mission was deviously clear, inoffensively intentional, and as innocent as a lamb—well, at least a leg of lamb on the barbecue. Usually I am an instigator. Simply all I had to do was interject the tainted phrase of "should have went" in conversation once in a while. The grammatically challenged masses would do all the heavy work for me by repeating the bastardized expression. It was brilliant!

One day, I revealed my plot to your mother. Her verbatim response was, "That is the biggest dumbass thing you have ever said!" and further noted, "And you have done a LOT of dumbass things!" She swore that if I pursued this, she promised to have the following engraved on my headstone:

HE SHOULD OF WENT TO HEAVEN, BUT HE'S JUST ANOTHER DUMBASS IN HELL

It was then I saw two flaws with my scheme. First, your mom would haunt me for the rest of my life reminding me how stupid I am—in this world and possibly beyond. I am confident I could have lived with that; it's par for the course most days. Second, and the fatal blow, I would be unable to manage how famous I might become if the arranged ruse was traced back to me. My lasting impact was mine to chase, but for others to judge. I didn't like that it was out of my control.

Because of this, it makes more sense for me to want to be rich. I know what I like, what I want, and what is important to me. I am not a selfish person and am gratified to share any excess of time, talent, or treasure I possess. My short stack of money may not be the envy of anyone. It's good enough for me and only a small part of how I measure wealth.

Epilogue to my master plan: I have not abandoned my quest for language infamy altogether. I have changed direction and intersperse the word "splendid" as often as I can into any conversation. So, please help your nearly splendid and dear old dad with this splendid new undertaking. It's splendidly low-key and low maintenance. It would be splendid if you would assist me. Can I count on your support? Yes? Splendid!

"Dad, do you believe in miracles?"

Wow, this is difficult to answer. Why couldn't you ask me something easy like which came first, the chicken or the egg? A miracle is a happening or event which defies reason and logic. Since I am neither entirely reasonable nor completely logical, I do believe in things I cannot see or understand fully. However, the spectrum is wide when it comes to the interpretation of what a miracle is. I consider childbirth, a rainbow, the pollination of flowers and plants by bees, and the 1980 U.S. Men's hockey team semifinal win over USSR as miracles. I would include the four-game miracle comeback by the Boston Red Sox over the New York Yankees in seven games in the 2004 American League Championship as beyond belief, however, I think we were due for a redemptive win—the cosmos and baseball gods owed us one. Beyond that, I believe all living things exhibit something miraculous at/from conception and I am in awe of the inherent drive to sustain and not be extinguished.

I do have difficulty believing in things that cannot be verified or explained, but I cannot say for certain that they do not exist. For instance, many religious phenomena have been revealed or stated as proof of miracles. I tend to side with Doubting Thomas on many of these as I don't think things happen for a reason other than cause and effect, but I am not the adjudicator of what is or isn't included in the realm of the impossible. However, I am a witness to an event beyond belief. There is no explanation, no soundness, no rationalization that one of my children is still alive today after falling out of a second-story window as a five-year-old child. You, my daughter, landed on your head and fractured your skull. There is no earthly justification for you to have survived the fall. Later at the hospital, when the wave of doctors had receded, we asked you about the accident. You didn't remember much. You told us you were awakened from a nap and leaned against the screen in your bedroom window. My heart soared that you could speak and were okay. You didn't remember falling, but you did say you felt like angels caught you before you hit the patio stones. My jaw dropped to the hospital floor with the revelation that you thought spirits cushioned your fall.

While I retain my reservation of logic-bending marvels, I admit I cannot state emphatically that miracles don't exist. How does a five-year-old kid have a frame of reference to comprehend an ethereal intercession? How do animals know to migrate hundreds of miles? How can a person be revived after drowning or many minutes without a pulse? How is it possible I re-met your mother within a one-in-a-million-chance-only single-minute window of opportunity after not seeing her for nearly fifteen years? There are just far too many things your dumb dad doesn't understand.

"Dad, speaking of things you don't understand, which did come first—the chicken or the egg?"

I am 100% certain it was the egg. You can quote me on that.

In My Humble Opinion

Well, kids, I have enjoyed this conversation. It is a memory I will treasure forever. There are many other topics we could have discussed as well, but hopefully we'll do this again soon. If our lives don't intersect for a while, I may write down my thoughts to share with you. I have always wanted to write a book so maybe I'll collect my experiences, stories, and opinions and compile them for you to read. It's just a thought. ☺

I am sure you have places to be, and I have some ribeye steaks in the smoker for guests coming to dinner. Who? Just some guys I met: Eric Cantona, Larry Bird, William Shakespeare, and Jesus. Tom Brady and Bobby Orr couldn't make it. In parting, if I can ask one favor, next time you have a question or an observation on life, give me a call or stop by. I love to hear from my kids.

PROCRASTINATION - DEAL WITH IT!

I know what you're thinking: *My dad thinks he's soooo clever. He wrote a chapter about procrastination and placed it near the end of his book. Mom is correct again; my father is an idiot.*

I am somewhat insulted if you thought I was trying to be crafty or flippant. I am further offended if you already perused the first paragraph for a lame joke about how I postponed writing this chapter only to compose it after much delay. Give your dad some credit! Despite your imagined protestations, I am astute and humorous. My level of cunning is beyond grasping low-hanging fruit from the procrastination branch of the joke tree. (**Dad Note/Confession:** Okay, I did consider it, but honestly, only briefly!)

I am often frustrated that I have not completed this book yet. In various stages and formats, this project began when I was nearly thirty years old. (**Dad Note:** The Big Three Zero is a frustrating mile marker on life's highway. It's a signpost warning which indicates either "Open Roads with No Delays" or "Potholes and Grooved Pavement Next 15 Miles," but there's no way to tell the difference because it's written in Sanskrit, so you silently curse yourself because you chose hieroglyphics as your Dead Language elective in college. At thirty, the roads are hilly and sometimes covered in thick fog. It's a time in your life when you are convinced your tastes have improved, your knowledge base has expanded, you've learned from mistakes, but when you finally notice the blaring sirens from behind, you're unsure if it's to slow down, pull over, or speed up. Additionally, turning thirty is as awkward as turning thirteen minus the zits. At thirty, you semi-grudgingly acknowledge there are many life lessons yet to be learned but have to 100% admit you thought you'd know more about them by then.)

The book's big-banging genesis initiated from numerous conversations I had had with an older woman I worked with at the mortgage bank in Michigan. Often/constantly/incessantly, I shared my views on life with her through ideas I had conceived and narratives I had written. Sometimes comically and sometimes seriously, I would "enlighten" her with my very unlearned and often unsubstantiated opinions and assessments of how a life—in this world and beyond—should be lived. At that time, she was married, had two grown children, and had lived in her own home for more than thirty years. At that time, I lived in a leased apartment, drove a station wagon, had approximately $1000 in savings, and lived 700 miles from my daughter. Needless to say, I amused her, but not nearly as much as I amuse myself now reflecting on what a boob I was for thinking I had somewhat deciphered and demystified any of life's mysteries. Sheesh! It shocks me how much I thought I knew. Yikes! It astonishes me how little I did know. I am emotionally and mathematically sheesh!-times-yikes!-squared stunned that I have two children nearly the same age as I was then, and that my two youngest are less than a decade from the Big Three Zero.

I continued to contemplate, write, and evangelize my developing, untutored thoughts and opinions. (**Dad Note:** I have embarrassed you often during your lifetime. Please don't be mortified for things I said and did, or the way I acted before you were born. You are more than welcome to feel pride in my accomplishments, but you carry no burden for any of my sins. Besides, more than half of them are untrue! When I say "evangelize," I wasn't speaking on pulpits in town squares. In my own way, and if someone asked, I offered my emerging points of view in conversation and/or debate, but mostly/mainly as entertaining rhetoric and humorous fodder for conversation as I gripped a double IPA in one hand.)

It would be years before I had written enough chapters, devised headings for sections, or even generated a title for the book. Thoughts existed, opinions were forming, personal theories were constantly being tested, and notes were being scribbled into speckled notebooks. I justified any delay with the notion that this book is about what I know so far. So, in fact and each day, I SHOULD learn something new or validate an idea to share. Fast forward a few decades and everything SHOULD be in place. In my head, it all seems lucid, compiled, and ready for your review. However, somewhere between the neatly formed information above my neck and the computer screen less than three feet away, there is a stall. Perhaps my fingers don't move quickly enough on the keyboard to keep up with the brilliant bits of wisdom I plan to relay. I am not procrastinating. I am not lazy. This is a labor of love. When the notions, feelings, and reflections align, I write. I don't fear rejection of my opinions; they are proudly mine. However, I hope to complete this project soon. I would like to finish before you get too world-wise to challenge everything I have written or before more than a couple of gray hairs sprout on my head. Now in my fifties and with you gaining valuable life experience, I am just tempting fate.

Laziness Is Not Procrastination

I assume each of my children will get married someday; one is already engaged. Since each of you will want my blessing, I have decided upon an unusual matchmaking fidelity test to gain my final approval. Besides all of the parental vetting I will do and the professional private investigator I will hire, I expect your intended spouse to briefly explain the difference between two commonly substituted, but misused words.

- Eldest Daughter: Jealousy and Envy. (**Dad Note:** Since you are already engaged, I temporarily withdraw the blessing I gave to your fiancé. I know it seems unfair and I apologize about blindsiding you with this engagement interruption, but a dad's gotta do what a dad's gotta do. I promise I will call or text him soon for his answer. Tell him not to be nervous, all he has to do is distinguish jealousy from envy. I have faith in him—there's a 60% chance he'll know the difference. I also apologize that your sister and brothers will have the advantage of reading this chapter before they become engaged. They will have time to advise/forewarn their future wife or husband about my "dad blessing" procedure or, at worst, time to caution them not to marry into our nutty little family.)

- Youngest Daughter: Accurate and Precise.
- Eldest Son: Further and Farther.
- Youngest Son: Concur and Agree.

I have no way of knowing if your marriages will last forever, so my little test is as good as any. Since I am such a magnanimous person, I will show you how easy it will be to answer. For example, I will differentiate the words "procrastination" and "laziness." (**Dad Note:** If it crossed your mind, "idiotic" is not a substitute for "magnanimous." Further, and as always, don't tell your mother about any of this. The marriage suitability vetting and new dad blessing test are between you, me, and the private investigator.)

Most people support procrastination as synonymous with laziness. Most people consider them identical character traits of idleness or equally adverse and undesirable. At the very least, most people recognize laziness as a symptom of procrastination. In my younger, much less clever days, those would have been my assessments as well; I would have been included in the crowd of "most people." But since you and I both know that I am always less smart than most people and very rarely compared to most people, forgive my youthful indiscretion of not knowing the meanings of the words or how to categorize them. I have since learned they seem similar, but impact life differently. I have also learned that indiscretion, unlike acne, isn't reserved only for the young. (**Dad Note:** For reference, see chapter "Boys Are Stupid. Girls Are …" or read the news headlines.)

Laziness and procrastination both involve making a decision to do something or to make a choice.

- Laziness is the choice of inaction or non-commitment if a) there is minimal threat not to participate, and/or b) the challenge lacks a perceived better alternative.
- Procrastination is conscious, intentional delay. The decision to postpone/defer is because a negative outcome is anticipated from the action.

(**Dad Note:** Pretty simple and straightforward explanations, right? For three of my children, now you see how easy it will be for the person who intends to marry you to gain the much sought-after dad blessing. Well ... that and whatever the private investigator includes in the inspection report.)

Good Side of Laziness - Yawning After the Morning

Unless slacking off is habitual, couch-potato laziness might/will only cause minor problems in life. It may even become an obstacle in forming a relationship, but the sloth-like behavior probably won't end one. Your mother has a wide selection of reasons to be exasperated with me because I do numerous stupid and annoying things. Being lazy is not one of them. (**Dad Note:** I'd list my puzzlingly delinquent qualities but fear she may read this book and be reminded how much I irritate her. I may be dumb, I've slipped up, stirred up, screwed up, and effed up in my lifetime, but never kicked up a hornet's nest and I'm not signing up to start today.) By now she has learned to live with me and my secular triumvirate of idiosyncratic, eccentric, and peculiar behaviors. Thankfully, she accepts me for who I am and accepts that I use big words when shorter ones would suffice or when I don't always know what they mean. However, one minor issue that bothers her is my love of a weekend siesta, especially if after a Saturday night fiesta. I religiously adhere to my Sunday afternoon ritual. I'm betting my customary catnap won't be the straw that finally breaks the camel's mattress, but you never can tell when you're married to a go-go-go girl.

Any weekend afternoon, I am easy to locate. Identified by drowsy eyes and inclined-to-recline body language, I am either headed towards the couch in the den or already plopped down on it. Warning: If I am trudging zombie-like, don't talk to me. Another warning: Unless the house is on fire and the flames have reached the room with the couch I am on, don't talk to me. My eyes are closing or closed. The television is probably on. The TV remote control is held in a death grip in my hand. I am already definitely or will be definitely snoring, so leave me alone for at least an hour. I look forward to forty winks worth of counting of at least sixty sheep.

Believe it or not, my body-planked-on-the-den-couch napping routine is pretty organized and consistent and although it is not a fixed event on your mother's color-coded calendar, it might as well be. But it takes some forethought on my part. For instance:

Early Fall – Early Winter: Mom commandeers the den to watch professional football and HER New England Patriots. It has the comfiest couches and largest television in our home, so I have to "work" around her schedule. Earlier in our relationship, I could nap in the den if the Pats had the 4pm afternoon game, but thanks to the SEVEN-HOUR broadcast of the NFL Network's *RedZone*, I'm relegated to the basement each Sunday. Actually, it's not so bad. I can't hear Mom shouting at the players or referees on television.

Late Spring – Summer: This is a tricky time period. Summertime napping has its unique glitches. Mom complains that there are only twelve weekends per summer and I shouldn't be lying on a couch indoors. She would rather be on a boat, at the beach, or at a pool. I tell her it's only logistics—wherever I am, I am going to nap so I'd rather not drive somewhere to get wet or sandy before I take one. When that argument fails, I reason with her using "dad math." It goes like this: 12x2=24-12=12-5=7-2= 5. Here is my logic:

- Twelve weekends equal twenty-four days. 12x2=24

- Half of those are committed to a family event or social obligation, twelve remain. 24x1/2=12
- Five of those will disappear at the last minute or coincide with one of my baseball games (**Dad Note:** Yup, your idiot dad is still playing hardball), so only seven days remain for napping. 12-5=7
- Another one or two disappear because one of our children decides to visit us for the weekend, so only five napping afternoons survive the summer attrition by subtraction.
- 7-2=5

As you might imagine, Mom stared at me in wide-eyed disbelief the first time I explained my answer using dad math. She duplicates the perplexed you-really-are-an-idiot look each time I provide my calculations with any solution, or I head towards a couch during summertime. My arithmetic or my choice to nap is counterintuitive to Mom's go-go-go way of thinking. She wonders why on God's green, blue skies earth would any reasonable person want to sleep when the sun is bright yellow and shining. I've never had a good comeback for her question, but I stick to my computation—which reminds her how unreasonable I am—and I avoid direct eye contact. I slink off to a couch on a Sunday afternoon as if I were invisible. There are possibly a million other things I could/should be doing, but inaction is preferred; I stand by my desire to lie down.

Laziness is a choice. Devoid of fear, when challenged or asked to show effort, there is a disinclination to participate or exert oneself. Asked by others to join an event, group, or activity, the decision is, "Nah, I'm not interested." There is no motivation other than nothing is preferred versus something. Even if the something might be good, participation is declined. For me, I stretch and yawn, moan and groan, but opt to be sloth-like on a couch.

Bad Side of Laziness - Deferring a Decision May Have Costly Consequences

I may have unintentionally indicated that all laziness is okay because it comes with no real consequences. SOMETIMES, it's okay not to engage or exert. Though your mother, who, weirdly, has NEVER taken a nap while we've been married, may disagree, I believe I have made a very strong "no harm, no foul" case on behalf of my napping. Mental and physical strain can be remedied by removing oneself from a situation or series of events. The intermittent choice to pull back and lay low can even have positive long-term effects.

It is ironic that I had planned to work on this chapter today. As I write this, I am experiencing the negative impact of laziness. It is late December 2018 and I just got off the phone with my dad. We regularly speak to each other at least once a week. Mainly we discuss sports, New England weather, and Florida weather. He half-heartedly listens when I talk about any sport I play, and I reciprocate by listening to only 50% of his golf stories. He constantly asks me for updates on your lives too. But recently, chats about God and religion have crept into the dialogue. Perhaps he notices that the pace of time for both of us has seemed to quicken like dog years and he wants to share with me the wisdom he's gathered to make sure I understand more about life than where the best local diners are, how babies are made, how to shave, and that he's proud of me. Perhaps he recognized our viewpoints on the score of a ball game or an impending weather pattern aren't nearly as important as perspective on God's Will, God's Plan, or an afterlife and that our sports talks don't hold the same importance in our lives as they once did. Whatever his reason, the father-son conversations have shifted slightly, but noticeably.

One day, a few weeks before Christmas, we were engaged in our usual routine of sports, weather, and family updates when he asked me a very non-sequitur question. He mentioned something was bothering him. Specifically, he was perplexed by the idea of a heavenly soul. More specifically, if indeed each of us has one, where does it reside in the body. I told him that I had never really thought about a soul in the context of location within a person. I told him I believe I have one, but my belief is a leap of faith kind of trust that one has been assigned to me. Whether it exists in me, around me, or somewhere else wasn't important. I am confident I have one, it will present as my body of evidence for my earthly life, and it will be judged. I thought I had given him a pretty solid answer; it was obvious, philosophical, and fleetingly hinted at the metaphysical and barely the ethereal. I was pleased, but he wasn't. He remained fixated on location within the body as if I could use a smartphone app to find it. I lied and said I was sure a soul inhabits the heart. He liked my answer but asked why. I took a deep breath; I wanted to give a satisfying answer because I felt like if I didn't, Papa would be pressing me all day asking why. "Because I said so," was my response. I had waited fifty years to turn the tables and use that argument-silencing, game-ending line on one of my parents. Honestly, the delivery of that immortal, focus-shifting parental one-liner didn't live up to the hype. It was more fun to use it with my own children.

In a conciliatory gesture, I told Papa I said the soul was in the heart only for context. It makes it easier for human believers of an afterlife to conceptualize a physical location. I offered if he could remove himself from the trappings of his own question, he would comprehend that a fixed GPS position of a soul is of zero value compared to the flawed, unfixed condition of one. To appease him further, I offered Papa a nearly finished rough draft of a chapter called "Relationship with God" which included my thoughts about the human soul. I printed it and asked him to read it as well as two other finished first draft chapters I had written and told him I would appreciate feedback. He read them and called me two days later. (**Dad Note:** I cannot remember if I was insulted or honored that Papa responded so quickly. I thought I had given him a few pages of weighty topics to consider. I'd like to think he read them ravenously, enjoyed them tremendously, and wanted to congratulate me on my efforts and views. I'd still like to think that, but …) As per Papa's usual routine, he marked up the pages with penciled scribble notes in the columns. He asked if I could come to his house and if

I would be willing to listen to his interpretation of what I had written. Semi-hesitantly I said yes.

He shared comprehendible thoughts and wise views from his incomprehensibly scrawled notes. I was with him for more than an hour; he did most of the talking. I told him I appreciated his insight and that it fascinates me to learn what other people think about subjects I have contemplated. As I was leaving, he suggested a few more ideas to include in the rough draft chapter about God. He also offered that I should talk to his cousin, Jeanette. He considered her one of the smartest people he knew. She was a former nun and a professor. He was convinced she could provide me with understanding for the chapter and clear up a few questions I might still have. Politely but defensively, I told him this book was being written from my perspective, however limited it may be. Papa pressed and insisted I could learn a lot from her. Half-heartedly, I promised the relentless badger that I would call her. (**Dad Note:** Very strange—I didn't think my computer had the capacity to autocorrect. I typed "my dad," but it came out "relentless badger.")

I delayed making the telephone call. I had my reasons. It was the holiday season and I hadn't started shopping for presents (ugh!), my kids were coming into town (yay!), our roof was being replaced (ugh!), a contractor was in the house doing a few improvements (ugh!), the dogs needed attention (ugh!), I had visits to make (yay!), errands to run (ugh!), and things to do (yay! and ugh!). With "ugh!" outpacing "yay!" by a two-to-one margin, projects on my to-do list slid into one another like cars on a black ice road in winter. I promised myself that I would call her early in January. I even wrote it down on a pad next to my computer in my office. Papa called me today. He was sad. Jeanette passed away two days before Christmas.

Perhaps I may have learned nothing from a conversation with her. Perhaps it may have been enlightening. One thing is for sure, I will never know because I never placed the call. I was lazy. I was a bit protective of my own opinions and theories, but I could have at least listened to someone else's.

Sloth - The Gray Area of Laziness

"Sloth" is an interesting noun. It is pronounced the same regardless of context, making it a unique homograph. (**Dad Note:** A word that is spelled the same, but with different meanings. For example, the word "lead" is a homograph. It can be a noun or verb, it has separate meanings, and can be pronounced differently depending on the application. I'm pretty sure "sloth," like "lead," is a homograph too. It's not a homophone, a homophobe, or a homeopathic therapy. If I'm wrong, don't report me to the language police; they have enough on me already. Besides, it would not be the first mistake I ever made in life, with your mother, or even in this chapter.)

Sloth can refer to an animal recognized for slow movement. They're pretty cute and not very aggressive or a serious threat to humans. Their lives seem enviable. They have a pretty easygoing lifestyle hanging around munching on leaves at their leisure. Large jungle cats and large birds are their only real predators and since they hunt by sight, sloths are difficult to detect because of their slow movement. Because I often watch nature shows on television, the only downside or gray area to being a sloth, besides not being able to order an IPA and a cheeseburger, is that pooping is quite an ordeal for them. They may defecate up to one-third of their own body weight which has to be pretty painful.

Sloth denotes lethargy and sluggishness. It is a choice to prolong or maintain contentment or ease. It is a determination to avoid discomfort. Protracted sloth can have serious negative effects by shunning responsibility or showing disdain for activity which may promote a healthy body and sounder mind.

Sloth is also designated as one of the heavy-hitting Seven Deadly Sins of Christian teachings. Sloth, as a sin, is a choice like laziness, but is defined by spiritual or emotional apathy and neglect of the soul God has gifted us. It's obvious why Christians place this in the un-holy Top Seven.

There is no consistency to my sidestepping of obligations. I realize I am accountable for my actions as well as my inactions. If ever I identify myself as "sloth-like," think cute, dark-streaked, heavy-lidded, smiling brown eyes, but don't try to take the TV remote from my hand.

The Good Side of Procrastination

There is no good side of procrastination unless a lucky result is the outcome. For example, someone told me a story of a person who was going to quit his job in New York City. He had been delaying telling his boss because he liked the people he worked with and the big city feel of his office in one of the Twin Towers, but felt it was time to move on to a new challenge. On the day he had finally prepared to reveal his plan to leave the company, he chickened out and stayed home. He decided he would do it the next day. The next day would have been September 12, 2001. Due to freakish chance, it is highly probable his procrastination saved his life.

The Hard Cost of Procrastination

Laziness is a choice not to engage or do something. Sometimes it can be okay, like my sloth-like naps. Other times, like my conversation which never took place, the consequences can be costly and immeasurable. Procrastination is a choice too and invariably the price is steep. It strains the budget of a good relationship. It can bankrupt your emotions and feelings. I know this because my marriage almost ended because I procrastinated.

I have four children. I am proud each of you has either graduated from college or is still attending and doing very well. The graduation ceremony is a happy day; the culmination celebrating four years of hard work by you and at least four years of paying for that opportunity by us. I am not complaining, but college is very, very expensive. Guessing what it will cost 20-25 years from now is a WTF, mind-blowing game of "What If?" However, I am pleased you had the same chance for a higher education I

WHAT I KNOW (SO FAR)

was given. It is presently vitally important and not two generations ago only one of my four grandparents completed a higher education.

My two daughters began college in the same year, but started on different days, at very unalike schools, in completely different climates, and chose entirely dissimilar courses to study. What are the odds you would graduate on the very same day? Though the probability was extremely low, the outcome was 100%. This was a logistical nightmare and logical impossibility.

Deciding which graduation to attend was an unbearable weight. I love you both so much and wanted to be there to watch each of you receive your diploma. I wanted to smile, wave at you, take pictures, and celebrate your collegial rite of passage along with all of the other proud and embarrassing parents. As unmanageable, dreadful, and intolerable of a choice it was, I made a decision. I thought about leaving it to the flip of a coin, but luck is a sour mistress and I concluded whether heads or tails, I lose. Before you graduated, I called both of you and revealed my dilemma. I am still gratified of how well each of you processed the information and tried to relieve my guilt. In case I never told you, you each were willing to sacrifice for the other. Basically, you both said, "Dad, it's okay. I know you really wanted to be there for me, but I understand." I was so sad and so proud of how you addressed and handled my unwinnable predicament. Emboldened by pride and the maturity of my daughters, I should have channeled those good feelings to bravely tell your mother. I didn't.

I knew at least six weeks before the double G-Day what I had decided. I said nothing to Mom. I anticipated telling your mother would be my own D-Day. Instead of sharing my problem with her and possibly solving it, I trudged on like a soldier toward the beaches at Normandy with a secret buried deep and weighing on my heart. I felt like my fate was sealed before I jumped out of the boat and into hot, hot water.

I told Mom just a few days before we planned to leave that I could not go with her. She was livid. The word livid is too shallow. She was enraged. The word enraged falls short as well. Is there a word to describe a flood of negative emotions banging, blasting, and erupting with the force of a short-triggered recently detonated atomic bomb? Whatever THAT word is, I was standing next to it. Angry and fuming, your mom asked me to leave the house immediately. When she calmed down, the message was the same, but delivered firmly and clearly that we should separate. I was devastated. I expected a bad reaction. I felt mired on a giant sheet of Teflon tilted towards a cruel, colloid of quicksand. I was sliding and going to drown from the moment I knew about my unsolvable jam of which graduation ceremony to attend. I had nothing to cling to, so I procrastinated. I delayed telling her because I knew the outcome would cause a big argument. I didn't think it would cost me my marriage.

Skipping past the ugly details, eventually she forgave me. I remain married to your mother because I would not relent; I believed in us. I was determined not to accept her unilateral decision for my mistake. It took a while, but that was acceptable to me. I am persistent and I loved her so much it hurt to imagine not being with her. I promised I would never hold and hide something that could be shared and solved if we talked about it. She needed me to understand why she was so angry with me. She was upset because I had shut her out and didn't communicate my predicament. She understood my untenable quandary and even felt sorry that I was in the situation. BUT, not consulting with her indicated I didn't value her input on how to resolve it. Your dumb dad had no idea. I was baffled. The word baffled is too insubstantial. I was perplexed. The word perplexed is frail as well. Are there two words to describe muddled, disordered, chaotic, and bewildered? Yes, there are: your dad. My fear caused indecision which bled into inaction and almost cost me my marriage and relationship with my best friend. Fortunately, I learned my lesson and am still standing next to my greatest source of emotional strength and dearest treasure, my wife.

In My Humble Opinion

I'll make this short because I think you understand.

Laziness is a choice. I believe I have made a strong argument to support my quest to rest. Laziness has its appeal, but if it becomes a habit it is personally detrimental and interferes with relationships and self-improvement.

Procrastination is a choice too. Its only similarity to laziness is delay. Procrastination interrupts or postpones an inevitable outcome. Its adjournment is the result of an anticipated negative reaction or result. I try very hard not to procrastinate; I remind myself of what it nearly cost me. As life hurls lemons at you, my advice is to be pre-emptive and think positively about the cold glass of lemonade that awaits you. Be practical, upbeat, and active. Meet life head-on and on your own terms. The results may not always go your way, but you know how to dust yourself off and stand tall again. Believe me—life is improved if it's in front of you. Life may bruise, bump, and snarl, but it's better to see it coming than to be a distant memory in someone else's rearview mirror.

CONFRONTING MORTALITY

(**Dad Note:** This note was added after the chapter had been completed. Completed means it had been written, self-edited, and dad approved by me. It was ready for submission to a grammar-wielding literary samurai (i.e., an editor) to be reviewed, chopped, and changed into literate sushi. Since you are (un)fortunate to read the unfiltered version, I had to add this Dad Note because it pointedly, sadly, and unfortunately confronts the issue of mortality directly: Today we had to put down our beloved dog, Cinder. Grammatically, you sensed no pause or pain between the words "beloved dog" and "Cinder" except for a required comma. Believe me, the punctuation may look like a blip on a page, but it took me more than ten despondent minutes to compose myself to compose those three words. I'm still crying. While I didn't mean to begin on such a somber note or reignite the traumatic ache of losing Cinder, I wanted you to understand that—if there's anything useful to learn in this chapter—I will be practicing what I preach.)

If I never told you, I asked your mother to marry me in a pseudo-seedy bar. To be fair and to moderate your my-dad-is-a-cheap-bastard gutter thoughts about me, the place was also a restaurant. Literally, it was a ten-minute car ride only a few miles from home. Figuratively, it was thousands of miles from the places she was accustomed to and a big step down from any place your mother had ever been. Literally, it was a sketchy, basement dive bar—and restaurant—in a poorly lit back alley in Providence, Rhode Island. Figuratively, Mom had to lower her usual standards to literally descend an even more poorly lit short flight of stairs to get into the joint.

Truth be told, the locale wasn't so bad even if the stairs outnumbered the online review stars. There was dancing, cheap beer, and no one made fun of us (at least I don't think they did) for wearing Lilly Pulitzer and Ralph Lauren clothing. It was best described as a fully-licensed, garden-level downtown restaurant and bar establishment. In fact, it was described as "a fully-licensed, garden-level downtown restaurant and bar establishment" by the real estate agent who had the property listed before the site was ultimately condemned by the city.

Regarding the actual proposal of marriage, I didn't get down on either of my bad knees to propose. Not because they were so damaged, but because there was too much debris and sawdust to navigate a clean landing spot for my khakis. We were seated on barstools. I held her hand, gazed into her beautiful blue eyes, and made my marriage pitch. It was exactly this: I held up the ring close to her with one hand and rested the hand that had been holding hers on her leg. (**Dad Note:** It's a sales technique to charm, disarm, and invade personal space. Feel free to use it at your own discretion.) I said, "You have made me the happiest man by being with me. Will you continue to make me happy forever by marrying me?" It was poetic, sweet, and almost made her forget the smell of stale beer and the exhaust fumes from cars passing by the dingy cracked windows. She immediately replied, "Yes! Of course I will marry you, you handsome, intelligent, and humorous man! YOU are my best friend!" (**Dad Note:** Upon reflection, those may not have been her exact words.)

Actually, her response wasn't immediate—and it's not because she was weighing better options. It's because I pressed my luck and made my proposal conditional before she could reply. I added, "I want to marry you provided that a) you never force me to join a social or country club, b) you always look good in a pair of jeans, and c) we have a son and name him Nick."

She paused and displayed a he-might-be-crazy-and-not-worth-the-trouble hesitancy. During her contemplative silence, I sweetly professed I had fallen in love-at-first-sight love with her when I first saw her gorgeous smile and heard her irresistible laugh. The pause lingered like a hydrogen-filled dirigible, and she held the match. I sweetened the deal with one final item to remove all doubt of my undying affection: I promised your mother I would live forever and always be with her. I didn't just promise it, I guaranteed it. I assured her of my immortality. Finally, she returned my gaze with sympathetic eyes. It was either the look of astonishing love or the uncertain thousand-mile stare or perhaps the effects of a third beer. Her mouth was slightly ajar. I couldn't precisely tell if she was going to kiss me or tell me to take a hike. And her balled fingers began to unclench, like she was going to hug me or smack me.

As a shoot-the-works-and-bet-the-farm final inducement, I made a final pledge. "Because I am immortal, I vow to love and appreciate you ceaselessly." I rested my case. I was confident she'd never receive a warranty in a marriage proposal like I had just offered. The enticement worked. Her caution dissipated and she replied enthusiastically, "Yes! Of course I will marry you, you handsome, intelligent and humorous man. You are my best friend!" (**Dad Note:** Again, possibly not her exact words.)

I was very confident she would ultimately say yes. Back then she adored me and always wanted to be with me. Now, not nearly as much or as often, but that's another story for a different chapter. Further, I was slightly amazed she agreed to my demands without protest and shockingly didn't contest my immortality claim. Also, and possibly from shock, she outlined no requirements for me. I thought to myself, *Hmm, well done, Anthony*. I learned something about myself on that life-changing/altering/improving day. As good-looking, smart, and funny as I am, I am an even better salesperson and negotiator. ☺

I've Got a Secret

For the first few years of our marriage, I often reminded her of my one-time timelessness pledge. I am sure she viewed "the immortality addendum" as an adorable inside joke just between the two of us. Privately, it was a serious issue for me. Against all doubts and logic, I believed in my eternal nature. For many years I remained a my-casket-will-never-be-more-than-half-full optimist because I had reasoned my claim of infinite intransience. I trusted the following facts and truths:

- Existentialism aside and to date, I haven't died yet.
- Your mother didn't murder me even after I added three conditions to a marriage proposal. (**Dad Note:** Seriously, what kind of moron does that? The answer: Exactly the same moron who insisted on "Love Shack" and "December 1963 (Oh, What a Night)" as our wedding songs.)
- Mom hasn't tested/challenged my immortality claim. For example, she has not pushed me out of a moving car or down the stairs—yet, or on purpose.
- Into my fifties, the one foot which should be nearing the grave is still firmly planted in my mouth.
- Most notably, I am still alive even after all of the stupid things I have said and done during my lifetime.

(**Dad Note:** While I can neither confirm nor deny that someone hasn't tried to kill me, if an attempt has been made, so far, they/he/she/Mom have been unsuccessful.)

Truth be told, though I told your mother I would live forever, I admit I bore a microscopically sub-atomic secret doubt that my body might not make the "togetherness journey" that I promised her. I'm not (entirely) stupid. I was aware of the science-y evidence indicating the temporary-ness of human corporal-ness. I recognized the hominid similarities between you, me, and the rest of (y)our species. I had to consider I MAY be human after all. And IF I was, I have a TBD expiration date like the rest of you. For instance, I noticed the similarities to the rest of you. I viewed them as physical warning signs.

- I remain handsome as all heck, but not as "all heck" as I once was.
- My birthday cake no longer supports the one candle per year tradition; lighting them together looks like a non-permitted bonfire.
- The number of gray hairs on top of my head, especially on my face, is beginning to exponentially exceed the number of knee operations I've had. I know this because one winter season in my fifties, your mom shockingly suggested I grow a beard. I believed her odd request was to show others that I am older than my adorable and youthful appearance. Even she admits I look younger than I am; she's always saying I am innocent, boyish, and that I don't look my age. (**Dad Note:** Hmm, possibly not her exact words. Or does she call me immature and childish and tell me that I don't act my age? That does sound more familiar.)
- When I descend our staircase, my body makes more creaks than the stairs do.
- I have wrinkles around my eyes when I laugh or smile. Hate me if you want, but sorry, this one surprised me.

Am I the Only One?

While I will not speak on behalf of my gender, mostly because they'd NEVER ask me to, I will make a representative statement: **Human males have difficulty with the concept of mortality; we do not readily accept and barely/rarely contemplate the inevitability of our own deaths.** We begin life believing we are superheroes, faster than speeding babysitters and able to leap tall tables in a single bound. Even after the millionth time of hearing our full three-word names yelled at us, we still run with scissors. Even when we've heard "Stop!" or "No!" or "Don't do that!" we steam ahead with our scissors and head towards any electrical outlet we see. In our teens, we have a fuzzy sense we are not a bird, a plane, or even Superman, but we associate the danger of our activities with an inferred and very distant mortality. We eventually discard the cape, and especially the clingy tights. In our "Me First, Me Only, Me Invincible" twenties, most men will even admit to a kryptonite or two when significant relationships, careers, and children enter our horizon. In our "What Can I Do for Them?" thirties, we trade the pace of Metropolis and happily settle into the suburbs of Smallville. We raise super kids with our beloved Lois Lanes. Color-coded schedules blur family, work, and social life faster than a speeding bullet. In our "How Am I Going to Pay for College Tuitions?" forties, while we gain intuition and insight into the hopefully distant mortal lens, we cross our fingers that no one notices we're still getting the hang of this parenting gig. We also hope we have done enough to teach our kids to be wary of the Lex Luthors in the world. In our "Why Am I Still Paying College Tuitions?" fifties, we notice our nests are as empty as the formerly jam-packed, colorfully-coded daily planner on the kitchen wall. We find new rhythms to a less structured life, like reading the *Daily Planet* in a comfy chair in our quiet home. With our super kids on their own, we pray more, and we worry more. My daily prayer remains, "Gosh, I hope you're making good decisions." In our "I'm Not There Yet So I Don't Really Know What I'm Talking About" sixties, contemplative issues replace strict daily calendars. Births, weddings, and funerals remind us how precious life is. Death is a niggling itch and fingers and toes crossed, hopefully as distant as Krypton is from Earth. In our "I'm Only Guessing" seventies and beyond, we hope we have been good examples of well-lived lives because mortality is as noticeable as Superman's cape and as constant as a bad case of poison ivy.

Early on in life, most men, and all women, gain self-awareness through the same births, weddings, and funerals that life is precious, short, and nothing lasts forever. But, not surprisingly, not your dad. I was in my forties before the inevitable, inescapable facts of (non)life hit me: I am like the rest of you and I will die someday. What can I say? I am a slow learner. Until then I WAS different; I was immortal.

But I am not as dumb as you think I am even though I believed I would live forever. I understood the math of life. There is a finite and equal number of breaths entering and exiting the body. I understood two basic scientific principles of life. One, a body in motion remains in motion until it doesn't, and two, what goes up must come down six feet underground.

As silly as my logic may seem to you about my own mortality, it wasn't borne irrationally of fear. Honestly, the concept of my own death has never frightened me. I admit I don't live each day to its YOLO fullest, but I do seek enjoyment in all that I do. I may not like the uncertainty of when or where, but it's like being in an amusement park's haunted house. I paid for the ticket and I knew what I was in for; I just hate not knowing the spooky details around the corner about to scare the bejeezus out of me. Yes, I comprehend the math and science of living. I know the cost of my admission.

Emotionally, my immortality was challenged when I became a dad. Actually, it was designed when my dadness was three-quarters full of kids with one on the way. Psychologically, my immortality claim had to sit on a back burner; I'd re-examine it someday, provided I was still here. But I had more pressing issues based on my newly adopted theory: If I am human, I will die someday. Guided by my then-recent acknowledgment, three persistently unanswered questions continually surfaced from the myriad of unanswerable questions in my head.

- Have I provided encouragement, inspiration, and guidance to make an impact?
- Will I have done enough to have a positive effect?
- Will I be remembered when I'm gone?

I accepted that death was one of the only sure things in life, but I avoided confronting it because there was no way to quantify the resultant effects caused by my death. My three base questions multiplied like two lonely field mice listening to Marvin Gaye singing "Let's Get It On (in the Barn)."

- Am I/was I a good enough father?
- Am I/did I live a good and well-meaning life?
- Have I taught you and raised you in the best manner?
- If I'm not around, how will my grandchildren know who I was?
- And finally, when I'm gone, how will I be sure my Last Will and Testament request to have a park, river, or street named after me was honored?

I became "haunted house" prepared for my own unknown "best if used by" date; it scares me, but it doesn't. However, I was still ill-equipped to be detached from emotional bonds I had made—most especially with you. I was not equipped to handle loss from which there is no return and creates a void that changes you forever.

Contrary to popular opinion, your dad, and other human males, actually can assess and process my/our surroundings; there is a degree of self-realization. However, it's in the context of our instincts: Death isn't in our character. It is a result, not an impulse. Our nature is to compartmentalize our lives into four categories. Either implicitly or explicitly, we ask ourselves or our mates daily:

1) What's for dinner?
2) Where am I going to sleep tonight?
3) Can I go play with my friends?
4) Do you have a headache tonight?
5) Am I sleeping on the couch again?

(**Dad Note:** Number 5 is the ensuing bonus question after asking question number 4.)

Forgive me for offering a male assumption: Though we are predisposed to be disposed of, death is not in our character. Throughout our lives, we receive, carry, consent, shoulder, and allow for things we understand and other things you all tell us we should understand. But death is the game-changer. It alters life and shakes its foundations. In real, up-close, three-dimensional life, each of us has had family members and friends die. On a larger, two-dimensional scale, we feel the impact of what we see in the news or in our action movies. Men accept mortality begrudgingly. We do not contemplate our own impermanence until something hits us hard and squarely in the Y chromosome. For me, two monumental things happened: My mom died and then my very dear cousin and very close friend, Natalie, was diagnosed with a rare, incurable disease.

Again, I wasn't unaware of death. I saw the clues etched on my own impressionable life. The notches, bumps, and bruises revealed it was precious, short, and carved in granite like a forever tattoo. The permanent marking of human transience read: "Someday, you will die," but I clung stubbornly to immortality. I remained forever resolute of my ceaseless-ness even as I watched *The Lion King* with my puzzled, horrified nieces as Mufasa teaches Simba about the life-death connection in the great "Circle of Life." I maintained my grip on my undie-able existence even though I knew that all of my grandparents had passed away and was thoroughly crushed when my mom's dad, whom I was named after, died. I remained tethered to forever even as I attended funerals for close relatives, dear friends, and friends of my parents. And I persisted, cleaved to my personal perpetual-ness even as I stared in horror and disbelief along with the rest of the world when the Twin Towers were struck by terrorists in New York City killing more than 2,600 people, including a high school classmate. But none of it could or would impact me. I KNEW I was immortal.

Body Blow #1 and What I Learned from That Punch

When I was forty-four, my mom passed away. She was the original YOLO poster child. Among the many stories I could tell you—and some I probably shouldn't—she ran away from home at age sixteen to join a convent two hundred miles away. After she was married and had four kids, she bought a motorcycle and even took lessons to get her airplane pilot's license. Among the craziest PG-rated stories I can relay about her, she drove her car about five miles one night on the bike path near our home. When she told us what she had done, our jaws hit the pavement of the street she should have been driving on. She added a logical twist to her mischief; she said if the police stopped her, she would have been happy to pay the $100 fine on the spot and tell the officer it was the best hundred she ever spent. With utmost reverence, the word "rebel" always comes to mind when I think of her. I just realized the first four letters in the word "rebel" correspond with the moniker we all called her, Rebe. Coincidence? I think not.

She died from a gruesome disease called pancreatic cancer. In her final two YOLO-intact years, her joyful and selfless live-life-to-the-fullest life was slowly stripped from her. The sickness took everything but her dignity. As bad as it was for her, selfishly, it was an awful time for me. She was my mother, mentor, and one of my best friends. I offer the playful teasers of her impish behavior because to speak only of her death would be an injustice to her life. She taught me so much about leading and living a good life. She demonstrated what good relationships meant. She showed me the importance of being around trustworthy people and more importantly, being a dependable, steadfast person for others. She was a whiz in the kitchen, a wizard in the boardroom, and her wisdom is partially the inspiration for this book. She was a person to emulate. But it wasn't until a few days before she died that she taught me anything about death. Not that she hadn't tried, I just never wanted to listen. I sloughed it off or changed the subject every time.

During her final days, I rarely left her alone. Since I can be very sensitive, it may not have been the wisest choice, but I wanted to be there if a miracle was going to happen. In her final few hours, I sat near her on her bed. Knowing I wouldn't leave her side, she pointedly and prophetically asked me if I remembered what she had always said about dying. This time it was impossible to escape the conversation or invoke my immortality clause, but I lied anyway and said no. She weakly smiled because she knew I was lying. She looked into my eyes and repeated the words for probably the thousandth time, "Anthony, when you die, the only things you take with you are your memories."

Until that moment, I ignored any conversation concerning death. It was taboo and had nothing to do with me personally. Until that moment, I thought she meant that material things do not matter as much as you think they do—her version of the commonly expressed "you can't take it with you" phrase. Whenever she'd speak her prophetic phrase, I never asked her for clarification of her "memories" catchphrase because I didn't care. Though for personal satisfaction, I should have pressed her, especially since I loved to debate with my mother. She was a master. She had a gift for listening to your side of the argument as long as you listened to hers. Alas, I regret I never pushed for a meaning to her enlightened mantra.

Her body was very weak, but the force of her words was strong. "Anthony, when you die the only things you take with you are your memories." She didn't force me to interpret or ask if I understood, she delivered the words a final time to me and to the universe. Sensing it would be our last conversation ever, she bravely continued and asked that I not mourn her passing too greatly. She asked me to stay close to my dad because "you know how he can be." She made me promise to watch over my brothers and sister because they would need me now more than ever. She told me she would miss me, but that she was happy and at peace to be going home to God. I tried to remain composed. I willed myself to be strong, quiet, and not too emotional, but I had to ask her, "How can you be so happy?" She reminded me, for the final time, that all of her good memories would be with her for eternity and THAT was heaven to her. I didn't understand completely, but I think she was telling me it was okay to let her go. I would always be with her, and she would always be with me.

It was a rough period in my life after she died. I couldn't keep up my end of the bargain to not mourn her too deeply. I survived the roughest patches because I was married to my best friend, your mom, and had the support of you (my children), close family, and good friends. I eventually rebounded, but without God in my life; I felt He abandoned me, so I abandoned Him. Selfishly, He didn't produce the miracle I—and many, many others—constantly prayed for and desperately wanted. I survived with many, many good memories of my mom, hundreds of her life lessons, and with her cryptic "memories" words, which I would not fathom until years later.

Body Blow #2 - How Do I Get Off the Canvas This Time?

(**Dad Note:** This too was written before Natalie passed away.) When I was forty-eight, my cousin Natalie was diagnosed with an irreversible, untreatable, and yet-to-find-a-cure-so-keep-the-Ice-Bucket-Challenge-going illness called amyotrophic lateral sclerosis, known commonly as ALS. Nearly seven years and many Ice Bucket Challenges later, as I bang away at this keyboard, I am fortunate she is still with us in mind, body, and spirit. I am more fortunate that I spend considerable quality time with her and her family regularly. I am most fortunate to consider her one of my best friends. As high a compliment as I can pay her, she reminds me of my mom. Both were blessed with the cutest laughs, most heartwarming smiles, and beautiful tumbly, curly brown hair. (**Dad Note:** Each might argue they were cursed with hair they were relentlessly straightening. As adults, the task was assigned to the hairdresser. As children, I remember Natalie wore a dish towel as a terrycloth wig to feign straight hair and I had heard stories that my mom did the same. Someday, ask me about Natalie wearing those awful rags when we were young. I'm smiling just thinking about it!)

I don't believe souls are reincarnated or spirits can be channeled by the living, but Natalie exhibits some of the best qualities my mom had. She possesses calmness when there should be agitation. She seeks to make the lives of those around her better by example and instruction. She prays to God, but rows towards shore. She recognizes her own limitations as a flawed human and lives to improve. And most importantly and similarly to my mom, she listens. Lastly, Natalie and my mom seemed to live by the code of the Serenity Prayer: "God, grant me the serenity to accept the things I cannot change, courage to change the things I can, and wisdom to know the difference." For many years I have repeated this prayer quietly to myself daily, but I ask God for strength instead of serenity because I am not at the same level of spiritual enlightenment as my mom or Natalie.

So, when I was forty-eight, four years after my mom died and with my spiritual legs still a bit wobbly, Natalie revealed to me soul-crushing, mind-numbing Body Blow #2. She had ALS. It was the second screamer of a punch to me and our entire family. I knew very little about ALS except that it was a knockout of a diagnosis from which no one recovers. I was floored and staggered to my knees, devastated that I would lose one of my best friends. I was literally down on the mat, but I wasn't praying because I had already stopped believing in God. Quietly, I had been without Him since a few months after my mom's death. You would not have noticed because we attended church services as a family, I encouraged you to find your path to God, and I urged you to lead good lives. But I swear that my heart, and mainly my soul, was not into it. At that point in my life, I was convinced a body was devoid of a soul so there was no way I could have committed that part of me to a relationship with a higher power. Trust me, my disassociation was complete. There was no person, thing, or word that would change my mind. Ever!

Down, But Not Out

Fortunately for me, "Ever!" was more malleable than I imagined and a more flexible concept than I had committed to. I am a man of faith again and my revived transcendent connection has allowed me to accept my own mortality. I rekindled my spiritual bond with the Almighty after a conversation with my cousin Natalie, stricken with the incurable soul-crunching disease ALS. It was one of the most influential moments of my life. I had asked her if a soul could be removed from a person, would she trade her own to regain her health. As quickly as a lightning strike, she told me no she would not. I sweetened my hypothetical challenge. What if the exchanged soul was anyone else's? Still she replied equally speedily and said no. Undeterred, I suggested a bargain. What if the soul belonged to an evil person already on the hot track to Hades? Again, her response was an emphatic "No!" I could not change her mind. She said the possibility of an eternal life in heaven was too precious and should not be forfeited no matter how I structured the deal to win back her health. I was knocked onto my proverbial haunches. She wouldn't budge. The weight and intensity of her resolute answer immediately forced me to rethink my agnostic approach to life. Though I wasn't close to relinquishing my immortality, I wanted to feel the way she felt about God and about heaven. After quiet contemplation, after serious but one-sided conversations, and after many car rides with the convertible top down, my faith was reawakened.

Renewed, Relit, Restored

Finding God again was a start, but three other things happened that allowed me not only to confront my own mortality but to accept it.

1) Natalie asked for a favor I never thought I would have the inner strength to complete.
2) I concluded a daily routine I had practiced for four years.
3) I finally discerned the words my mom had always said.

(**Dad Note:** Same as before. Natalie was alive when I first wrote this.) First, I have been visiting with Natalie every Tuesday since soon after her diagnosis of ALS. As of today, it's been more than six years. At fifty times per year plus holidays, she has seen me in excess of three hundred times during that span. (**Dad Note:** I admit I am annoying and most people would have found a way to stop me by now, but not Natalie.) Despite her condition, we have a blast together. She is grateful for my attention, but I am ten times as thankful for what she has given me—a path back to God and incentive to write this book for you. On one of our Tuesday visits a few years ago, Natalie revealed to me that she had been given some particularly discouraging news about the progress of her affliction. The doctor indicated her future plans should be limited in sight, scope, and outlook. The degeneration from the ALS disease had accelerated and she was advised to have all of her legal affairs in order. When it came time to tell me, she was sad and reticent. She had accepted her fate, but she was troubled only because she knew how negatively the news would affect *me*! Before I could dwell on the findings of her doctor or even digest his opinion, she asked me a favor: Would I help her write a letter to her family and friends? I was honored and devastated by her request because I knew exactly what she was asking for—a goodbye letter. Without hesitation, but with tears in my eyes, I said yes. (**Dad Note:** Anyone who really knows me understands how difficult it is for me to block out my feelings. Generally, I wear them on my sleeve and every other piece of clothing I own.) Over the next few days, I summoned inner resolve I did not know I possessed and wrote a thoughtful message which she lovingly approved and graciously accepted as her own. It is my greatest hope that nobody reads this letter for a long, long time.

Natalie indirectly forced me to examine my own mortality. While she accepted her own destiny and knew what was coming, I am convinced she had an inkling I had not considered my own. Perhaps it was intentional on her part. She knew my faith was staggered but recovering. The key element to me living a good and well-lived life had not been knocked out, but it had been given a standing eight count. She figured I could recover once I cleared my head. My dear cousin and inner circle friend was correct.

Second, and I don't know exactly why, but Natalie's request compelled me to immediately cease an interminable daily routine. I stopped asking myself two persistent and poisonous questions.

-   "Why does someone have to die?"
-   "Why is this happening to her/them/us/me?"

Natalie saved me from the boundless, murky edge of Dante's Purgatorio which my brain had skirted for years. The instant I stopped asking, Paradiso appeared, and the answers emerged. I discovered a simple resolution through a science/God connection that constantly eluded me like the Road Runner outdistancing Wile E. Coyote. With rhyme and/or reason, shit happens. AND sometimes *without* rhyme and/or reason, shit happens. I appropriately named my philosophical realization the Shit Happens theory. Here's how it works. However you believe it transpired, the world is in motion. Personally, I am convinced it was by a higher power and not science acting independently. For argument's sake, it doesn't actually matter; the fact is we are here and we are spinning. I am confident God did it AND that He does not control my destiny as I rotate. His gifts to mankind were life and free will. **Since I make the choices, there is no special fate or design for me. I am at the mercy of the cause and effect of natural order, of the resolutions of others, and of my own decisions, but so is everyone and everything else.** Shit happens. For instance, there is no ethereal interference in the form of a prayed for winning run to score in the bottom of the ninth inning nor does heaven influence weather patterns seeking death like vengeance. Shit happens. I admit there is a level of unpredictability and sometimes random occurrences reward and sometimes they penalize. Succinctly and perfunctorily: Shit. Just. Happens.

I became able to pause, reflect, and move forward. Inspired with new insight and enthused by novel awareness, I felt almost clairvoyant. And as sad as I was about the task, I could write what Natalie requested. She made me realize there is but one alternative to life and that is death. Given the choice, from this day forward, I was going to swim in the living pools, seas, and oceans of life. I would no longer fear the sharks of doubt and anxiety.

Third, after I finished the letter for Natalie, I was able to revisit my mother's lifelong message about death, dying, and an afterlife. With my newly constant mindfulness, the meaning of "Anthony, when you die the only things you take with you are your memories," unraveled like a poorly knit sweater.

For years, whenever I had tried to solve exactly what she meant, I became as frustrated as a Mac user on a Windows platform. To relieve stress and to think, I have always liked to ride in my convertible car, especially with the top down. The whipping wind frenzies my thoughts, not just my hair. I would drive countless, aimless, lonely-crying, top-down miles to contemplate questions of "Why her/them/us/me?" and to understand my mom's point of view. Surprisingly, I figured it out one night in the stillness and quiet of our basement where my hair only moves if I sit near enough to the oscillating floor fan.

I considered that memories are more than chemical imprints in a well-oxygenated brain; they are in your soul's luggage when you die. If your life was well-lived and well-intentioned, you keep the transcendent photographs from your past life when you check in with St. Peter at the Pearly Gates concierge desk of heaven. If the reservation is valid, you get a room key to your comfy, puffy forever cloud fully stocked with an endless top-shelf minibar, an eternal supply of clean linens, and your good memories. Your spirit is enveloped forever in the goodness and purity of your priceless, vault-safe recollections. They never grow stale, they can be recalled instantly, and they comfort and please through all eternity. Further, the bliss is more rapturous than sensing the grandest of those memories for the first time on Earth. I am convinced my mom was correct. I have no idea how she knew it, but she understood what heaven is. (**Dad Note:** I have considered that hell is the opposite. That is, if your life was impure, you will relive and be reminded of awful and sad images from it. I discarded the theory because that would make God evil and vengeful. I think heaven is earned and hell is its absence.)

With peace in my heart and clarity of mind, I am able to accept my own mortality because:

- My mom showed me there are some things you can take with you when you die.
- I am stronger because my cousin Natalie asked me to write a goodbye letter. I faced my unopposed and certain hubris of immortality.
- I am at peace because I stopped a daily negative routine.
- I finally consented to a cosmic theory that shit just happens.

So It's True? Today Really Is the First Day of the Rest of My Life?

My new agreement with the universe sounds neat, tidy, and easy, but it wasn't. It was assembly-line processed rather than a mystic-like conversion. On the one hand, I assented I will die and my soul may experience eternal heaven. On the other hand, where both of my hands presently reside, I was scared. It is going to sound stupid, but I had never anticipated not being here with you. All of my prior go-forward plans involved me perspiring and not expiring, joking and not croaking. I mow my lawn. I play baseball and softball with friends. I drink beer with those same friends. I planned to move heavy furniture when you buy your first home and then mow your lawn while I drink your beer and throw a ball with your new neighbors. I envisioned repeating this cycle for generations to come. I needed a new plan, especially one with less heavy lifting.

Questions were scattered in my head like Lego blocks and Lincoln Logs jumbled together by messy toddlers on a family room floor. I needed to pick up those pieces, separate them, and construct something I could live with for the rest of my life—no matter how long that was going to be.

First Step: Accept my own mortality.

This may be easy for you to do, but not for me. I had to imagine (gasp!) a world without me. I produced a working thesis to guide me: The Multiple Perspectives of a World Starved for AND Devoid of Anthony. It began with a sort of "pros and cons" list.

- My physical impact on the planet:
  Pluses: My carbon footprint is pretty good. I drive a high mileage car and am a steadfast recycler.
  Minuses: I consume a lot of food and breathe a lot of air.
  Verdict: No clear advantage if I'm here or not.

- My social impact on society:

  Pluses: I am a good neighbor, dependable family member, trusted confidante, and I make friends easily. I make a lot of people smile. My friends would suffer the loss of my humor and personality.

  Minuses: I have the ability to unnerve friends and neighbors with my brand of humor. I make a lot of people smile, but they seem to smile uncomfortably. I can be acerbic and stinging like eye drops.

  Verdict: By the razor thinnest of margins, the scale tips in favor of getting rid of me.

- My financial impact on commerce:

  Pluses: I support local businesses. How many burgers will go uneaten and buffet restaurants will close without me around? Markets, actual food and supermarkets, may cease operations without me here.

  Minuses: I haven't bought new clothes for myself in twenty years.

  Verdict: Slight nod to keeping me around, but my excessive food consumption may be the thing that finally does me in.

This internal debate progressed as a stalemate. Carefully and carelessly considering advantages and disadvantages of having me around was yielding very little. A gained benefit was volleyed easily by a sharp hindrance. The dispute raged back and forth, hit and miss, point and counterpoint. My conclusion was the world would neither suffer nor be remarkably better with or without me. I moved on.

<u>Second Step: Sort through worrisome financial and emotional questions.</u>

When I finally acknowledged my limited humanity, it felt freeing—sort of. I felt like Leif Erikson discovering Vinland on the east coast of Canada. "Wow, I'm here! This is great! Umm ... where is here because I don't see anyone playing hockey, eh?" Initially, it was satisfying to ultimately solve the "Will I or won't I live forever?" conundrum, but questions arose quickly as my mind's internal compass readjusted for reading a new map.

My working theory for this part of the process was "Have I Prepared You Well Enough to Handle What Lies Ahead for You?" For a dad, "enough" is a panicky word because enough is never enough. An overwhelming number of questions raced around my brain like Erikson's crew around Greenland.

- Did I teach you the significance of non-verbal communication while negotiating a deal?
- Have you memorized "buy low and sell high?"
- Did I explain all of the nuances of individual effort in the context of a team sport?
- Who will take care of my 1965 Mustang convertible and my meat smoker?
- Will you remember to pursue your passions?
- Do you know where my sports memorabilia, cash, and other collectible items are hidden?
- Will you always be proud of who you are?
- What will happen to my album collection?
- Will you remember to get up one more time than you get knocked down?

The list was growing faster than a line of people outside a bank giving away $20 bills. Before I could answer one question completely, two more would sprout inside my head. The mice were multiplying in the barn again while the Legos and Lincoln Logs were getting mixed up once more. I moved on.

<u>Third Step: Take a step back to look at the big picture of my little life.</u>

Inhale. Exhale. Inhale. Exhale. Repeat until my brain senses the rhythmic rapture of listening to my Howlin' Wolf/Muddy Waters/T-Bone Walker playlist instead of being frustrated staring at a disorienting pile of blocks on the floor. (**Dad Note:** I should have started my mental journey with the repeated deep breathing and listening to favorite songs.)

As helter-skelter as my organizational skills and time management may appear, I appreciate structure and being prepared. I like to be on time for meetings, for meals, and for church. Don't be confused; beneath my muddled countenance, I have vision. Beyond my vacant dad stare, I make plans. The blueprint for my initial clarity and subsequent success includes three schematic stages: assess, adapt, overcome.

Inhale. Exhale. "Smokestack Lightning" is playing in my head.
Inhale. Exhale. "Mannish Boy" is queued up to play next.
All is good.

When confronting mortality, the "assess" part is simple. If you are able to assess your life and your surroundings, then you are alive and able to transform it, maintain it, or improve it; if you cannot, you are not. But by divine design "adapt" and "overcome" had to be discarded from the blueprint—death cannot be adapted and it cannot be overcome. Casting aside metaphysical debate, there is but a singular alternative to being alive and that is being dead. There is no planning to conquer or overwhelm; the odds are clearly stacked in favor of the house of the Lord. I would stick with "assess" to create my success for the rest of my life.

Not in the least bit selfishly, I figured dying doesn't really matter when I apply the Shit Happens theory. While I'm here—and for the benefit of me and the society I live in—I will change the things I can change. While I'm here—and for the benefit of me and the society I live in—I will begrudgingly accept the things I cannot change. While I'm here I will cherish and pursue happiness, not because I know I will die, but because living is a gift to me. Inhale. Exhale. I live. I will die. Inhale. Exhale.

When I die, I hope my conscious, corporal life had a positive impact on those who knew me and that my spirit and essence will be judged as having been good-intentioned and well-meaning. I want my good memories to transcend with my soul. I revisited step number 2. I sorted what I could; this book is a testament to those answers.

From my fresh perspective, I have accepted historical data and hard evidence I had previously spurned. My revolutions around the sun are finite; it's a fact that my body will die someday. (**Dad Note:** I write "body" because I believe I have an infinite soul and it will be judged. If I have lived a good and just life, my soul will enter heaven; if I have not, I had better pack some spiritual sunscreen.)

It remains my hope and dream to be in your lives for a long time. I want to cheer your successes. I want to beam when you find your soulmate. I want to meet my grandchildren and coach them to properly throw and hit any kind of ball. I want to be your biggest cheerleader and remind you that "you can do anything you set your mind to." I would like to be here, body and soul, for a very long time. I will die and I don't know when. I have always been inwardly and implicitly nervous for you. Now, and explicitly I tell you, while I am here with you, let's make the most of our relationship. When I am gone, I hope you remember me fondly and I am saved in many of your good memories. I hope you retain what I have taught you; if you haven't, I am super confident you're smart enough to figure it out. I am no longer confused or sad about death. Shit happens then you die. I accept I cannot change this earthly harsh truth, not even for you. It is my intention that I will live to impact myself, your lives, and our planet for the better.

In My Humble Opinion

I realize you may have been looking for this chapter to reveal new dad-invented clues or fresh dad-contemplated evidence on how to better deal with death. Sorry, but the stages are what they are in their various forms and lengths: denial, anger, deal-making with a higher power, depression, and finally, acceptance. I'll add my own two cents' worth of dad-reasoned psychology: Don't force yourself to rush towards acceptance, feel how you feel, revel in the memories that initially are painful because eventually they will be cherished more than you currently realize. Reminding myself of my own advice helped when Cinder died.

Dealing with the loss of a loved one is a private assessment of a broken bond. To cope with bereavement by yourself is difficult. Unchartered feelings are stirred and raw emotions surface. Weirdly, but fortunately, experience with death is communal as well; everybody has lost someone they love. Your grief rouses empathy and sympathy from others who feel/felt grief and want to improve your condition. It's a wonderful human attribute. For me, passion is my first reaction. All other sensitivities wait their turn while prudence and logic sit on the sidelines until the fervency subsides. Thankfully I am surrounded by people who offer support and help me manage my pain.

Confronting mortality is a personal test as well, but it commences with logic and the realization that except for gum stuck on the sole of your shoe or a stain on the front of your favorite shirt, nothing lasts forever. To fathom your own mortality challenges you to examine an intrinsic false belief that horizons are limitless. The self-awareness shapes your reasoning, judgments, and personal outlook that endless sunrises don't exist and every living being has a TBD expiration date. It's not sad or defeatist; it just is what it is.

When I die, I am confident I will be missed. Though I never had a street or park named after me, or wrote a song people will remember, I think I will be grieved and reminisced (mostly) affectionately. I know your lives will change for a little while. Be sad, but just for a little while. Here's what I'd like you to do. First, if there are any bottles or cans remaining in my beer fridge in the garage, you have my permission to drink my good double IPAs I keep in the back. (**Dad Note:** Can't find them? They're hidden behind the crappy stuff I bought for you when you visited me and right next to those awful wheat beers Mom likes.) Next, raise your bottle or can and offer an inappropriate toast to me. Next, arrange an event to celebrate me and what I meant to you. Invite my friends. Swap some funny stories about the uniqueness of your dad, BUT do not believe the stories my friends will tell you—remember they only came to the memorial service to make sure I was really dead and to drink and eat for free. Lastly, I have prepared a playlist of music for my final party. Play it too loudly in my honor.

I believe in a higher power. I believe in the reward of heaven for a life well-lived. If I ever make it there, I don't believe I will be able to watch over you as your guardian angel. My guess is any communication will be impossible. Though it's very interesting and inviting to imagine me protecting you or us conversing, I don't think those are line items in the "It's A Wonderful Afterlife" brochure. I am already—and always will be—with you in your heart, on your mind, and in your soul. You possess the best of my debatable intelligence and off-beat humor which you are free to use or to discard. I showed you how to love, to be loved, and how to live a good and just life. By example, I showed you how important it is to get up at least one more time than you fall down. When I'm gone, and I don't know the ethereal mechanics, but I promise I will miss you. I feel badly that I don't know when it will happen so I can't give you any notice, but I imagine heaven is so special it will compensate for the loss of our physical relationship so don't be too sad for me.

I know how difficult it is to have faith in a higher power these days, especially at your age with so many earthly decisions consuming your day and all indications that there is no such thing as an afterlife. Considering the alternative of an eternity of nothingness, I choose to believe in an earned heaven. It's actually pretty inviting. Imagine being in a place where the good images of your life are retold to you, all of the time, and you enjoy the sensory reception as much as you did the first time you saw or heard it. Even better, it may even be like retelling someone else about a fond memory and instead of being told "You've said that before," or "How many times do I have to hear this one?" you sense a great appreciation from them for sharing a wonderful anecdote. Wouldn't that be splendifer-ously outstanding? Imagine every story you sense or share has the magic of an earthly first kiss—that would be heaven to me. Because here on Earth, I am hyper-frequently reminded, "Dad/Husband, we've heard that one before." I would be the happiest married man on the planet to tell a story and not see anyone rolling their eyes at me. (**Dad Note:** By the way, don't tell your mother I said that. Also, please don't tell your mother I have changed my opinion on my own mortality. I don't want her to worry. Besides, a tiny, nagging, infinitesimal portion of my brain that fires on the same set of neurons clinging to the thought of a real Santa Claus clings to the immortality proposition. If you have to tell her anything, tell her there's still a chance.)

Death isn't really under your control, but life is. If it sucks, change it. If it is just okay, improve it because you deserve better. If it is great, maintain it. It may sound corny, but life is a once-in-a-lifetime amusement park ride spinning on an axis at 1,000 miles per hour while revolving around the sun at nearly 70,000 miles per hour. How cool is that? Do me a favor and try to grab the brass ring while you go round and round.

And one more thing—I don't fear death the way I once did. I still have some anxiety about my body physically dying and some trepidation with the unknown departure date, but I kinda like the prospect of an eternity of favorable weather, two good knees, and an audience who will laugh at my habitually often repeated jokes.

MY THREE-PART PERSONAL SUCCESS FORMULA:
- BE PASSIONATE, PERSISTENT AND PERSONABLE
- FEAR LESS
- KNOW YOUR AUDIENCE

This is the last chapter in the book, the veritable and literal literary finish line. It is scarcely a closing argument, hardly my final lesson, and, like I am, not nearly a complete and ultimate resource. As the title of the book suggests, it is what I know so far. There will be further contemplation, working hypotheses, trial, error, and offered opinions open for discussion.

Since your dad-weary brain and father-bleary eyes have made it this far, I wanted to end in remarkable, microphone-dropping, stage-diving style. Though I am unsure of what you expect when you read my Last Will and Testament—which foolishly remains unwritten—I figured I owed you some fireworks, some verbal pyrotechnics as a grand finale.

Like your anticipated inheritance, I became anxious. "Have I done enough to leave you plentiful wisdom, ample comfort, and/or sufficient awareness?" The anxiety felt like an avalanche of burdensome "what ifs" resting on a precipice.

I stepped back from the worrying, proverbial brink of uncertainty all dads find ourselves on at some point. From time to time, our toes balance unsteadily on that nervous-sweat, slippery edge. Searching for poise and equilibrium, all we find are shadows of the irrational and unlikely. We watch the irrational and unlikely morph from murky shadows to take shape. Surrounded by the quicksand of a depthless valley of doubt, we ask ourselves, *Did I improve my children's lives by way of good examples, positive words, and honorable actions? Was my intent always decent, fair, and moral?* I can't answer for all dads, but I find steadiness in remembering I wasn't handed a playbook when your life began and that, sometimes, the best I can do is to try to do the best I can.

Since I continue to ponder, ask questions, form opinions and working hypotheses, and reach conclusions, I will be forever dispensing "wisdom" to you. This is but another chapter in a book in a pseudo-complete body of dad-formed evidence presented for your review, for your assessment.

"Wisdom" is a strange word. It sounds as if I have it all figured out when I talk or write. I promise you, I do not. Wisdom encompasses truth and fact; it is not wholly objective. It includes views and estimations. It embraces platitudes and beliefs. Wisdom runs the gamut and through a gauntlet of acumen, understanding, good judgment, and perception.

I had hoped to provide ultimate insight for the roads most, more, and less travelled. I wanted to provide a map so that each time you came to a fork in the road of life you instinctually knew which way to turn. Since no confirmation exists to deliver an all-encompassing compass, my highest level of expectation is that my children are prepared to reach the proverbial fork in the road and are bold/smart/courageous enough to take it no matter which way it leads.

Through my own optimism, I anticipated the book ending with a summary of "best and highest use" material.

- Eat your vegetables.
- Drink lots of water.
- Buy low, sell high.

- Live a well-lived and well-meaning life.
- Never discuss benefit until need has been established.

I stopped the summation; it seemed as banal as a fortune cookie is prudent. There is self-styled, semi-sagacity, but the list would have rambled and its importance would have been forgotten, tossed, or lost.

I changed tactic, knowing full well my own limitations. Since two is my favorite number, I tried desperately for the sake of brand recognition of my voodoo for the number two to make this a two-part success formula.

- I worked a weak philosophical angle of the perfection of a synergistic, symbiotic pair like peanut butter and jelly, or Will Ferrell and John C. Reilly. I realized a faultless twosome still needs a third part, like bread or a buddy movie, to make it milking-stool successful. Besides, my poetic attempts turned cheesy, and my prose read like baloney.
- I switched writing gears and employed even more poetic license like Virgil did with *The Aeneid*. Minus the dactylic hexameter, I failed epically to elide the words properly to keep their meaning intact.

  1) Be Pass'istent-able.
  2) Fear no your audience.

- I attempted misdirection with an "all-in" gamble using the number in writing a haiku.

  "To succeed in life:
  Three Ps. Fear Less. Gauge viewers.
  Gladdened, well-lived life."

(**Dad Note:** I chuckled when I wrote this. I was pleased that the three lines/phrases of 5/7/5 functioned correctly in verse but figured that unless you know what the three Ps are, the meaning is ineffective as a message.)

My Three-Part Formula

Two is still my favorite number. My good mojo connection remains intact. I was wary of a three-part formula because I have always foolishly believed when a second bad thing happens, a third whammy is right around the corner. I couldn't see a way around the enchantment, but I resisted the voodoo. There are plenty of good combinations that come in threes, though for the life of me I couldn't produce more than a few. I was re-energized and emboldened to offer a three-part formula to live a good and well-lived life to add to this list.

This formula is my own invention, but like my mom's Sunday gravy recipe, it isn't necessarily precise and includes ordinary and common ingredients. (**Dad Note:** "Sunday gravy" is customarily called "spaghetti sauce" by Americans without tomato paste coursing through their veins). My procedure and method are neither in equal parts nor are they featured in an exacting order. The simple ingredients for success are:

- passion, persistence, and being personable
- fearing less
- knowing your audience

But sometimes, like salt, pepper, or other spices, the quantities, quality, or intensity will change.

Success By Definition

Success is the measured achievement of an intended goal. A dictionary or other resource may propose a slightly different version of the simple definition I provided, but they exist within the same spectrum. Generally and objectively, success can be qualified, quantified, and achieved without feeling or emotion. (**Dad Note:** Feelings/emotions may factor in the success equation but are not necessarily required.)

A plan is set. Action is intended. Results are evaluated. For example, a scientist hypothesizes a theory. She performs a test or series of tests to conclude the success or failure as an outcome. Without passion, the theory can be reexamined, refined, and retested until the desired answer is achieved: yes or no, pass or fail.

Success is not lucky, though luck may play a part in the timeline of the result. Luck is passionless and coincidental. Lucky is being in the right-place-right-time kind of result. A lucky bounce happens in sports contests and can affect a final score. However, if your goal is to lose twenty pounds in a year, decide how you will do it, and then step on a scale 365 days after you started; there is no luck involved. But if your goal is to win the lottery, your plan had best include purchasing tickets for the chance to win. However, there are factors you cannot control or predict.

Success is about planning. It is said, "People don't plan to fail, they fail to plan." A blueprint to succeed includes ideas, strategy, implementation, margin for error, and ability to reassess and re-execute until the desired objective is met.

Personal success incorporates the same factors as "regular" success, but it is achieved with feelings like passion, it assesses fear, it is flexible, it can be measured by degrees, and it is based on a vision or mission statement. Fear is a driving force in every decision we make. It incorporates our fight or flight instinct, it initiates uncertain outcomes, it can provide a basis for our greatest triumphs.

These are my versions cobbled together from online research of dictionary definitions. Most descriptions lacked clarity, exactness, and didn't get to the essence of how I assess the two subjects. For me, the two are intertwined; one cannot achieve success without the presence of fear.

Success is not limited by the notion of specifically acquiring more stuff and more dollars. I do not gauge my life by how large a pile of money I obtain. I view the singular goal to attain wealth in order to measure success as unbalanced, too consuming, and it will never resonate with how I want my life to be. My plan is to live a good and well-lived life; everything I TRY to do fits in with this vision. It is not limited by profit, riches, or a favorable result. For example, one of my dearest desires is to own a 1965 Pontiac GTO tri-powered convertible, but if I never have one, my life will not be a failure. I perceive disappointment if I am not surrounded by people I love and admire, whose trust I deserve, and whose respect I have earned.

Success is also about aiming, but not always scoring. It is a desired achievement, not necessarily reaching an apparent summit. It is more about the journey than the destination. Learning something new and useful is what success means to me.

Be Passionate, Persistent, and Personable

The first part of my success formula came to me by way of a seminar I attended. Each person was told that they would have to stand in front of the assembly and talk about themselves at the next meeting. Some of the attendees audibly gasped when the instructor made the request. I wasn't worried because I don't mind speaking in front of a group. When I went home that night, I outlined a brief speech. I included a few humorous anecdotes and a quick synopsis about myself personally and professionally. Besides basic facts, I wanted my presentation to reveal who I think I am. As I wrote the short sentences on index cards, I noticed three words kept popping up: passion, persistence, and personable. I used the words repeatedly for the speech just as I had used them many times before in conversations, interviews, or communicating to a team I coached. It dawned on me that these were not just adjectives to describe myself or qualities necessary to achieve a goal, they were the goal.

It isn't necessary to define the words for you. You've done enough reading and I've done enough lecturing. Besides, if you don't know what they mean by now, then I sucked as a role model and parent. However, here is my variably fixed view of the combination: **Uncover and become inspired to be passionate about what life offers, remain persistent even when the mountain seems too high to climb, and radiate to the world that you are personable and approachable.**

Fear Less

The second part of my success formula was garnered from a motto I had seen written on a throw pillow in a small home goods shop in Bermuda. Mom was looking at things to buy to remind us of our wonderful trip; I was harrumphing around the store like a 260-pound bored, hungry baby. While actual and imagined bellyaching, I noticed a hand-stitched message on a cushion. It read: "Once you become fearless, life becomes limitless." I was dumbfounded by the sutured, spot-on revelation of one of life's mysteries.

Any fool—especially this old fool—realizes life will always have limits. The promise of the potential of "limitless" is in the attempt rather than the accomplishment. For if "limitless" is ever fulfilled, isn't it just like counting to infinity and then adding one? The promise of fearless translating to actual limitless is irrational, but perhaps I was reading too much into seven words sewn onto a small pillow.

After some post-vacation contemplation, I realized the words beckoned me to follow my dreams and passions. They implored me to stand up for what I believe in. They compelled me to do what was right rather than what was convenient. If I really wanted to live a good and well-lived life, a life my children would respect and one worthy of every breath I take, then I must fear less.

Fear is healthy and instinctual, but when it causes procrastination, apathy, or disinterest it becomes too strong a factor to improve, to help, and to act responsibly. Without question, life is challenging and demanding; it is full of risks and rewards, littered with potholes and smooth roads. If fear forces you to ride shotgun in your own life, then it is time to reassess.

I have taught you to be willing to get up at least one more time than you are knocked down. Fear will always be there, whether you are high on the horse or dusting yourself off on the ground. Be brave and courageous enough to grab the reins to ride again. The journey is the goal; the attempt is what inspires the promise of "limitless."

Know Your Audience

The third part, know your audience, might sound like the weakest and ineptest piece of my three-pronged approach. It may seem predictably trite and not worthy of the end of a thought/chapter/book. I imagine you wondering, *Has my dad lost it? Is he stuck for material? Is he just tired of typing?* Surprisingly, I am neither stumped nor weary, though the jury is still deliberating the number of marbles I retain.

Knowing your audience is the inexact but essential science of learning, not assuming, the significance viewers will place on your words or actions. It is intelligence-gathering research of beliefs, recon of opinions done in advance, and anticipation of consequences for and from your recipients/ addressees. All with the awareness that despite best efforts, a message may still fall flat on its face, especially now in an era of heightened social sensitivity, a shifting mainstream, and an unusual intolerance for differing views. Today, knowing your audience is probably the most frightening and difficult part of my formula.

My outlook on life includes acceptance of the dissimilar and divergent. As conservative and buttoned-down as I appear, my viewpoint embraces the contrary and conflicting. I want to grow and improve personally and spiritually. I cannot if I adhere solely to unexamined dogma or unconfirmed opinion. Even at my age, I must ask questions if I want to develop as a person. I must inquire to increase my social awareness. I must query to strengthen my own intelligence. As dad-corny as it sounds, I feel duty-bound as a citizen of this planet to transform what needs to be changed, to maintain a high moral code, and to enrich the lives of others. My hope for you and my fellow earthlings is that reasonableness and tolerance become acceptable, because right now we sit on the precipice of an off-the-rails, no-going-back failure and I want to believe that the intent of actions and purposeful words will be judged more critically than the results.

Remember this is a three-part success formula to attain success in the manner I define it. Individually, each part is good advice, not ultimate, not penultimate, and not best-in-class blue ribbon guidance, but worthy to verify and experience. To be passionate, persistent, and personable is an admirable and worthy recommendation. To fear less, i.e., to challenge more, is valuable and commendable. But without the component of knowing your audience, the success of living a good and well-lived life will elude you.

In My Humble Opinion

As I have proven repeatedly, I am not the smartest person. Even as I sit alone in my basement office with our two dogs gnawing on marrow bones, I am still uncertain if I am the wisest in the room. I aim to live a good and well-lived life. I hope to leave an imprint, however light, on your lives. I aspire to change the things I can and should change and be blessed with enough wisdom to recognize the difference. To paraphrase Dr. Martin Luther King Jr., I wish to be "judged by the content of my character" and nothing else. I desire to have a fulfilling relationship with each of you.

I have no idea if my goals are lofty or low, but I know they are mine and I do not view them as targets. I see them as ambitious works in progress steeped in purposeful, personal satisfaction. My unyielding but malleable goal is to live a good and well-lived life. I will travel, arrive there on the wings of my passion, on the steadfastness of my persistence, and with my aptitude for being personable intact. I will do my dad darndest to face my fears so that I pass none of them on to you. I will estimate my audience, knowing my words and actions may fall on deaf ears and closed minds, but confident they were delivered genuinely and with the best of intentions.

Love, Dad

P.S. Now that you've finished reading the book, you're thinking, *Wow, Dad is smarter than he looks.* Or, *Not bad, Dad. That wasn't as awful as I thought it would be.* Or, *We got off easy. There are plenty of other things I remember Dad rambling on about.* Put your minds at ease—I have much more dad wisdom and plenty of advice to dispense in my next volume(s).

CPSIA information can be obtained
at www.ICGtesting.com
Printed in the USA
JSHW030137080822
29013JS00002B/10